W9-BWU-522

continued

EDUCATING EMERGENT BILINGUALS

POLICIES, PROGRAMS, AND PRACTICES FOR ENGLISH LEARNERS

SECOND EDITION

OFELIA GARCÍA AND JO ANNE KLEIFGEN

Foreword by Jim Cummins

TEACHERS COLLEGE PRESS

TEACHERS COLLEGE | COLUMBIA UNIVERSITY
NEW YORK AND LONDON

Published by Teachers College Press, 1234 Amsterdam Avenue, New York, NY 10027

Cover design by Patricia Palao. Cover photo by timsa / Getty Images.

Table 3.1 adapted from *Educating English Learners: Language Diversity in the Classroom* by James Crawford. Copyright © 2004 by James Crawford. Reprinted by permission.

Figure 6.1 is used with permission from Kyle Borlase, designer. Figure 6.2 is used with permission from McGraw-Hill Education, *New York Science, Grade 8, 1st Edition*, 2006.

Library of Congress Cataloging-in-Publication Data is available at loc.gov

Names: García, Ofelia, author. | Kleifgen, Jo Anne, author.
Title: Educating emergent bilinguals : policies, programs, and practices for
   English learners / Ofelia Garcia, Jo Anne Kleifgen ; foreword by Jim
   Cummins.
Description: Second edition. | New York : Teachers College Press, [2018] |
   Includes bibliographical references and index. | Description based on
   print version record and CIP data provided by publisher; resource not
   viewed.
Identifiers: LCCN 2017061242 (print) | LCCN 2018000019 (ebook) | ISBN
   9780807776766 (ebook) | ISBN 9780807758854 (pbk. : alk. paper)
Subjects: LCSH: Education, Bilingual. | English language—Study and
   teaching—Foreign speakers. | English language—Acquisition. | Second
   language acquisition.
Classification: LCC LC3715 (ebook) | LCC LC3715 .G37 2018 (print) | DDC
   370.117/5—dc23

LC record available at https://lccn.loc.gov/2017061242

ISBN 978-0-8077-5885-4 (paper)
ISBN 978-0-8077-7676-6 (ebook)

Printed on acid-free paper
Manufactured in the United States of America

25 24 23 22 21 20 19 18   8 7 6 5 4 3 2 1

For all those emergent bilingual students around the world who have come through our classroom doors and enriched our lives as educators.

Contents

Foreword

Perhaps once or twice a decade you read a book that is so lucid, convincing, and inspirational that you want to order copies for every teacher, administrator, and policymaker across the nation. Ofelia García and Jo Anne Kleifgen have written such a book. Their message is very simple: If you want students to emerge from schooling after 12 years as intelligent, imaginative, and linguistically talented, then treat them as intelligent, imaginative, and linguistically talented from the first day they arrive in school.

Woven throughout the pages of *Educating Emergent Bilinguals* is the reminder to educators and policymakers that effective schooling has much more to do with the quality of human relationships orchestrated between teachers and students than with the simple transmission of content. These relationships are obviously influenced by the conditions within which educators work—the curricula they are mandated to teach, the standardized tests that often operate as a proxy curriculum, the language(s) and varieties thereof that are considered legitimate within the ideological space of schooling. Yet, despite the myriad constraints within which educators (including administrators) operate, there are always degrees of freedom that permit and require them to make choices on a continuing basis.

Thus, individual educators are never powerless; they always exercise agency, understood as the power to act. Although they rarely have complete freedom, educators do have choices in the way they structure the interactions in their classrooms. They determine for themselves the social and educational goals they want to achieve with their students. There are always options with respect to educators' orientation to students' language and culture in the forms of parent and community participation they encourage and in the ways they implement pedagogy and assessment.

The choices we make in the classroom are infused with images: images of our students as we perceive them now and in the future, and images of our own identities as educators. To what extent are we communicating to the students in our classrooms an image of themselves as capable of becoming bilingual and biliterate? Capable of higher-order thinking and intellectual accomplishments? Capable of creative and imaginative thinking? Capable of creating literature and art? Capable of generating new knowledge? Capable of thinking about and finding solutions to social issues?

As García and Kleifgen point out, when students see themselves (and know that their teachers see them) as emergent bilinguals rather than as English language learners (or some other label that defines students by what they lack), they are much more likely to take pride in their linguistic abilities and talents than if they are defined in deficit terms. Similarly, when students are given opportunities to engage in critical inquiry with their peers aimed at generating knowledge, they are likely to adopt what Patrick Manyak (2004) has called identities of competence. These identities of competence propel students into active engagement with literacy and learning.

Unfortunately, far too few low-income students in North American classrooms are given opportunities to engage in cognitively powerful and identity-affirming learning experiences in comparison to their higher-income peers. The No Child Left Behind legislation institutionalized high-stakes standardized testing as the simultaneous gauge of student learning and teacher effectiveness, thereby reinforcing the pedagogical divide between schools serving economically privileged communities and those serving the impoverished and dispossessed. Frequently, the dispossession continues within the school as emergent bilingual students are further stripped of their home language and culture. Defined by their limited English skills and their low standardized test scores, emergent bilingual students struggle, often un-successfully, to escape from the externally imposed identity cocoon within which they find themselves.

One of the most powerful messages woven into this book is that, as educators, we do have the power to push back against myopic and irre-sponsible policies that ignore the research evidence in relation to bilingual students' academic development. When we articulate our choices, individu-ally and collectively, we will find ways of connecting academic content with our students' prior knowledge; we will identify ways of enabling students to engage in higher-order thinking through the translanguaging instructional strategies outlined in this book; we will explore how technological tools can be used creatively by students to generate knowledge; and we will infuse a sense of pride and affirmation of identity into the projects that our students undertake. In this process of articulating and acting on our choices, our own identities as educators will expand. The classroom interactions we orches-trate with our students will shape, rather than simply reflect, our society.

—Jim Cummins

Acknowledgments

The preparation of the first edition of this book could never have happened without the help of Heidi Batchelder, then a graduate student at Teachers College, Columbia University, who prepared the chapters for submission and collected missing references. We are very grateful to her for her attention to detail and for keeping up with our tight schedule. We also thank Meg Lemke from Teachers College Press for her encouragement and support. For this second edition, we are especially grateful to Emily Spangler from Teachers College Press for convincing us to work on this second edition, Jennifer Baker for her attention to the manuscript, and Tara Tomczyk for her copyediting. Several doctoral students, who read and commented on different parts of the first edition, continue to deserve our heartfelt thanks—Laura Ascenzi-Moreno, Nelson Flores, Kristin Gorski, Laura Kaplan, Briana Ronan, Karen Velasquez, and Heather Woodley—as does our colleague, Ricardo Otheguy. For work on this second edition, we wish to express our gratitude to Khanh Le and Gladys Aponte, doctoral students at The Graduate Center, CUNY.

This book is an extension of a report we originally wrote for the Campaign for Educational Equity at Teachers College, Columbia University. We thank the Campaign; its executive director, Michael Rebell; its research director, Amy Stuart Wells; and its policy director, Jessica Wolff, for giving us the opportunity to write the report and for offering excellent suggestions. In particular, we owe a special debt of gratitude to our coauthor in the report, Lori Falchi, who supported our original thinking and writing as the report took shape.

A number of people contributed significantly in the preparation of the review we conducted for the Campaign for Educational Equity. We are most grateful to Jim Crawford for his willingness to share his expertise from the very beginning and to continue to support us as we updated the information for the first edition. Besides Crawford, a number of people read and commented on parts of the original review—Jamal Abedi, Bruce Baker, Luis Moll, and Terry Wiley. And others provided us with essential pieces of information—Lyle Bachman, Tim Boals, Ellen Forte, Margot Gottlieb, Luis Reyes, Roger Rice, Pedro Ruiz, Mariano Viñas. For this second edition, we want to express our gratitude to Michel DeGraff, who provided us with feedback about his project on Haitian Creole and technology in Haiti; we also thank David Wible for suggestions regarding the digital writing platform developed in Taiwan. Our gratitude also goes to Robert Linquanti, who was most helpful in helping us understand the recent policy changes. Chris Bacon and his students from Boston University also provided us with feedback on the first edition so that we could improve this second one, and we are grateful. Finally, we want to express our gratitude to our partners—John Borghese and Ricardo Otheguy—who have exercised much patience while we engaged again with the preparation of this second edition.

Gracias to all for contributing to the efforts to improve the education and lives of language-minoritized students in the United States.

Preface

In the 10 years since the publication of the first edition of *Educating Emergent Bilinguals,* much has changed in educational policies. However, little has changed in inequitable practices that continue to be used to educate emergent bilinguals. Meanwhile, new research continues to confirm and extend the importance of the role of students' home language in education.

At the time we write, we are experiencing unprecedented uncertainty in the ways that federal and state policies are being interpreted and implemented. The federal Every Student Succeeds Act (ESSA) supplanted the No Child Left Behind (NCLB) act in 2015, but we are unsure of how the ESSA regulations will be implemented, and what impact this will have on state education policy and on the education of emergent bilinguals. The Common Core State Standards (CCSS) Initiative, a set of rigorous standards for K–12 mathematics and English language arts that was introduced with much fanfare in 2009, was being questioned in 2017. States that had previously adopted the Common Core have repealed or are in the process of repealing their participation. States are scrambling to figure out how emergent bilinguals are to meet standards.

With regard to the students who are the subject of this book—emergent bilinguals—the socioeducational climate has never been less auspicious. For newcomers and immigrants, stern immigration policy is affecting how they are viewed in schools and society, with talk of "walls" and "keep them out." Many are afraid of walking home from school, fearful that they will be deported. Children of immigrants, and even grandchildren of immigrants, are also afraid that their loved ones might be deported.

Despite changes in policies that affect the education of emergent bilinguals, research findings in the past 10 years have only continued to assert the importance of leveraging *all* the linguistic and cultural practices of emergent bilinguals to educate them. In the past decade, a considerable literature on translanguaging has emerged, and this edition pays attention to its potential. Also in the past decade, new technologies have emerged altering the ways in which we educate. This second edition includes a new chapter on the affordances that multimodal resources and technology provide to educate emergent bilinguals. Despite the availability of alternative language and literacy practices in education today, these often elude emergent bilinguals. Schools continue to educate emergent bilingual students as if their different linguistic and cultural practices did not exist.

There has been one noticeable change concerning bilingualism in schools in the past 10 years. We have witnessed a growing acceptance of programs that educate students bilingually. However, the term *bilingualism* is silenced by naming these programs "dual-language" programs, thus implying that bilingualism can only receive its legitimacy from the presence of White, English-monolingual, middle-class students.

When we wrote the first edition of this book, we chose to call the students who are the object of our attention "emergent bilinguals," mainly to emphasize their bilingualism rather than their lack of English, as signaled by other terms (*English language learner, limited English proficient*). But the growing popularity of two-way dual-language programs (what we call here dual-language bilingual education, or DLBE, to emphasize its bilingual nature) has complicated the term, for language-majority students learning languages other than English can also be considered emergent bilinguals. In this book, however, we reserve the term *emergent bilingual* for *minoritized* students—usually Brown and Black students, whose emergent bilingualism educational policymakers often prefer to neglect rather than nurture.

Little has changed in the education of minoritized emergent bilingual students in the past 10 years, as we make obvious in the text. In fact, the reality of educational practice for them is that there is less bilingual education and more English-only education. Despite our growing knowledge of the value of dynamic bilingual practices in the world today, we minoritize emergent bilingual students precisely by ignoring their dynamic bilingualism.

The central idea in this second edition continues to be what we stated clearly at the end of the first chapter of the first edition—that there is a growing dissonance between research on the education of emergent bilinguals, policy enacted to educate them, and the practices we observe in schools. What these 10 years have taught us is that this dissonance only exists when the students are those who are minoritized and excluded from social and educational opportunities. We are not ignorant about the assets that bilingualism can bring in a globalized world. But this privilege seems to be granted only to those whom political and educational institutions really want to educate well—White, middle-class, English-speaking monolinguals. Minoritized emergent bilinguals continue to experience the educational inequities that we identify in this book. We write this second edition hoping that our work will raise awareness of the inequities in which emergent bilinguals are educated. And we write hoping that educators develop *the will* to change, transform, and imagine the possibilities.

—Ofelia García, The Graduate Center, CUNY
Jo Anne Kleifgen, Teachers College, Columbia University

CHAPTER 1

Introduction

> There is no equality of treatment merely by providing students with the same facilities, textbooks, teachers, and curriculum; for students who do not understand English are effectively foreclosed from any meaningful education.
>
> —*Lau v. Nichols*, 1974

This introductory chapter:

- Discusses the labels used for students who are not yet proficient in English and advocates for using the term *emergent bilingual,*
- Gives reasons why thinking of students as emergent bilinguals can result in a more equitable education for these students, and
- Provides an overview of the book.

EMERGENT BILINGUALS

One of the most misunderstood issues in prekindergarten to 12th-grade education today is how to educate students who are not deemed proficient in English. These students are often called English language learners (ELLs) or, as in the 2015 Every Student Succeeds Act (ESSA), simply English learners (ELs). Before 2015, the federal government referred to these students as limited English proficient (LEP). The designation refers to students who speak a language other than English and are acquiring English in school. Although local and state education agencies may use different definitions (see Chapter 2), the official definition in ESSA is of students "ages 3–21, enrolled in elementary or secondary education, born outside of the United States or speaking a language other than English in their homes, and not having sufficient mastery of English *to meet state standards and excel in an English-language classroom*" (Title III, Elementary and Secondary Education Act [ESEA], as cited in National Research Council, 2011, p. 5). No Child Left Behind (NCLB) had described these students as those "whose difficulties in speaking, reading, writing, or understanding the English language

1

may be sufficient to deny the individual the ability to meet the *State's proficient level of achievement on State assessments*" (2001, Sec. 9101[37]; emphasis added). Although the change is subtle and holds the same meaning, it is indicative of the greater emphasis in ESSA on meeting academic standards in English, rather than simply doing well on state standardized tests.

According to 2015 data from the National Assessment of Educational Progress (U.S. Department of Education, 2015c, NAEP), the difference in reading and mathematics performance between students designated as ELs and others is striking. In the 4th grade, the scale score for students designated as ELs was 189, representing a below-basic level in reading, whereas the average scale score of those considered English proficient was 226, representing almost a proficiency level in reading (a difference of 37 points). In the 8th grade, the scale score for ELs was 223, whereas for English proficient students it was 268 (a difference of 45 points). In mathematics, 4th-grade ELs had a scale score of 218, representing basic proficiency; those who were considered English proficient had a 243 average scale score, representing proficiency level (a difference of 25 points). All 8th-graders did more poorly in math, with ELs having a 246 average scale score, representing below-basic proficiency in math, whereas those considered proficient in English had a 284 average scale score, approaching the proficiency mark, but not quite (a difference of 38 points). Although many have sounded a voice of alarm over the scores for ELs, we have to remember that those who are learning English are being assessed in English only—that is, they are prohibited from using most of their language repertoire. It should not surprise us, then, that only 4% of 8th-grade students who are designated as ELs were seen as having achieved grade-level proficiency in reading, and 6% in math (U.S. Department of Education, 2015c). These percentages have remained the same since 2007, when Batalova, Fix, and Murray (2007) reported that only a very small percentage of these students in the 8th grade was proficient in reading (4%) and in math (6%).

Students designated as English learners are also not graduating in proportionately the same numbers as those who are English proficient. The 4-year national graduation rate for the class of 2014 was 82%, whereas for ELs the rate was 62.6%, a slight increase over the past, but trailing other groups, including students with disabilities and students from low-income families (EDFacts, 2015). Many educators and scholars blame two factors for the low graduation rate. On the one hand, some argue that students learning English require more than 4 years to use English in ways required in school assessments. In fact, many educators argue that some may need 6 years to pass assessments given in English. On the other hand, some scholars blame the English language skills-based curriculum, often used to educate English learners, for their poor performance (Callahan, 2016).

Referring to these students as English language learners (ELLs) or English learners (ELs)—as many school district officials and educators presently do—signals the omission of an idea that is critical to the discussion of equity in the teaching of these students.

English learners are, in fact, *emergent bilinguals.*[1] That is, through school and through acquiring English, these students become *bilingual*, able to continue to function with their home language practices,[2] as well as in English—the new language practices that they acquire in school. The home language is a significant educational resource for these students as they develop their English for academic purposes. When officials and educators ignore the bilingualism that these students can and must develop through schooling in the United States, they perpetuate inequities in the education of these students. That is, they discount the linguistic and cultural practices and understandings of these students and assume that their educational needs are the same as those of a monolingual child. Or they assume that these students are inferior and need a remedial English language, skills-based education, thus robbing them of meaningful academic content and of ways to use their entire language repertoire to make meaning.

There is little agreement about what name best describes these students. In addition to the terms *limited English proficient* (LEP), *English language learner* (ELL), and *English learner* (EL), students who are acquiring English in the nation's schools are also variously referred to in the literature as *culturally and linguistically diverse* (CLD), students with *English Language Communication Barriers* (ELCB), *English as a Second Language* (ESL) students, *language minority* (LM), *language minoritized, dual language learner*, or *bilingual/multilingual learner.* Each label has different connotations and most are problematic.

Critics of the LEP label used formerly by the federal government argued convincingly that it focuses on the students' limitations rather than their potential. The terms CLD and LM students can also include culturally and linguistically different minority students who are already bilingual, although the language-minority (LM) label may better offer a legal basis for rights and accommodations (May, 2011). The recent use of the term *language minoritized* (used without abbreviation in critical scholarship of bilingualism) points to the power of language-majority groups over those they deem inferior, and resists a categorization of "minority." English as a Second Language (ESL) refers to a subject and not to people; also, this label does not encompass students for whom English is a third or fourth language. Furthermore, to tell students that they are learners or speakers of English as a Second Language robs them of the opportunity to appropriate "English" features as part of their very own linguistic repertoire.

Since 2010, the term *dual language learner* (DLL) has gained much currency. This has to do first and foremost with the silencing of the term *bilingual* in the United States since the late 1990s (for more on this history, see especially Crawford, 2007; see also Chapter 3, this volume). It also has to do with the rise of what in the United States are increasingly called "dual-language" programs, bilingual programs that typically teach language-majority and language-minoritized students together. But referring to these students as "dual language learners" constructs them as having two discrete language systems that have to be developed separately, when in fact, as we will see later, bilinguals develop one complex linguistic system that they use at all times to learn.

Recently, the term *dual language learner* has been increasingly used to refer to young learners, under 8 years of age, who are learning English in school while continuing to develop basic proficiency in their home language (Williams, 2015). The Dual Language Learners National Work Group, a group dedicated to raising awareness about very young bilingual learners, reserves the term *English language learner* for those who are older than 8 and who are said to have basic proficiency in their home language (Williams, 2015). Although we applaud the efforts of early childhood educators to bring attention to the capacities of very young emergent bilinguals, we take exception with the unequivocal adoption of the term *DLL* for very young children. Many children entering early childhood educational settings and preschools today are simultaneous bilinguals (see Escamilla et al., 2014), being raised in bilingual and multilingual homes and in communities where more than one language is spoken and heard. The way in which the DLL label has been constructed around very young children leaves out the recognition of the complex bilingualism of those who grow up bilingual from birth, and who also need development and expansion of their entire language repertoire, and not just "dual" languages as if they were two autonomous entities.

The terms *bilingual/multilingual* learner or *multilingual learner* has many advantages over the *English learner* label. Identifying students as bilingual/multilingual learners does not focus on the needs of these students to learn English. Instead, it celebrates these students for their bilingual/multilingual capacities.

State and local educational authorities prefer the term *English language learner* (ELL) or *English learner* (EL) because these are protected labels. That is, once students are given this label, their English learning needs are recognized and funds are allotted to their education. But the ELL/EL label has serious limitations: It devalues other languages and puts the English language in a sole position of legitimacy. It also focuses solely on the development of what is referred to as "academic English," ignoring other parts of students' language and education.

We prefer, and use here, the term *emergent bilingual* because it has become obvious to us that much educational inequity is derived from obfuscating the fact that a meaningful education will not only turn these English learners into English proficient students, but more significantly, into bilingual and multilingual students and adults. *Emergent bilingual* most accurately indexes the type of student who is the object of our attention—those whose bilingualism is still emerging.

WHAT'S IN A NAME?

Thinking of these students as emergent bilinguals has important consequences not only for them, but also for teachers, policymakers, parents, the language education profession, and U.S. society at large (García, 2009b). The use of the term *emergent bilinguals* allows us to imagine a different scenario. Instead of being regarded as "limited" in some way or as mere "learners of English," as the terms *limited English proficient* or *English language learner/English learner* suggest, students are seen instead for their potential to become bilingual or even multilingual. Their emergent bilingualism begins to be recognized as a cognitive, social, and educational resource to be leveraged, which is consistent with research on this topic (see Chapter 4).

For teachers, working with these students as emergent bilinguals means holding higher expectations of them rather than simply remediating their limitations and focusing on their English learning. In recognizing the emergent bilingualism of students, educators are building on their strengths—their linguistic and cultural practices. They are thereby making positive use of the students' home language and bilingual practices, rather than suppressing or ignoring them.

In naming these students as emergent bilinguals, policymakers can begin to require a more rigorous curriculum and more challenging instructional material for them and recognize that language development takes time. Educational policymakers become more patient, understanding that, as research has clearly shown, it takes students 5 to 7 years to develop features of what is considered an additional language.[3] And, it becomes easier to demand that assessment be valid for *all* bilinguals. A more flexible norm can then be adopted that includes all students along a bilingual continuum, instead of insisting on a rigid monolingual standard.

The term *emergent bilingual* recognizes the fact that our linguistic performances are always emerging, depending on the task that we are asked to perform. Our linguistic performances are never done, completed, finished. Teachers of emergent bilingual students are thus challenged to provide rich affordances that will encourage students to use suitable language features to perform academic tasks for a particular audience.

Giving emergent bilinguals a name that does not focus on their limitations means that their family and community language practices are seen as an educational resource. Instead of assigning blame to parents and community for language practices that may not include English, the school can begin to see the parents and community as the experts in the students' linguistic and cultural practices, which are the basis of all learning. As a result, family and community members will be able to participate in the education of their students from a position of strength, not from a position of limitations.

The language education profession is presently compartmentalized in ways that do not support the holistic education of students. Focusing on students' emergent bilingualism/multilingualism facilitates the integration of four approaches to language education that presently exist separately in the United States—the teaching of English to speakers of other languages (TESOL), bilingual education (BE), the teaching of the heritage language (HL), and the teaching of a foreign language (FL). As a result of a more unifying focus, teaching begins to be centered on *the students* rather than on a profession or on a curriculum.

Finally, we know that bilingual practices in the 21st century are more important than ever, and thus important for U.S. society. It is clear that having flexible language practices, being able to use language bilingually in ways described by many scholars as *translanguaging* (García, 2009a; see also García & Wei, 2014, and Chapter 4, this volume), can become an important resource for all in the future. The linguistic resources of the United States have never been greater. Despite the insistence on being identified as a monolingual nation-state, the United States has perhaps the world's most complex multilingual practices. The benefits of harnessing the lived multilingualism of Americans are more evident than ever.

THIS BOOK

The central idea that we present in this book is that there is a growing dissonance between *research* on the education of minoritized emergent bilinguals, *policy* enacted to educate them, and the *practices* we observe in schools. Whereas research has consistently shown the importance of building on students' home language practices as they develop ways of using English, whether in ESL instruction or bilingual education,[4] U.S. educational policy has often ignored these research findings. In fact, in recent years in the United States—as we explain below—educational policy toward minoritized emergent bilinguals has become more rigid, embodying a view of these students solely from a deficit perspective and increasingly demanding that English alone be used in their education. It is interesting to note, however, that language-majority families have had a growing interest in making their children bilingual, accounting for the growth of immersion programs in languages other than English, as well as two-way dual-language bilingual education programs where language-majority students participate. This book focuses on emergent bilingual students who because of race, poverty, immigration status, and English language proficiency are subjected to an impoverished education that contradicts research on language acquisition, bilingualism, and learning in general.

Educators, who are closer to the ground than many policymakers and researchers, are often caught in the middle of the dissonance between research, policy, and the immediacy of having to educate emergent bilinguals. As a result, educators' teaching practices sometimes suffer as they strive to find alternative ways of acting on top-down national and local educational policies that are plainly misguided for the education of these students. This frequent incompatibility between research, policy, and teaching practice is responsible for much of the miseducation of emergent bilinguals in the United States and their failure in school.

Chapter 2 in this book characterizes the students who are the subject of our attention: emergent bilinguals. We raise questions regarding the ways in which demographic data on these students are collected at state and national levels and used to identify them for educational purposes. Chapter 3 briefly reviews the policies and practices targeted toward this group of students that have been developed over the past 50 years. We then turn to the chapters of the book that include theoretical constructs, empirical evidence, and practices related to what we think are the five most important aspects of the education of emergent bilinguals—language and literacy considerations (Chapters 4 and 5); multimodalities, digital technologies, and learning (Chapter 6); curriculum and pedagogy (Chapter 7); family and community engagement (Chapter 8); and assessment (Chapter 9). The objective of these chapters is to expose the educational inequities that directly affect the education of emergent bilinguals and to provide descriptions of alternative practices that alleviate these injustices. Most of the inequities stem from policymakers' and often educators' lack of understanding of bilingualism/multilingualism itself. Thus, we will discuss how misunderstandings of the nature of bilingualism have educational equity consequences for some of the most disadvantaged students. Finally, Chapter 10 offers recommendations for advocates, policymakers, educators, and researchers.

STUDY QUESTIONS

1. Discuss some of the issues that emerge from the different labels that have been assigned to students who are developing English proficiency in schools.

2. What are the reasons why García and Kleifgen name these students emergent bilinguals? Discuss how using this term affects students, teachers, policymakers, parents, the language education profession, and U.S. society.

3. What is the central idea in this book?

CHAPTER 2

Who Are the Emergent Bilinguals?

This chapter provides background information on emergent bilinguals. Specifically, the chapter asks the following key questions:

- How do we know who they are?
- How many are there?
- How are they designated?
- How are they reclassified?
- Where do they live and go to school?
- What languages do they speak?
- What are their demographic characteristics with respect to:
  - ➢ Ethnicity/race and socioeconomic status,
  - ➢ Age distribution and access to pre-K programs, and
  - ➢ Nativity?
- How do they use language?
- Who are the Latinx students?
- What do all emergent bilinguals have in common?

In this chapter, we address the issue of how students are identified, counted, and designated as English learners, as we elucidate their sociolinguistic characteristics. The chapter also brings to the forefront the mismatch between the policy that dictates how data on their characteristics are collected and considered, the reality of the students themselves, and what research tells us about how best to educate emergent bilingual students. In other words, the dissonance between the research and the policies and practices enacted, which is the central theme of this book, begins with descriptive data that have shaped the way these students are defined. As we consider the data, we will point out these contradictions.

HOW DO WE KNOW WHO THEY ARE?

Part of the difficulty in understanding the characteristics of emergent bilinguals results from the great inconsistency in the data that purport to describe them. Primary data on students needing services are collected using a variety of measures across different states. As we will see, states use different assessments for the identification of emergent bilinguals, sometimes measuring different abilities. The federal government, in its most recent legislation (ESSA, 2015), has not resolved the inconsistencies in the data.

HOW MANY EMERGENT BILINGUALS ARE THERE?

However inaccurately these students are counted, we do know that the numbers of emergent bilinguals are increasing and growing much more rapidly than is the English-speaking student population. Between 1995 and 2005, the enrollment of emergent bilinguals in public schools nationwide grew by 56%, whereas the entire student population grew by only 2.6% (Batalova et al., 2007). Although the total enrollment of students has remained flat, the number of emergent bilinguals continues to increase (Batalova & McHugh, 2010).

Table 2.1 shows the growth of this population between 2008 and 2014, according to data gathered by the U.S. Department of Education, National Center for Education Statistics (2015e). One out of 10 students in the United States is an emergent bilingual, accounting for 4,929,989 students.

The large number of emergent bilinguals is consistent despite the different methods used to identify these students. For instance, the U.S. census provides information about the number of students between the ages of 5 and 17 who speak a language other than English (LOTE) at home. The census also asks families who report that they speak a LOTE at home to indicate their ability to speak English as either "very well," "well," "not well," or "not at all." Students who live in households where English is spoken less than "very well" are considered eligible for English language support. Table 2.2 indicates the number of 5- to 17-year-olds who speak

Table 2.1. Emergent bilingual students (EBLs in table) enrolled in public and elementary U.S. schools

Year	# of EBL students	% of EBL students as % of total enrollment
2008–2009	4,685,746	9.7%
2009–2010	4,647,016	9.7%
2011–2012	4,635,185	9.6%
2012–2013	4,850,293	10.0%
2013–2014	4,929,989	10.1%

Source: U.S. Department of Education. NCES. 2015e, Table 204.27.

languages other than English at home, as well as the number who live in families that speak English less than "very well."

According to the American Community Survey (ACS) of the U.S. Census Bureau (2014), there were 2.4 million 5- to 17-year-old emergent bilinguals in 2014; in contrast, the states reported a total of 4,929,989 million ELLs for the same year. This discrepancy has to do with the fact that the Census Bureau relies on self-reports and asks only whether or not students speak English, but not whether they can read and write English. In addition, the census undercounts the undocumented population, which the states are more likely to count because they collect their data through the schools themselves.

But Table 2.2 tells an even more interesting story. It is important to note that, although the percentage of youths who speak languages other than English at home is increasing (21.9% in 2014 compared to 20.5% in 2008 and 8.5% in 1979), the percentage of LOTE speakers who are also emergent bilinguals is decreasing (17.7% in 2014 compared to 24.7% in

Table 2.2. Speakers of LOTEs and emergent bilinguals (EBLs in table), 5 to 17 years old

Year	Total 5–17 yrs*	No. Speakers of LOTEs*	% Total Speakers of LOTEs	No. EBLs**	% Total who are EBLs***	% Speakers of LOTEs who are identified as EBLs
1979	44.7	3.8	8.5%	1.3	2.8%	34.2%
1989	42.3	5.2	12.3%	1.8	4.3%	34.6%
1995	47.5	6.7	14.1%	2.4	5.2%	35.8%
2000	52.5	9.5	18.1%	2.9	5.5%	30.5%
2004	52.9	9.9	18.8%	2.8	5.3%	27.9%
2008	53.0	10.9	20.5%	2.7	5.1%	24.7%
2014	53.8	11.8	21.9%	2.4	3.9%	17.7%

* Numbers are given in the millions.

** Emergent bilinguals here are those designated by the federal government as English learners. They are those who speak languages other than English at home, and speak English less than very well.

*** This number represents the number of English learners in the entire population.

Sources: U.S. Census Bureau, 1979, 1989, 1995, 2005; U.S. Department of Education, National Center for Education Statistics, 2006; U.S. Census Bureau (ACS, 2008); U.S. Census Bureau (ACS, 2014).

2008 and 34.2% in 1979). That is, there is a rise in the number of *bilingual* students who are both speakers of other languages and also fluent speakers of English.

In fact, as Table 2.3 shows, the increase in the number of bilingual students who are proficient in both English and another language in the U.S. school population has been considerable. From 1979 to 2008, while the number of LOTE students who spoke English less than very well increased by 107% (from 1.3 million to 2.7 million), the number who were proficient in English, and thus considered fluent bilinguals, increased by 220% (from 2.5 million to 8.1 million). The increase in the number of emergent bilingual students from 1979 to 2014 was 85%. But during the same period, the number of fluent bilingual students increased by 292%.

Certainly, the growth in the number of bilingual English proficient students is greater than that of emergent bilinguals, making bilingualism a central educational topic for teachers of *all* U.S. students, not just those who are learning English, since nearly one out of every four students in the U.S. speaks a language other than English at home.

Although the growing bilingual student population is an important resource in a globalized world, our focus in this book is on minoritized emergent bilinguals because they are the students who need the most support from the educational system. We warn, however, as García (2006b) noted, that English learners are "only the tail of the elephant"—2.4 million of the 11.8 million bilingual and multilingual U.S. students in 2014. When educators and policymakers use the term *bilingual students* to refer only to the elephant's tail, or those students who are not yet proficient in English, they lose sight of the incredible potential of the millions of multilingual students in this country. Focusing narrowly on the beginning points of the bilingual continuum blinds them to the strength and potential of bilingualism. This makes all bilingualism suspect for policy and practice, when,

Table 2.3. Speakers of LOTEs, both emergent bilinguals and fluent bilinguals, 5 to 17 years old

LOTE Speakers	1979	2008	2014	% Change 1979 to 2014
Emergent bilinguals	1.3*	2.7	2.4	85%
Fluent bilinguals	2.5	8.1	9.4	292%
Total speakers of LOTE	3.8	10.8	11.8	

*Numbers are given in the millions.

Sources: U.S. Census Bureau (1979); U.S. Census Bureau (ACS, 2008, 2014).

instead, being bilingual/multilingual is becoming the norm for students in an increasingly multilingual United States.

HOW ARE THEY DESIGNATED?

The question of how many emergent bilinguals there are has to do with the ways in which they are designated and then reclassified as a specific category of student. Unlike other categories of identification such as ethnicity, race, and gender, the English learner (EL) classification is fluid—that is, students move in and out of being classified according to their progress. And we emphasize that being classified as an English learner or reclassified as a "fluent English speaker" is based on a cutoff score that sometimes has little relationship to the actual academic performances of these students in school tasks.

Since the 1970s, based on federal civil rights legislation and federal case law, states have had to identify emergent bilinguals and ensure that their schools serve them (Linquanti, 2001). Guidance from the U.S. Departments of Education and Justice in January 2015 reminded schools of their obligation to "identify English learner students in a timely, valid and reliable manner" (U.S. Department of Education, 2015b). ESSA requires that emergent bilinguals be identified 30 days after the beginning of a school year, or 2 weeks after enrollment if students enter during the school year. But the criteria used to identify emergent bilinguals continue to vary by state and sometimes even by districts within a state (Linquanti & Cook, 2013; Zehler, Fleischman, Hopstock, Stephenson, Pendizick, & Sapru, 2003).

Because so many studies have pointed to the variations across states in ways of identifying those classified as English learners, the U.S. Department of Justice Civil Rights Division and the U.S. Department of Education Office for Civil Rights (2015b) published a set of guidelines to ensure the adequacy of identification and classification. In addition, also in 2015, the U.S. Department of Education's National Center for English Language Acquisition (NCELA) published an "English Learner Toolkit," providing guidance on how to identify English learners (U.S. Department of Education, 2015a).

An initial step in identifying students as ELs usually takes place when students first register for a new school: They are given a *home language survey*, which contains questions for students' parents or guardians about the language used at home by students and others. But as Bailey and Kelly (2013) have demonstrated, states vary in what is asked in the home language survey. Almost half the states have a single form and mandate its use in schools statewide; other states, however, allow school districts to create their own surveys.

Home language surveys tend to view bilingualism through a monolingual lens and ignore the complexity of linguistic practices of multilingual populations. For example, many states' and schools' home language surveys ask which was the first language the student learned, ignoring the fact that many students are simultaneous bilinguals, growing up in homes with complex language practices where members of families use their multilingual repertoire flexibly. The surveys also often ask which language is spoken to the child in the home, overlooking the bilingual/multilingual practices of parents and caregivers when interacting with one another and their children.

Moreover, because of the monolingual bias in many states' home language surveys and the stigmatization that often follows a student's designation as an English learner, many bilingual parents hide their bilingualism, refusing to acknowledge their home bilingual practices. The construction of inferiority that accompanies being categorized as an emergent bilingual in many schools means that some parents prefer to say that the child only speaks English. Only by changing the negative perception in which speakers of languages other than English are held will schools be able to offer beneficial instruction by building on students' bilingual capacities.

Students identified by the home language survey as potentially needing services are then referred for an English language proficiency assessment (Linquanti & Bailey, 2014). According to a report by the National Research Council (NRC, 2011), more than half the states use a screener/placement test for identification as English learner. Of these, the majority use the screener test for designation called the Access Placement Test (W-APT). Some states, however, use their own screening assessment. At the time of this writing, California, for example, uses the California English Language Development Test (CELDT). New York has developed the New York State Identification Test for English language learners (NYSITELL). Still other states provide their school districts with a list of tests from which the districts can select (Linquanti & Cook, 2013). The NRC's (2011) report concludes the section on the identification of English learners by saying:

> Because of the differing state policies, practices, and criteria for initially identifying students as linguistic minority and for classifying them as an English language learner (ELL), individuals who are classified as ELL students in one state may not be classified as ELL students in another. In states that permit local control, students classified as ELL in one district may not be classified as ELL in another district in that state. (p. 86)

School districts classify students as English learners through a combination of information on the home language survey and formal assessment/screening.

HOW ARE THEY RECLASSIFIED?

Equally important to the question of how many students are designated as emergent bilinguals in U.S. public schools is the question of how these students get reclassified as English proficient. Even though *language proficiency* should be the focus for designation as English learner, *academic achievement in English* is key to students' reclassification as English proficient (Linquanti, 2001). This means that the assessment used for the reclassification process should be much more complex because multiple dimensions of communicative competence have to be considered (Bachman, 2001; Canale & Swain, 1980). In other words, to be reclassified, students must not only be able to comprehend and communicate effectively, but also do cognitively demanding work in the content areas at the appropriate grade level in English (Bachman, 2002; Linquanti, 2001).

One of the advances toward the educational equity of emergent bilinguals made since No Child Left Behind (more in Chapter 3) has been the requirement that states develop English language proficiency standards for emergent bilinguals, as well as an assessment instrument aligned to these standards that measure listening, speaking, reading, writing, and comprehension. In addition, grants have been made available to develop, validate, and implement such assessments. As a result, the states' English language proficiency tests used in reclassification of students have improved dramatically.

Furthermore, the Common Core State Standards (CCSS) in English language arts and mathematics released in 2010 (more on this in Chapter 3) have led to efforts to develop standards for English learners, as well as assessment systems. The states that make up the largest consortium, called WIDA (no longer an acronym),[1] use WIDA's standards-based, criterion-referenced English language proficiency test for reclassification (Assessing Comprehension and Communication in English State-to-State, ACCESS for ELLs 2.0). WIDA is in the process of building a comprehensive and balanced technology-based assessment system for English language learners. The other smaller consortium of states is ELPA21[2] (English Language Proficiency Assessment for the 21st Century). ELPA21's assessment system consists of a screener to assess baseline English language proficiency, as well as a summative assessment.

Some states have not joined consortia as of 2017 and use other English proficiency tests. In 2016, some of the "big states" with large numbers of emergent bilinguals used their own assessments for English language proficiency: California—California English Language Development Test (CELDT); Texas—Texas English Language Proficiency Assessment (TELPAS); New York—New York State English as a Second Language Achievement Test (NYSESLAT); and Arizona—Arizona English Language Learner Assessment (AZELLA).

Not all tests focus on the same skill domains or weigh each skill domain equally. For example, California's CELDT assigns equal weights to listening, speaking, reading, and writing. However, ACCESS for ELLs weighs its overall composite in favor of literacy. As a result, students reclassified in one state would not be considered reclassified in another state.

On average, emergent bilinguals are reclassified 3 years after school entry, in 2nd grade (Slama, 2014). Reclassification rates are lowest in kindergarten through 2nd grade as well as in grade 9, when many emergent bilinguals first enter the school system.

An important finding is that Spanish-speaking emergent bilinguals are reclassified at half the rate of those who speak other languages, even after controlling for income (Slama, 2014). That is, emergent bilinguals who speak Spanish are twice as likely as those who speak other languages to remain categorized as English learners. There may be many reasons why this is so, but it might be important to consider causes that have to do with what some scholars call *raciolinguistic ideologies* (see Alim, Rickford, & Ball, 2016; Flores & Rosa, 2015). The field of raciolinguistic ideologies explores how language and race have been mutually constitutive, with language used to construct race, and ideas about race being shaped by language. In the United States, Spanish-speaking students have traditionally been considered non-White. The Spanish language has been used often as a proxy for race, a way to segregate and exclude the minoritized Spanish-speaking students from rich educational opportunities.

Reclassification of English learners is as problematic as identification. On the whole, reclassification criteria are left up to states and school districts, although they must be based on test scores. But as we have seen, assessment systems differ widely.

WHERE DO THEY LIVE AND GO TO SCHOOL?

Eight states accounted for more than two-thirds of the emergent bilingual population in the United States in 2012–2013: California, Texas, Florida, New York, Illinois, Colorado, Washington, and North Carolina. Table 2.4 gives the number of public school emergent bilinguals in 2012–2013 in these eight states, as well as the percentage of students they represent.

Emergent bilingual students make up a large proportion of the total pre-K to 12 population in several other states, even if their actual numbers are not as large as in these eight states. After California, where 24.5% of the total school enrollment is designated as English learners, schools in New Mexico (18%) and Nevada (17%) have the greatest *proportion* of students categorized as English learners. They are followed by Texas (15.1%), Colorado (13%), and Alaska (11.3%) (Kena et al., 2016; Ruiz Soto, Hooker, & Batalova, 2015a).

However, the greatest *growth* in the number of students who are developing English proficiency in the past decade has been clearly outside all

Table 2.4. Number of public school emergent bilinguals (EBLs in table),
2012–2013

State	Number	% of EBLs among students
California	1,571,772	24.5%
Texas	773,732	15.2%
Florida	277,802	10.3%
New York	237,499	8.8%
Illinois	190,172	9.3%
Colorado	114,415	13.3%
Washington	107,307	10.2%
No. Carolina	102,311	6.8%

Source: Ruiz Soto, Hooker, & Batalova, 2015a.

these states, in a new set of southeastern and midwestern states. South Carolina experienced an 800% growth in its emergent bilingual population from the period between1997–1998 and 2007–2008, and Indiana experienced a 400% growth during the same period. From 2004 to 2014, four states had an increase of more than 200% of emergent bilinguals—Louisiana, Maryland, Michigan, and West Virginia (Gil, 2016). Other states with recent dramatic growth include Alabama, Arkansas, Delaware, Georgia, Kentucky, Nevada, North Carolina, Ohio, Tennessee, and Virginia (Batalova & McHugh, 2010).

Emergent bilinguals overwhelmingly attend urban schools. In 2012–2013, the Los Angeles Unified School District had the largest population of emergent bilinguals (152,592), closely followed by New York City (142,572) (Ruiz Soto et al., 2015a). However, percentage-wise, the Santa Ana Unified District had the highest proportion of emergent bilinguals in the nation (56.2%), and three other school districts in California had an over 30% emergent bilingual population—Garden Grove Unified (43.2%), San Bernardino City Unified (32.3%), and San Francisco Unified (30.3%). The other two school districts that had over 30% emergent bilinguals in their schools were Dallas Independent (36.0%) and School District 1 in Denver (31.4%) (Ruiz Soto et al., 2015a, 2015b).

Despite the spread of emergent bilinguals across the United States, they seem to be concentrated in fewer than half the school districts in the country. In 2005, nearly 70% of all emergent bilingual students were enrolled in 10% of elementary schools (De Cohen, Deterding, & Chu Clewell, 2005). Further, school districts that have more than 5,000 emergent bilinguals enroll 54% of all English learners in grades K to 12 (Zehler et al., 2003). This points to the high degree of racial and linguistic segregation in the United States (Orfield & Frankenberg, 2014). De Cohen et al. (2005) report that nearly 70% of emergent bilinguals in elementary grades are enrolled, on average, in just 10% of the public schools in a metropolitan area.

As a result of this residential segregation, the majority of emergent bilinguals—53%—go to schools where more than 30% of their peers are also emergent bilinguals (Fix & Passel, 2003). In contrast, 57% of students who are English proficient attend schools where less than 1% of all students are emergent bilinguals (Van Hook & Fix, 2000). Thus, emergent bilinguals often attend schools with others who, like them, speak little English. The level of linguistic segregation in the United States has risen steadily (Arias, 2007; Carnock & Ege, 2015).

WHAT LANGUAGES DO THEY SPEAK?

Emergent bilinguals in the United States are speakers of many different languages, although Spanish remains by far the language spoken by the highest number of them. Estimates of the percentage of emergent bilingual students who speak Spanish at home range from 70% (according to the 2014 American Community Survey) to 76.5% or 3,770,816 Spanish speakers who are emergent bilingual students (U.S. DOE, NCES, 2015d).

Table 2.5 provides the distribution of the languages other than English spoken by students in the United States, including those who are emergent bilinguals, according to calculations from the U.S. Census[3] (U.S. Census Bureau, ACS, 2014). It shows the number of youth who speak a language other than English at home, as well as those who speak English less than very well and are considered emergent bilinguals. The table also shows the percentage of emergent bilinguals speaking a given language group compared to others. In addition, the last column of the table shows the percentages within each language group who are emergent bilinguals.

Despite the fact that the greatest proportion of emergent bilinguals as shown in Table 2.5 is Spanish speaking (70%), it is important to point out that, proportionately, Spanish-speaking youth are *not* less proficient in English than Asians. In fact, the proportion of speakers of Asian/Pacific languages who are emergent bilinguals (26%) is greater than that of the Spanish-speaking group (20%).

After Spanish, and based on the 2013–2014 state reports of who their emergent bilinguals are and what their commonly reported home languages are (U.S. Department of Education, NCES, 2015d), the most common language spoken by emergent bilinguals in 2013–2014 was Arabic, spoken at home by 2.2% of all emergent bilinguals (109,170 students). Chinese followed as the third most spoken language by emergent bilinguals (107,825 or 2.2%), although this category includes speakers of Mandarin, Cantonese, and other Chinese languages, such as Fuzhounese, Wu, and Taiwanese Hokkien. Interestingly enough, a year later, 2014–2015, Chinese (97,117)

Table 2.5. Numbers and percentages of languages spoken by emergent
bilinguals (EBLs in table), 5 to 17 years old

Language group	Number of LOTE speakers	Number of EBLs	% of all EBLs	% of EBLs within language group
Spanish	8,520,957	1,687,451	70.2%	20%
Indo-European[4]	1,467,490	284,297	11.8%	19%
Asian/Pacific[5]	1,270,332	324,440	13.5%	26%
Other	529,975	106,637	4.5%	20%
Total	11,788,754	2,402,825	100.00%	

Source: U.S. Census Bureau, American Community Survey, 2014, 1-year estimate,
TABLE B1604.

had surpassed Arabic (96,572). This change might reflect changes in immigration patterns, with fewer Arabic speakers entering the United States and with more leaving after September 11, 2001.

A surprising result in the 2013–2014 data for reported home languages of English learners in schools is that English is the fourth most common reported home language of English learners (91,669 students). The U.S. Department of Education attributes this to "students who live in multilingual households and students adopted from other countries who speak English at home but also have been raised speaking another language" (U.S. Department of Education, NCES, 2015e, Table 204.27, Footnote 3). However, this is another indication that many emergent bilingual students increasingly are speaking English at home, as well. It also accounts for the change in immigration that has brought many bilingual English-speaking students from Africa and Asia to the United States. This points to the growing complexity of language use, including the use of English, that we describe in subsequent chapters.

After Spanish, Arabic, Chinese, and English, the most common home language for emergent bilinguals is Vietnamese (89,705 in 2013–2014, and 75,529 in 2014–2015). The languages that follow, all having between 20,000 and 25,000 speakers, are Haitian Creole, Hmong, Somali, and Tagalog. (U.S. Department of Education, NCES, 2015d; Office of English Language Acquisition [OELA], 2017).

Spanish is the leading language of emergent bilinguals in all but five states, where other languages dominate: Alaska (Yup'ik), Hawai'i (Ilokano), Maine (Somali), Montana (German), and Vermont (Nepali) (Ruiz Soto et al., 2015b). Maine and Vermont have large settlements of Somali and Nepali refugees. Yup'ik is a major indigenous language in Alaska. Ilokano is the language spoken among most Filipino immigrants to Hawai'i. Most surprisingly, the variety of German spoken by the Hutterites, a religious group in Montana, is the leading home language of emergent bilinguals in that state.

WHAT ARE THEIR DEMOGRAPHIC CHARACTERISTICS?

Ethnicity/Race and Socioeconomic Status

When we look at racial/ethnic classifications according to the categories of the U.S. Census,[6] emergent bilinguals are overwhelmingly Hispanic or Latino (78.1%). Asians account for 10.6% of the emergent bilingual population, whereas Whites account for 5.8% and Blacks for 3.5%. There are many emergent bilinguals who are categorized in the census as American Indians and Pacific Islanders, although their numbers pale in comparison with those of the other racial/ethnic categories. The growing proportion of emergent bilinguals who are of two or more races points to the greater number of racially and linguistically mixed families in the United States. Table 2.6 presents the ethnic/racial characteristics of emergent bilingual students in 2014.

Although the percentages of each racial/ethnic category have not shifted much over the past decade, there is much more racial and linguistic

Table 2.6. Emergent bilinguals in public schools, by race/ethnicity

Race	Number of EBLs	% of total
Hispanic	3,648,211	78.14%
Asian	496,359	10.63%
White	270,854	5.80%
Black	163,588	3.50%
American Indian*	45,687	.098%
Pacific Islander	25,616	.055%
Two or more races	28,445	.061%

*Figures for fall 2014 (includes students from Bureau of Indian Education Schools).

Sources: Taken from U.S. Department of Education, National Center for Education Statistics, 2016. EDFacts file 046, Data Group 123, extracted April 24, 2016, from the EDFacts Data Warehouse (internal U.S. Department of Education source); Common Core of Data (CCD), "State Nonfiscal Survey of Public Elementary and Secondary Education," 2009–10 through 2013–14; and National Elementary and Secondary Enrollment Projection Model, 1972 through 2025. Table 204.25.

heterogeneity among emergent bilinguals than ever, with Brown and Black students predominating. For example, among emergent bilinguals who are counted as French speakers, we now find students from all over West Africa who are multilingual. The Africans arriving in the United States have brought their many languages (and their various multilingual practices), the most numerous being Ibo, Yoruba, Kru, Amharic, Cushite, Swahili, Bantu languages, Fulani, and Mande. And among emergent bilinguals from the Indian subcontinent, we find not only students who speak Hindi and Urdu, but also substantial numbers of speakers of Gujarati, Bengali, Punjabi, Telugu, Malayalam, and Tamil, who are also multilingual. In addition, emergent bilingual students in large numbers are found among Native Americans, especially Navajos (Diné), but also Yup'ik, Keres Pueblo people, Apache, Cherokee, Choctaw, Dakota, and Ojibwa.

Turning now to the socioeconomic characteristics of emergent bilinguals, Zehler and colleagues suggested in 2003 that more than 75% of emergent bilinguals were poor, and they estimated that 54% of the parents of emergent bilinguals had not completed 8 years of schooling. In 2013, Grantmakers for Education noted that 60% of emergent bilinguals in every state live in families whose income falls below 185% of the federal poverty line.

As we noted above, De Cohen et al. (2005) report that nearly 70% of emergent bilinguals are enrolled in only 10% of the schools within a given metropolitan area. These schools are predominantly located in urban poor areas. Their study shows that 72% of students in what they call "high-LEP schools" (schools with a high proportion of limited English proficient students) qualify for free and/or reduced-price school lunches compared to about 40% in "low-LEP schools."[7] Forty percent of the principals at the high-LEP schools in the study by De Cohen et al. (2005) cite poverty as a serious issue and identify student health problems as "serious" or "moderate." In describing schools that have high concentrations of English learners, De Cohen et al. (2005) summarize:

> High-LEP schools are more likely to be located in urban areas and therefore have many characteristics associated with urban schools: larger enrollments; larger class sizes; greater racial and ethnic diversity; higher incidences of student poverty, student health problems, tardiness, absenteeism, and lack of preparation; greater difficulty filling teaching vacancies; greater reliance on unqualified teachers; and lower levels of parent involvement. (p. 19)

Gender, Age Distribution, and Access to Pre-K Programs

According to Office for Civil Rights data (U.S. Department of Education and Office for Civil Rights, 2016), slightly more than half of emergent bilinguals in the nation's schools are males (53%), with just less than half female (47%).

The growing population of emergent bilingual students in the United States is younger than the average K–12 student and thus clustered more in elementary schools. In 2000–2001, for instance, 44% of all emergent bilingual students were in pre-K through grade 3, and only 19% were enrolled at the high school level (Kindler, 2002). In 2001–2002, 70% of emergent bilingual students were in grades pre-K to 5, pointing to the potential of having bilingual citizens if we truly cultivated this aspect of these young students' education (Hopstock & Stephenson, 2003a). Moving higher up in the grades, we find that the number of emergent bilinguals decreases; in the same period, over a quarter (26%) were in grades 4 through 8, and only 14% were in secondary school (grades 9 through 12) (Hopstock & Stephenson, 2003a).

In 2013–2014, the same pattern emerges. In kindergarten, 17.4% of students nationwide were emergent bilinguals. That figure remains fairly constant in the first 3 years of school (17.1% in 1st grade, 16.6% in 2nd grade, 15.0% in 3rd grade). In 4th grade, it drops to 11.9%; in 5th grade to 9.8%; in 9th grade to 6.6%; and by the 12th grade, emergent bilinguals constitute only 4.6% of the graduating class (U.S. Department of Education, 2015a, 2015b).

The drop in the number of emergent bilinguals as we move up the grades reflects two important trends. On the one hand, at the elementary level, the change points to the success of educators in moving emergent bilinguals along the bilingual continuum, so that they can "test out" of the English learner classification. But the reasons for the decline in the numbers of emergent bilinguals in middle school and high school should be interrogated. The decline might reveal the high dropout rate in this age group, as well as the secondary schools' policies of "pushing out" students who might not succeed in the standardized tests and graduation tests that are required so that schools can claim "success." We return to this below.

Finally, although the total number of emergent bilinguals is increasing and more of these students are moving up in the educational pathway, we see evidence that relatively few of these students are getting the kind of head start they need prior to entering school in kindergarten. In 2000–2001, only 1.5% of all emergent bilinguals were in prekindergarten (Kindler, 2002). In 2005, 43% of Hispanic students 3 to 5 years old attended some form of center-based child care or preschool, compared to 59% of White students and 66% of Black students (Education Law Center, 2007; National Task Force on Early Childhood Education for Hispanics, 2007). These numbers suggest that there is a dearth of public preschool programs available for these students and, thus, a disturbing gap exists in the early childhood education of most emergent bilinguals (Ackerman & Tazi, 2015; E. Garcia & Frede, 2010).

In 2011–2012, the Office for Civil Rights reported that of the total 1,390,422 students enrolled in early childhood and prekindergarten education nationwide, a growing percentage was made up of Hispanics or Latinos (29.3%), whereas 43.6% were White and 18.5% were Black. Furthermore, 11.9% of all students in early childhood were labeled English learners. Although there has been progress, young emergent bilinguals are not enrolled in quality early childhood and pre-K programs (Espinosa, 2013a, 2013b). Most are not being provided with the bilingual early childhood experiences that the growing number of very young bilingual Americans need and deserve.

More emergent bilinguals need to be enrolled in educational programs in their prekindergarten years. If there is no funding available for the types of bilingual preschool programs that are most effective at helping the youngest ones achieve an equitable education, then it is no wonder that we often see these same children falling behind as they grow older (E. Garcia & González, 2006; Kindler, 2002; Tazi, 2014).

Nativity

Despite popular perceptions, emergent bilinguals are by no means all immigrants or foreign born. Zong and Batalova (2015a) report that 77% of emergent bilinguals are *U.S. born.* In prekindergarten to 5th grade this proportion is even greater, 85% (Zong & Batalova, 2015b). The high number of American-born children who enter U.S. schools and are designated as English learners points to the greater multilingualism in the United States; American children are increasingly growing up in homes where English is not the only language spoken at home. Bilingualism is not a *foreign* phenomenon. It is an American sociolinguistic reality, chosen by many who see it as important to family and community life. The fact that U.S. schools do not understand the value of bilingualism to families points to how out of touch they are with their communities.

It is important to point out that at the middle and high school level, U.S.-born students still account for 57% of all students designated as ELs (Grantmakers for Education, 2013). This has to do with three factors— the complex nature of immigration and family settlement, the presence of individual disability, and the failure of our school system to meaningfully educate emergent bilinguals.

The complex nature of immigration and families today refers to the fact that, although in the past children born in the United States have grown up in the United States, travel across national borders is currently more frequent. And this is not happening only with migrant rural families. Urban families are increasingly moving back and forth across borders, and their U.S. children often end up being schooled in languages other than English. Additionally, many families send their U.S.-born children to live with grandparents in other countries while they work long hours in the United States. Only when the children are older and able to care for themselves do they return to live with their parents.

Many of the U.S.-born children who remain emergent bilinguals after middle school have language disabilities. Some students who are designated as emergent bilinguals when they enter school are afterward referred for evaluation to receive special education services. Because they have been designated as English learners, they then have to pass the state's exam—which assesses performance in listening, speaking, reading, and writing—for reclassification as English fluent. Despite being quite fluent in English, many students with disabilities cannot be reclassified because of poor scores on exams that have been normed on students without disabilities. Therefore, their designation as English learners travels with them throughout their education.

The failure to provide an equitable, rigorous, and consistent education to emergent bilinguals results in much academic failure. Despite excellent English proficiency, many students are unable to pass English proficiency exams for reclassification because these exams rely heavily on reading and writing skills. The number of students who are designated as English learners for more than 6 years has increased over time, leading to the creation of another subgroup of emergent bilinguals—those known as long-term English learners (Menken & Kleyn, 2009; Menken, Kleyn, & Chae, 2012; Olsen, 2014). They represent one in four of all emergent bilinguals. This points to the failure of the U.S. education system to provide a meaningful and equitable education to these students, often stemming from the system's refusal to see their bilingualism as a resource for learning.

The majority of emergent bilinguals who are born in the United States (77%) are the children of immigrants or have at least one immigrant parent (Zong & Batalova, 2015a, b). Although some may continue to speak languages other than English at home, this fact does not explain why so many others continue to be designated "English learners" when, in fact, they may not speak anything but English.

On the other end of the spectrum are *foreign-born emergent bilinguals.* They vary in the number of years they have been in the United States, but almost three-fourths of all foreign-born English learners have been in the United States for less than 5 years (Zehler et al., 2003). It is difficult to determine the number of foreign-born emergent bilinguals who are children of immigrants, refugees, temporary sojourners,[8] or migrant workers.[9]

Of the 41.3 million immigrants in the United States in 2013, approximately one-fourth (11.4 million) were undocumented. Of those who were documented, approximately half were naturalized citizens and the other half were permanent residents. A total of 2.3 million were refugees or asylum seekers, the majority of whom come from Iraq, Burma, Myanmar, and Bhutan. Finally, 1.5 million had legal temporary status (mostly foreign students and temporary workers) (Zong & Batalova, 2015a). But we know little of how these figures relate to students enrolled in schools.

In 2013, there were 41.3 million immigrants in the United States, the majority of whom were from Latin American countries (46%). Sixty percent of immigrants come from the following countries of origin: Mexico, 28%; India, 5%; China, 5%; Philippines, 4%; Vietnam, 3%; El Salvador, 3%, Cuba, 3%; Korea, 3%; Dominican Republic, 2%; and Guatemala, 2%.

Some foreign-born students, mostly from the middle class, come to the United States from well-resourced schools and often have had some instruction in English. But other foreign-born students come from societies torn by war and poverty, where the educational system has declined or collapsed. Some come from poor rural communities where it has been difficult to go to school consistently. These students, often classified as students with interrupted formal education (SIFE), have minimal literacy in their home language (see Klein & Martohardjono, 2009; Menken & Kleyn, 2009; Menken, Kleyn, & Chae, 2012). For them, achieving proficiency in the ways of using English for academic tasks is a struggle, because they have little familiarity with these tasks.

We know that approximately 1.1 million to 1.6 million students under the age of 18 are undocumented immigrants, and an additional 3 million are native-born U.S. citizens who have undocumented parents (Jensen, 2001; Passel, Capps, & Fix, 2004; Suárez-Orozco, Suárez Orozco, & Todorova, 2008; Zong & Batalova, 2015a). But again, we do not know how many of these students are emergent bilinguals. The education of undocumented students in K–12 classrooms was guaranteed by the Supreme Court in 1982, when it ruled in *Plyler v. Doe* that a K–12 education is a fundamental and protected right that needs to be provided to all students, regardless of citizenship or residency status.

From October 2013 to September 2014, 53,515 unaccompanied minors came into the United States (U.S. Department of Health and Human Services, 2017). The states into which they were released tells the story of the changing demographics of the United States. As expected, Texas received the most unaccompanied minors (7,409) in the same period; New York, California, and Florida each received between 5,955 and 5,445; Virginia and Maryland each received almost 4,000; and New Jersey received 2,680. But states generally not characterized as having a large immigrant population—North Carolina, Georgia, Louisiana, Massachusetts, and Tennessee—received upwards of 1,300 unaccompanied minors. Although the number of accompanied minors dropped to about half in the year that followed, from October 2015 to September 2016, more than 50,000 unaccompanied minors entered the United States.

It is important to understand that, although important, the education of emergent bilinguals is not just about immigrant or refugee education alone. Their education is, in fact, an educational issue that also concerns a large proportion of native-born U.S. citizens, who represent anywhere from half to nearly two-thirds of all emergent bilinguals.

WHAT IS THEIR USE OF LANGUAGE?

Approximately 85% of emergent bilinguals are able to communicate orally in English; however, they have difficulty using English for literacy and for completing academic tasks (Zehler et al., 2003). This is important to keep in mind as we debate whether census figures are reliable in identifying this population. The U.S. Census Bureau only asks families about spoken English, but what is at issue for educational attainment is the ability to complete academic work, which requires written, along with spoken, proficiency. Therefore, relying on census figures may be misleading and may underestimate the population of students who are emergent bilinguals.

Estimates of the percentage of emergent bilinguals who can use their home language in complex academic tasks also vary, but school coordinators think that approximately 39% of these students nationwide have lower levels of literacy in their home language compared to what might be expected of students going to school in a country where it is the language of schooling (Zehler et al., 2003). This fact should be of vital importance to those who coordinate and plan for the education of these students because it turns out that the benefits of what is known as "linguistic transfer" of literacy skills from one language to another will not be completely enjoyed by emergent bilinguals who have not learned literacy practices for academic purposes in their home language.

Linked to the issue of many emergent bilinguals' poor literacy performances with their home language practices is the group of students, most commonly found in secondary school, referred to as students with interrupted formal education (SIFE) or students with limited or interrupted formal education (SLIFE). It has been estimated that between 11% and 20% of emergent bilinguals in middle schools and high schools have missed more than 2 years of schooling since the age of 6 (Ruiz-De-Velasco, Fix, & Clewell, 2000; Zehler et al., 2003). This group also has very high dropout rates, with estimates as high as 75% at the secondary level (Montero, Newmaster, & Ledger, 2014). Furthermore, even students who have consistently attended school in their countries of origin have often learned to use language for literacy purposes that are very different from those literacies required by U.S. schools (Menken, 2013; Yip, 2016; more on this in Chapter 4).

WHO ARE THE LATINX EMERGENT BILINGUALS?

We start by contextualizing our use of the term *Latinx* in this book, when up to now we have used the terms preferred by government agencies and much scholarship—*Latino/a* or *Hispanic*. In 1970, the U.S. census used the term *Hispanic* for the first time, although much of the population of Latin

American origin in the United States preferred the term *Latino/a*. In 1997, the census expanded the category to "Hispanic or Latino origin," legitimizing the use of the word *Latino*. At the same time, a battle was brewing over who was included as Latino and whether the masculine ending "o" was gender normative. The alternatives—*Latino/a* or *Latin@*, introduced by many scholars—were not satisfactory for many because the terms reified the gender binary. In the past decade, the term *Latinx*, a gender-neutral alternative to *Latino*, *Latina*, or *Latin@*, has been increasingly used by scholars and the community to include those who are trans- or gender nonconfirming. Because, for us, the act of naming is important in offering ways of seeing beyond traditional categories of all types, we use the term *Latinx* in this book, except when referring to the work of others.

In 2016, the U.S. Latinx population numbered 58 million, and it is projected that by 2060 that figure will be 119 million. In 2011, Latinx students made up 26% of the country's prekindergarten and kindergarten pupils, 25% of elementary school students, and 21% of high school students (Fry & López, 2012). That is, in 2011, 23.9% of all U.S. students in prekindergarten through 12th grade was of Latinx origin (Fry & López, 2012). In California and Texas, the Latinx school-age population is already about one-half of all students (Gándara & Contreras, 2009), and in 2006, Latinx students in Arizona and New Mexico constituted more than 40% of all public school students. Latinx students also constituted between 20% and 40% of all public schools in five additional states in 2006—Nevada, Colorado, Illinois, Florida, and New York (Fry & Gonzales, 2008). The U.S. Census Bureau has forecasted that Latinx students will make up a third of the nation's 3- to 17-year-old learners by 2036.

Two of the five largest school districts in the country are Los Angeles and Miami Dade County. Seventy-three percent of students in Los Angeles, and 60% of students in Miami Dade County, are of Latinx background (KewalRamani, Gilbertson, Fox, & Provasnik, 2007).

The Latinx population is complex. Almost two-thirds have been born in the United States (64% in 2014), and a little over one-third have been born abroad (35%). Of the Latinx students in K–12 in 2006, 16% were foreign born, and 84% native born (Fry & Gonzales, 2008).

The Latinx group also represents many national origin groups, although almost two-thirds are Mexicans (64%). Regardless of where Latinx people have settled and the sociohistorical circumstances of their settlement, U.S. schools have rarely built upon their funds of knowledge (Moll, Amanti, Neff, & Gonzalez, 1992; see also Chapter 8) or used pedagogy that leverages their cultural practices (Ladson-Billings, 1995; Paris & Alim, 2014; Villegas & Lucas, 2002). Speaking specifically about the importance of leveraging Latinx cultural and linguistic practices in their education, Pedraza and Rivera (2005) use the image of *sankofa*, a Swahili word that refers to going back to the source, and suggest that it is important for Latinx students to explore their "historical, sociocultural and familial traditions and legacies" (p. 234). The education system's lack of attention to Latinx students' sociohistorical context has resulted in these students not faring well in U.S. schools (Gándara & Contreras, 2009).

In 2007, there was a total of more than 7 million Latinx students in U.S. elementary and secondary schools, of which more than 5 million were of Mexican origin. The sheer number of Mexican-origin students makes them the group with the most Spanish-speaking students, as well as the group with the most emergent bilinguals. Mexicans are, however, neither the group that speaks Spanish the most at home nor the group that has the most emergent bilinguals, comparatively speaking. The Latinx national groups with the highest percentages of students who are emergent bilinguals are the following: Honduran (17.3%), Salvadoran (17.1%), Guatemalan (16.7%), Paraguayan (16.7%), Dominican (16.6%), Venezuelan (15.6%), Mexican (13.2%), and Ecuadorean (12.6%) (Office of English Language Acquisition, 2015).

Latinx students make up the overwhelming majority of all emergent bilinguals. In Arizona, Delaware, Kansas, New Mexico, and Texas, over 81% of all emergent bilinguals are Latinx students (Office of English Language Acquisition, 2015). Seventy-seven percent of Latinx emergent bilinguals have been born in the United States (Office of English Language Acquisition, 2015). Among the foreign born, 60% of Spanish-speaking emergent bilinguals were born in Mexico, followed in number by children from South America (14%), Central America (10%), Puerto Rico (8%), and Cuba (2%) (Zehler et al., 2003). These numbers exclude the 6% of Spanish-speaking emergent bilinguals who are said to be from places other than these countries. Of first-generation Mexican K–12 students, almost half, or 47%, are emergent bilinguals (Fix & Passel, 2003).

Latinx immigrant students account for more than half (58%) of all immigrant youth in the United States, and more of these students are in the upper grades than in the lower grades. Although we do not have good data on undocumented immigrant students, we know that many Latinx immigrant students are undocumented or are the children of undocumented immigrants (Capps et al., 2005), since about three-quarters (76%) of undocumented immigrants are of Latinx origin (Passel & Cohn, 2009).

One of the most alarming facts about Latinx emergent bilinguals is that more than 59% end up dropping out of high school; in comparison, only 15% of Latinx students who are proficient bilinguals drop out of high school (Fry, 2003). They mostly attend all-minority schools where over 57% are students like them. Forty-five percent of Latinx emergent bilingual students attend high-poverty schools compared to 8% of White students (Carnock & Ege, 2015). Clearly, practitioners, researchers, and policymakers must redouble their energies toward better serving Latinx students, who constitute the overwhelming proportion of the emergent bilingual population.

EDUCATING EMERGENT BILINGUALS: KNOWING WHO THEY ARE

Despite the differences among emergent bilinguals that we have identified in this chapter, a few generalizations can be gleaned from our prior discussion:

- Their numbers are increasing overall, but so is the number of fluent bilingual students.
- There are discrepancies regarding how they are identified and reclassified among state and local educational authorities.
- Most are poor, Brown, or Black.
- Most live in urban areas and attend underresourced schools that are segregated.
- Three-fourths were born in the United States.
- Although approximately half are in elementary schools, the greatest increase in the number of emergent bilinguals is in high school–age students, although many of them do not graduate.
- There is a dearth of early childhood programs for them, and few are enrolled in school prior to kindergarten.
- Most are of Latinx origin, despite the great linguistic diversity that characterizes this population.

STUDY QUESTIONS

1. Identify some of the contradictions in counting, classifying, and reclassifying emergent bilinguals. What are some of the inconsistencies in the data?

2. Describe the population of emergent bilinguals in the United States. What do all students have in common?

3. Find out who the emergent bilinguals are in your school district. How many are there? What are their characteristics, and what languages do they speak? How have they been counted? What method is used to identify, classify, and reclassify them?

4. Why is bilingualism a vital topic in the education of *all* children in the United States?

CHAPTER 3

Programs and Policies for Educating Emergent Bilinguals[1]

This chapter:

- Considers programs and policies for educating emergent bilinguals;
- Describes types of educational programs for emergent bilinguals;
- Reviews educational policies for these students in a historical context, including:
  - ➤ The antecedents,
  - ➤ Title VII: The Bilingual Education Act,
  - ➤ Legal precedents,
  - ➤ The 1990s,
  - ➤ No Child Left Behind (NCLB),
  - ➤ Common Core State Standards (CCSS), and
  - ➤ Every Student Succeeds Act (ESSA); and
- Presents a critical review of the present.

Since the 1960s, language-minoritized students have been the focus of many U.S. educational policy decisions at the national, state, and local levels and in all three branches of government. As a result of top-down education-al policies and negotiations with teachers and communities, different types of educational programs for these students exist in the United States. In what follows, we first review the educational programs that are available for emergent bilinguals. We then turn to a brief historical section in which we discuss the evolution of policies to educate these students. It will become evident that federal bilingual education policy has changed over the past 5 decades from taking into account the students' home language practices and being flexible about educational approaches to being far more rigid in em-phasizing English-only instruction for those labeled as English learners. As we also illustrate, the high-stakes standardized testing movement, spurred by NCLB (2001) and continued under ESSA (2015), despite the greater flex-ibility afforded to states, has had much to do with this new rigidity. At the same time, there has been a discourse shift in terms—from *bilingual education* programs to *dual-language* programs. The latter term focuses, not on leveraging and developing the bilingualism of emergent bilinguals who are progressing toward spoken and written skills in English along with their home language, but on programs that most often also include language-majority students, speakers of English who are learning an additional language for "enrichment." (We discuss the consequences of this discourse shift in more detail later in this chapter.) These developments mean that there is even greater dissonance today between policy and research on the education of emergent bilinguals than there has been in the past.

EDUCATIONAL PROGRAMS FOR EMERGENT BILINGUALS

Within the U.S. public educational system, there are different educational programs used in schools for working with emergent bilinguals. These programs range from those that expect students to learn English after simply exposing them to it and treating them like all other students, to those specifically designed to support students' academic and linguistic development through the deployment of their home language practices. The educational policies we discuss in this chapter are critical to the form of instruction that emergent bilinguals receive.

As we will see, the tendency over the past decade has been for policymakers, and the public more generally, to provide more English-only programs and move away from programs that use students' home languages. Before we discuss this shift and its (dis)connection with the research literature, we briefly describe these different programs/approaches and display them in Table 3.1.

In the first category, *nonrecognition*, often referred to as *submersion* or *sink-or-swim* programs, schools and educators provide emergent bilinguals with exactly the same educational services that are provided to monolingual English speakers. That is, they neither provide alternative educational services, nor do they use the students' home language practices to teach them. These submersion programs were prevalent before 1970 and still are used in many parts of the country, especially in light of recent English-only initiatives in certain states.

A second category of educational programs falls under the umbrella of English as a Second Language (ESL) programs, also called English as a New Language (ENL). There are pull-out ESL/ENL programs, which provide some support for students in special sessions outside of the regular classroom. Although these programs are meant to provide instruction exclusively in English, some home language support is allowed. There are also push-in ESL/ENL programs, in which an ESL teacher works collaboratively with the content-area teacher to support emergent bilingual students in the class. Some home language support is also possible in these programs. Still another type of program, called structured English immersion, also known as sheltered English or content-based ESL, provides emergent bilinguals with a great deal of pedagogical support and scaffolding in a program tailored specifically for these students. Usually, instruction is only in English in these programs, although some teachers do provide home language support.

The federal government has recently made a distinction between English as a Second Language programs and *high-intensity language programs* (see U.S. Department of Education, NCES, 2015d). This latter term is being used in some localities for programs that focus on intensive instruction in the features of English (lexicon, phonology, morphology, syntax). Usually, this is combined with sheltered English content courses or with mainstream classes in English only. This type of instruction is used especially in middle schools and high schools. These programs are also used in states that have abolished bilingual education. For example, in Arizona, emergent bilingual students spend 4 hours a day in these high-intensity language classes (Gándara & Orfield, 2010; Johnson & Johnson, 2015). Because of their focus on the structure of English, and not its use, these programs fail to provide students with adequate opportunities to use English meaningfully and develop proficiency.

Moving toward the other end of the pedagogical spectrum, there is a third category of programs that takes a more *bilingual* approach, in that students' home languages are used to teach subject matter for a variety of reasons—sometimes to support their transition to English and other times to develop their bilingualism and biliteracy. The first such type is known as transitional bilingual education, also known as early-exit bilingual education. This transitional program does use students' home languages to some degree, but the focus is on students' acquiring English as quickly as possible and exiting them into "mainstream" English-only classrooms. Another type of bilingual program is known as developmental bilingual education, or simply as maintenance bilingual education[2] (also known as late-exit bilingual education or one-way dual-language education). This type of program supports students' acquisition of both English *and* the development of their home languages. In some localities, these developmental bilingual education programs or one-way dual-language bilingual programs serve students of one language group who fall along all points of the bilingual continuum. That is, these programs may serve emergent bilinguals as well as more experienced bilinguals. In some cases, the emergent bilinguals are developing English, and in others, more experienced bilingual students are developing what is considered their heritage language. Developing students' bilingualism and biliteracy is the goal of these programs. A great deal of attention has been given recently to two-way bilingual education (also called two-way dual-language or sometimes simply dual-language, two-way immersion, or dual immersion). This type of bilingual program pushes the developmental

Table 3.1. Types of educational programs for emergent bilinguals

PROGRAM	LANGUAGE USED IN INSTRUCTION	COMPONENTS	DURATION	GOALS
I. Nonrecognition				
Submersion (sink-or-swim)	100% English	Mainstream education; no special help with English; no teachers qualified to teach emergent bilinguals	Throughout K–12 schooling	Linguistic assimilation (shift to English only)
II. ESL/ENL				
English as a second/new language (ESL/ENL) Pull-out (submersion plus ESL)	90–100% in English; may include some home language support or not	Mainstream education; students pulled out for 30–45 minutes of ESL daily; teachers certified in TESOL	As needed	Linguistic assimilation; remedial English
English as a second/new language (ESL/ENL) Push-in	90–100% in English; may include some home language support or not	Mainstream education; ESL teacher works alongside the subject teacher as needed; teachers certified in TESOL	As needed	Linguistic assimilation; remedial education within mainstream classroom
Structured English immersion (sheltered English, content-based ESL, stand-alone ESL)	90–100% English; may include some home language support or not	Subject-matter instruction at students' level of English; students grouped for instruction; teachers certified in TESOL; should have some training in immersion	1–3 years	Linguistic assimilation; exit to mainstream education
High-intensity English language training	100% English; focus on English features; usually combined with mainstream or sheltered English for content	Focus on features and structures of the English language, usually combined with mainstream or sheltered English for content; teachers certified in TESOL/ELA for language instruction	1–3 years, especially used in high school and middle school and antibilingual education school districts	Linguistic assimilation; remedial English focus; exit to mainstream education

PROGRAM	LANGUAGE USED IN INSTRUCTION	COMPONENTS	DURATION	GOALS
III. Bilingual				
Transitional bilingual education (early-exit bilingual education)	Initially 50%–90% home language and 10–50% English; home language gradually reduced to 10% and English increased to 90%	Initial literacy usually in home language; some subject instruction in home language; ESL and subject-matter instruction at students' level of English; sheltered English subject instruction; teachers certified in bilingual education	1–3 years; students exit as they become proficient in English	Linguistic assimilation; English acquisition without falling behind academically
Developmental bilingual education (late-exit bilingual education, one-way dual-language bilingual)	90% home language initially; gradually decreasing to 50% or thereabouts; home language subject instruction always available OR 50/50 from beginning	Initial literacy focus is in home language, although English simultaneously introduced; always some subject instruction in home language; ESL initially and English subject-matter instruction at students' level of English; teachers certified in bilingual education	At least 5–6 years	Bilingualism and biliteracy; academic achievement in English
Two-way bilingual education (two-way dual-language bilingual, dual-language bilingual, two-way immersion bilingual, dual-immersion bilingual)	90/10 model: 90% home language, 10% additional language in early grades; 50/50 model: parity of both languages	English speakers AND speakers of a LOTE taught literacy and subjects in both languages; teachers certified in bilingual education	At least 5–6 years; more prevalent at the elementary level	Bilingualism and biliteracy; academic achievement in English
IV. Blend				
Dynamic bi/plurilingual education	English and students' home languages in dynamic relationship; students are the locus of control for language used; peer teaching	Teacher-led whole classroom in English, coupled with collaborative project-based student learning using home language practices	Suitable at the secondary level, when students have already developed literacy in their home languages	Bilingualism, academic achievement in English

model even further by supporting fluency in both English and the home language within classrooms that enroll two types of emergent bilinguals: LOTE speakers and English speakers. In these linguistically and ethnically integrated settings, students with two different linguistic backgrounds learn through both languages. The goal is for both the language-minoritized students and the language-majority students to become bilingual and biliterate.

Notice that throughout this book we explicitly name the *bilingual* condition of all types of dual-language programs (whether one-way or two-way). We refer to them as "dual-language bilingual education," or DLBE.

All the programs described above develop from institutional structures that see themselves as being either monolingual or bilingual. In contrast, programs we call dynamic bi/plurilingual programs function as a *blend* of ESL and bilingual education programs. In these programs, most often found at the secondary level, students are given agency to negotiate their linguistic repertoires, although the teaching, at least when the teacher leads the whole-group discussion, is in English. The schools of the Internationals Network for Public Schools, which we describe below, fit this category (García, Flores, & Chu, 2011; García, Seltzer, & Witt, 2018; García & Sylvan, 2011).

To help differentiate programs in terms of their pedagogy, philosophy, and focus, we display all programs in Table 3.1, which is adapted and expanded from Crawford (2004). Readers are encouraged to study this table carefully, as it expands our descriptions of the programs (for other categorizations of programs, see Baker & Wright, 2017).

Although we present different program categories, in practice, the most innovative and committed educators start with designing a program for their actual community of students. In reality, we have found many times that educators blend features to fit their students' needs.

As Table 3.1 illustrates, students' home languages can be used in a wide variety of ways within educational programs. For instance, the home language practices can either be used *fully,* as in the case of bilingual education programs in which the students' home language is a medium of instruction and the goal is biliteracy, or *partially*, as when teachers teach only in English but use the students' home language practices for support. Sometimes students' home language practices are used to ensure comprehension or scaffold instruction in English; other times, they are used to support emergent bilinguals' work on collaborative projects. For example, the Sheltered Instruction, Observation Protocol model, a widely used program of sheltered English instruction for English learners, supports the use of the students' home language to clarify concepts and assignments. The developers of this approach state:

> [W]e believe that clarification of key concepts in students' L1 [first language] by a bilingual instructional aide, peer, or through the use of materials written in the students' L1 provides an important support for the academic learning of those students who are not yet fully proficient in English. (Echevarría, Vogt, & Short, 2004, p. 107)

The schools in the Internationals Network for Public Schools[3] encourage their students to work collaboratively on projects using their diverse home languages to deepen comprehension and critical thinking, although the schools then expect English to be the language used for oral and written reports. As students develop English language proficiency, however, their many home languages do not merely support English language acquisition, but also facilitate content-rich, interdisciplinary, and collaborative work.

Whether to use students' home language as a medium of instruction as in bilingual education or simply as a scaffolding mechanism in many ESL classrooms often depends on the number of students of the same language group in the same school and classroom, as well as the ability to find teachers who speak that language. Clearly, in classrooms where emergent bilinguals are from different language backgrounds, traditionally structured bilingual education is not feasible, although some form of bilingualism in education always is, as demonstrated, for example, by the work of the schools of the Internationals Network for Public Schools (Sylvan & Romero, 2002) and other schools that are said only to have forms of ESL instruction (García, Flores, & Chu, 2011; García, Flores & Woodley, 2015; García & Kleyn, 2016; Manyak, 2004). But, as we noted in Chapter 2, approximately three-fourths of all emergent bilinguals in the United States speak Spanish as their home language. Therefore, the recent shift toward increased efforts to teach Spanish-speaking emergent bilinguals exclusively in English, thereby omitting the use of Spanish to transform their learning, can be attributed to a lack of public knowledge about the nature of bilingualism and its benefits (detailed in Chapter 4), as well as cultural politics that have little to do with what is educationally sound for the students.

Further, Table 3.1 shows that the duration of different programs for emergent bilinguals varies considerably. These variations need to be considered in light of the research evidence that we introduce in Chapter 4, which suggests that to be able to use an additional language successfully in academic contexts takes considerably longer than to become conversant in that language. But first, we demonstrate how American language-in-education policy changes have placed limits on these program options.

A BRIEF HISTORY OF
EDUCATIONAL POLICIES FOR EMERGENT BILINGUALS

The Antecedents

In 1954, the U.S. Supreme Court ruled in *Brown v. Board of Education* that segregated schools were unconstitutional, ushering in a new era in the struggle for civil rights in the United States. Congress passed the Civil Rights Act in 1964, prohibiting discrimination on the basis of race, color, or national origin. According to Title VI of this act: "No person in the United

States shall, on the ground of race, color, or national origin, be excluded from participation in, be denied the benefits of, or be subjected to discrimination under any program or activity receiving Federal financial assistance" (Civil Rights Act, sec. 601, 1964). Thus, Title VI of the 1964 Civil Rights Act has played an important role in protecting the educational rights of language-minority students in the United States (see Crawford, 2004; E. Garcia, 2005; O. García, 2009a; and especially the National Clearinghouse for English Language Acquisition [NCELA], 2006). In addition to Title VI of the Civil Rights Act, the Equal Educational Opportunities Act of 1974 requires states to ensure that education agencies take "appropriate action to overcome language barriers that impede equal participation by its students in its instructional programs" (20 USC Sec.1703(f)).

Title VII: The Bilingual Education Act

In 1968, the U.S. Congress reauthorized the landmark Elementary and Secondary Education Act (ESEA), the largest and most influential federal education policy to date. Title VII of that act, known as the Bilingual Education Act, established a federal goal of assisting "limited-English-speaking" students in the acquisition of English. At first, only poor students were eligible to participate. Title VII of the Elementary and Secondary Education Act did *not* require bilingual education. Rather, Congress put aside money for school districts enrolling large numbers of language-minoritized students that chose to start bilingual education programs or create bilingual instructional materials. The Bilingual Education Act (1968) stated:

> In recognition of the special educational needs of the large numbers of children of limited English-speaking ability in the United States, Congress hereby declares it to be the policy of the United States to provide financial assistance to local educational agencies to develop and carry out new and imaginative elementary and secondary school programs designed to meet these special educational needs. (Sec. 702)

When the Bilingual Education Act was first reauthorized in 1974, eligibility for educational services was expanded to include students of any socioeconomic status who had limited English-speaking ability (LESA). The 1974 reauthorization also defined bilingual education for the first time as "instruction given in, and study of, English and (*to the extent necessary to allow a child to progress effectively through the education system*) the native language of the children of limited English speaking ability" (quoted in García, 2009a, p. 169; emphasis added). The subsequent 1978 reauthorization of the Bilingual Education Act expanded eligibility for services even further, from students with LESA to students with more general limited English proficiency (LEP), while reinforcing the "transitional" nature of bilingual education. The central focus during this time of expanding access was to ensure that students who needed bilingual education services were receiving them; the pedagogy was left to the educators who were tasked with carrying out "imaginative" programs.

By the mid-1980s, the tone and focus of the federal Bilingual Education Act had begun to shift support to English-only programs. For the first time, the 1984 reauthorization of the Bilingual Education Act also provided funding for programs that used only English in educating English language learners, although only 4% of the funding was reserved for these kinds of programs. The 1988 reauthorization of the Bilingual Education Act further expanded the funding for programs in which only English was used to 25% of programs funded. Additionally, it imposed a 3-year limit on participation in transitional bilingual education programs, meaning that schools had 3 years to move English language learners to fluency in English.

In 1994, Congress reauthorized the provisions of the Elementary and Secondary Education Act, including the Bilingual Education Act, this time under the new Improving America's Schools Act. Although this reauthorization gave increased attention to two-way bilingual education programs, the cap for English-only programs that was previously legislated was lifted.

These legislative efforts, beginning with ESEA in 1968, were the first to focus on the need to provide language-minoritized students with an equal opportunity for an education. Not long after the 1968 legislation, a series of legal battles began for an equitable education for emergent bilinguals.

Legal Precedents

In the early 1970s, a group of Chinese American parents brought a judicial case against the San Francisco school board on the grounds that their children were not receiving an equitable education. The case was brought under the equal protection clause of the Fourteenth Amendment of the Constitution and Title VI of the Civil Rights Act. The case, known as *Lau v. Nichols*, was eventually appealed up to the U.S. Supreme Court and was decided on the basis of Title VI. Justice William O. Douglas wrote the majority opinion of the Court, stating:

> [T]here is no equality of treatment merely by providing students with the same facilities, textbooks, teachers and curriculum; for students who do not understand English are effectively foreclosed from any meaningful education. . . . Basic skills are at the very core of what these public schools teach. Imposition of a requirement that, before a child can effectively participate in the educational program, he must already have acquired those basic skills is to make a mockery of public education. We know that those who do not understand English are certain to find their classroom experiences wholly incomprehensible and in no way meaningful. . . . No specific remedy is urged upon us. Teaching English to

the students of Chinese ancestry who do not speak the language is one choice. Giving instructions to this group in Chinese is another. There may be others. (*Lau v. Nichols*, 1974)

The Court offered no specific method of instruction as a remedy. It merely instructed school districts to take "affirmative steps" to address the educational inequities for these students and called upon the federal Office for Civil Rights, as part of the executive branch, to guide school districts. The Office for Civil Rights set up a task force that eventually promulgated guidelines for schools and districts. These guidelines eventually became known as the Lau Remedies (1975). In addition to instructing school districts on how to identify and serve emergent bilinguals, these guidelines specifically required bilingual education at the elementary level and permitted the introduction of ESL programs at the secondary level. Emphasizing that English as a Second Language was a necessary component of bilingual education, the guidelines continued, "since an ESL program does not consider the affective nor cognitive development of the students . . . an ESL program [by itself] is not appropriate" (as cited in Crawford, 2004, p. 113). In 1979, the Lau Remedies were rewritten for release as regulations. However, they were never published as official regulations, and in 1981, were withdrawn by Terrel Bell, the incoming secretary of education under Ronald Reagan, who called them "harsh, inflexible, burdensome, unworkable, and incredibly costly" (cited in Crawford, 2004, p. 120).

Yet, even as the executive branch of the federal government was signaling retrenchment from meaningful bilingual education, emergent bilinguals continued to have the courts on their side. In another important federal court case (*Castañeda v. Pickard*, 1981), the U.S. Court of Appeals for the Fifth Circuit upheld the *Lau* precedent that schools must take "appropriate action" to educate language-minoritized students and that such action must be based on sound educational theory; produce results; and provide adequate resources, including qualified teachers and appropriate materials, equipment, and facilities. The case, however, did not mandate a specific program such as bilingual education or ESL.

English-Only Education at the Polls: The 1990s and the Aftermath

In the 1990s, the use of the child's home language to support learning came under political siege (see Gándara & Hopkins, 2010). The most effective attack against bilingual education was spearheaded by Silicon Valley software millionaire Ron Unz. Proposition 227 (California Proposition 227, 1998, sec. 300-311), also known as the English for the Children Initiative, was presented to California voters in June 1998. The proposition prohibited the use of home language instruction in teaching emergent bilinguals. It mandated English-only instruction for a period not to exceed a year, after which students were put into mainstream classrooms. Parents were able to request a waiver from the 1-year English immersion program if the child was over 10 years of age, had special needs, or was fluent in English. Sixty-one percent of Californians voted in favor of this proposition, making it state law. The vote of the Latinx population was two to one against the initiative.

This proposition passed despite the fact that only a minority of emergent bilinguals were in bilingual programs in California in the first place. Prior to the passage of Proposition 227, only 30% of emergent bilinguals were in bilingual programs, with the rest in either ESL programs or regular classrooms (Crawford, 2003). Of the 30% of California English learners in bilingual programs, less than 20% were being taught by a credentialed bilingual teacher (Cummins, 2003). A year after the passage of Proposition 227, California students in bilingual programs declined from 29.1% to 11.7% (Crawford, 2007). Four years after Proposition 227 was passed, only 590,289 emergent bilinguals (just 42% of the total in 1998) had become proficient in English, and annual redesignation rates—that is, the rates of English acquisition—remained unchanged. According to the California Department of Education (2006a, 2006b), as of 2006, only 7.6% of English learners in California were in transitional bilingual education classrooms because their parents signed waivers requesting these programs (California Department of Education, 2006a, 2006b; Rumberger & Gándara, 2000). Baca and Gándara (2008) attest to the inadequate English-only instruction that emergent bilinguals in California were receiving, as well as their poor assessment results. In fact, the number of students who were not able to become proficient in English for 6 or more years increased dramatically as a result. A space for bilingual education was found during this time in the implementation of "dual-language" programs, a label that, as we have said, does not name its bilingualism, and in programs where "English learners" are taught with "fluent" English speakers.

A year after California's Proposition 227 was passed, Unz took his English-only efforts to Arizona. In 2000, 63% of Arizona voters approved Proposition 203, which banned bilingual education in that state. Arizona's statute is even more restrictive than California's. It limits school services for emergent bilinguals to a 1-year English-only structured immersion program that includes ESL and content-based instruction exclusively in English. Waivers are almost impossible to obtain. And in 2006, the Arizona Legislature passed HS2064, which reshaped the structured immersion programs into a 4-hour-a-day block of instruction specifically on English language development (Johnson & Johnson, 2015).

In 2002, a similar proposition to outlaw bilingual education in Massachusetts (Massachusetts Question 2, G.L. c. 71A) passed by 68%. Emergent bilinguals continue to be the lowest-performing subgroup in the state by every measure—English language arts and math, and graduation rates. After 5 years in English immersion programs, only 20% of emergent bilinguals in Massachusetts had achieved grade level (Karp & Uriarte, 2010).

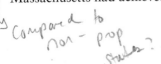

Compared to non-prop. states?

important

In 2002, Amendment 31 to Colorado's state constitution, which would have made bilingual education illegal, was defeated, with 56% of voters opposing it. Ironically, the campaign to defeat the amendment focused on the threat to parental choice and local control of schools, as well as the possibility that non-English-speaking children would be in the same classrooms as other children. A TV commercial warned that the Unz-backed English-only amendment would "force children who can barely speak English into regular classrooms, creating chaos and disrupting learning" (Crawford, 2004, p. 330).

No Child Left Behind

An important stage of the policy movement away from bilingual education and toward an English-only approach was the reauthorization of the Elementary and Secondary Education Act under the more ambitious No Child Left Behind Act (NCLB), which was signed into law by President George W. Bush in January 2002.

As we said in Chapter 1, NCLB's definition of *limited English proficient* as referring to those who could not meet proficiency levels in English on state assessments signaled a significant shift in political culture and ideology. From an earlier era that provided language-minoritized students and their families with greater access to educational resources and more equal educational opportunities to become truly bilingual, NCLB heralded a period focused solely on closing the achievement gap through testing and English immersion.

NCLB (2001) mandated that, by the 2013–2014 school year, all students would achieve the level of "proficient" in state assessment systems. To accomplish this lofty goal, NCLB required schools and districts to ensure that all their students meet specific state-developed annual targets of adequate yearly progress (AYP) for reading, math, and science. In addition, it was not enough for schools or districts to meet their goals in terms of their aggregate data; they also were required to show that all subgroups of students—meaning students of different races, ethnicities, income groups, gender, and so on—were meeting AYP goals.[4] One of the subgroups that NCLB required schools and districts to keep track of was "limited English proficient students." As a result, local school officials had to pay attention to their emergent bilinguals' yearly progress in English proficiency (Capps et al., 2005).

NCLB (2001) required assessments for emergent bilinguals under Title I (funding for poor students)[5] and Title III (funding for limited English proficient students) of the Act. Under Title I, which, as we noted, is the federal compensatory education program for poor students, if English learners or other subgroups did not meet their test score targets, their schools could be subject to interventions. Parents whose children attended schools in need of improvement were permitted to send their children to an alternative school in the same school district, provided that the school had room and the services each student required. Parents of students in schools designated as in need of improvement were offered supplemental services such as after-school tutoring programs. If the schools continued to fail to meet the performance targets, they were to be eventually restructured or closed (NCLB, 2001).

Meanwhile, the purpose of Title III of NCLB, then called "Language Instruction for Limited English Proficient and Immigrant Students" (the old Title VII under ESEA) was "to help ensure that children who are limited English proficient, including immigrant children and youth, attain English proficiency" (2001, sec. 3102). Schools were required to evaluate the English proficiency of all students enrolling for the first time in school, establish criteria to determine eligibility for programs and services for emergent bilinguals, and implement appropriate educational services. States were to hold schools receiving Title III funding accountable for meeting annual measurable achievement objectives for their emergent bilinguals, which placed unprecedented demands on the states for improvements in both the academic proficiency and the English proficiency of emergent bilinguals. From the beginning, NCLB regulations proved problematic for emergent bilinguals. Unlike other subgroups, emergent bilinguals eventually become bilingual, and thus, they move out of the "English learner" category. Therefore, emergent bilinguals' progress toward proficiency is difficult to demonstrate, because only those who fail to progress remain in the category. By 2010, the difficulties inherent in NCLB were obvious: States lowered their standards so that more students would appear proficient, schools that missed a single target were considered failing, interventions were one-size-fits-all, and the focus was on tests, forcing teachers to teach to the test and eliminating subjects such as history and the arts (Duncan, 2013). The Obama administration called on Congress to reauthorize a revamped Elementary and Secondary Education Act. Arne Duncan, then secretary of education, started granting states waivers from some NCLB provisions and giving them greater flexibility in exchange for commitments to adopt higher standards, target the lowest-performing schools, and choose teacher and principal evaluation and support systems that take into account student growth.

The state waivers were coupled with the 2009 announcement of Race to the Top, the $4.35 billion U.S. Department of Education competitive grant that created incentives for states to adopt common standards (see the next section), performance-based evaluations for teachers and principals, and data systems, as well as to give increased attention to the lowest-performing schools. Race to the Top also gave extra points to states that expanded high-quality charter schools; this competitive grant officially ended in July 2015.

Common Core State Standards (CCSS)

In 2009, the Common Core State Standards (CCSS) in English language arts and mathematics were released. This was an initiative of the National Governors Association and the Council of Chief State School Officers, which outlined what students were expected to know at the end of each grade. But the CCSS document devoted only two and a half pages to English language learners and acknowledged that "these students may require additional time, appropriate instructional support, and aligned assessments as they acquire both English language proficiency and content area knowledge" (www.corestandards.org, n.p.). By 2016, all but four states had adopted the CCSS; however, by October 2017, 10 states had either rewritten or replaced the CCSS. The withdrawal of states from the CCSS signals increasing opposition to the role of the federal government in supporting the adoption of the CCSS and its attendant emphasis on testing. The passage of ESSA (see the next section) explicitly forbids the federal government from requiring adoption of the CCSS by states. Texas, the state with the second highest number of emergent bilinguals in the country, has never adopted the CCSS.

With respect to emergent bilinguals, the problem with the CCSS is that the standards don't seem to have a coherent theory of language. At first glance, the English language arts standards seem to support a view of language as human action in the standards related to listening, speaking, reading, and writing. García (2016) summarizes this by saying:

> Students are asked to use a greater variety of complex texts—oral, visual, quantitative, print and non-print—that technology has enabled. The purposes for which language is used have also changed—from recreation or factual declaration giving way to analysis, interpretation, argument, and persuasion. Even language itself has gone from being acknowledged as simply grammar and vocabulary of printed texts to include its many levels of meaning—figurative language, word relations, genres, and media. Finally, students are now being asked to perform language socially through cooperative tasks. It is not enough to organize information on one's own and write as an individual; it is important to build upon others' ideas, whether those of peers, teachers, or authors of texts, to find evidence to articulate one's own ideas, adjusting the presentation according to the different purposes or audiences. (p. 48)

All of these are lofty goals, ones that emergent bilinguals can meet with the appropriate support, especially by leveraging their home language practices (for an analysis of the CCSS from a multilingual perspective, see García & Flores, 2014). However, on closer inspection, the strand of the CCSS known as the Language Standards requires something completely different. These standards reinforce the learning of grammar and vocabulary in English only—that is, of English as a system of structures that are to be taught in progressive and linear order. As we will see later on, emergent bilinguals need experience using English in legitimate academic tasks; they do not benefit by simply analyzing the structure of the English language. Linguistic features are acquired in authentic use, not by focusing on them in isolation.

When the CCSS were adopted, educators immediately had to scramble to put together resources to help prepare emergent bilinguals for the new ways in which language was being assessed (see, for example, Heritage, Walqui, & Linquanti, 2015). As we said in Chapter 2, WIDA and ELPA21 emerged as two consortia of state departments of education, which focused on developing English language proficiency standards to indicate progression of language development. Both California and New York developed their own progression standards toward English language proficiency for emergent bilinguals. A Bilingual Common Core Initiative, with progression standards in both English and the home language (see Velasco & Johnson, 2014), was adopted by New York State, whereas California adopted the California English Language Development Standards. All of the standards for language progression of emergent bilinguals support the use of the home language to help emergent bilinguals meet academic standards. This is especially so for students situated along the beginning points of the English language progression.

Every Student Succeeds Act (ESSA)

On December 10, 2015, President Barack Obama signed the new reauthorization of the Elementary and Secondary Education Act (ESEA) of 1968, which was called the Every Student Succeeds Act (ESSA). This law continues the goal of preparing all students for success in college and career, while providing flexibility for some of NCLB's more prescriptive requirements.

As with NCLB, the needs of English learners are addressed in ESSA under Title III, "Language Instruction for English Learners and Immigrant Students." According to Section 3003, "English Language Acquisition, Language Enhancement, and Academic Achievement," the purposes of Title III of ESSA are:

1. to help ensure that English learners, including immigrant children and youth, attain English proficiency, and develop high levels of academic achievement in English;
2. to assist all English learners, including immigrant children and youth, to achieve at high levels in academic subjects so that all English learners can meet the same challenging State academic standards that all children are expected to meet;
3. to assist teachers (including preschool teachers), principals, and other school leaders, State educational agencies, local educational agencies, and schools in establishing, implementing, and sustaining effective language instruction educational programs designed to

assist in teaching English learners, including immigrant children and youth;

4. to assist teachers (including preschool teachers), principals and other school leaders, State educational agencies, and local educational agencies to develop and enhance their capacity to provide effective instructional programs designed to prepare English learners, including immigrant children and youth, to enter all-English instructional settings;

5. to promote parental, family, and community participation in language instruction educational programs for the parents, families, and communities of English learners (Section 3102, 129 STAT. 1954).

ESSA not only reauthorized Title III, but also increased the authorization levels to $63 million in 2017. As with NCLB, ESSA requires that states establish and implement standardized statewide entry and exit procedures for emergent bilinguals.

As we said in Chapter 1, whereas NCLB focused on emergent bilinguals' achievement on assessments, ESSA looks at their achievement on academic standards, taking the onus off standardized tests, although not quite. It continues the requirement that states administer assessments in English language arts and mathematics aligned with their standards annually in grades 3 to 8 and once in high school. It also requires testing of science content once in grades 3 to 5, once in grades 6 to 9, and once in grades 10 to 12.

One major change between NCLB and ESSA is that the accountability provisions for English Learners were moved to Title I, incorporating the English language proficiency of these students not as an add-on, but as part of the general life of the school. Schools are now required to have an "English language proficiency indicator" as part of Adequate Yearly Progress (AYP), and to have goals and interim targets for emergent bilinguals. But as in NCLB, ESSA requires states to have standardized statewide entrance and exit procedures for identifying emergent bilinguals. It also continues the requirement that states annually assess emergent bilinguals' English language proficiency and specifies that it be "aligned with their academic standards in a valid and reliable manner" and provide "appropriate accommodations (including, to the extent practicable, assessments in the language and form most likely to yield accurate information on what those students know and can do in the content area assessed" (ESSA, 2015, n.p). A noteworthy new requirement is that states identify languages that are present to a "significant extent" as well as those languages for which there are no assessments (CCSO, 2016; ESSA, 2015).

As with NCLB, the English language arts and math scores of emergent bilinguals who have been enrolled in U.S. schools for less than 12 months are excluded for accountability purposes. ESSA, however, does not require states to count the scores of emergent bilinguals until their third year of enrollment. Furthermore, ESSA expands NCLB in allowing states to include for accountability purposes students designated as English learners for 4 years after reclassification. ESSA also adds that states report not only the data for emergent bilinguals, but also the data for two subgroups of emergent bilinguals: those with disabilities and those who have not achieved English proficiency after 5 years (now labeled long-term ELs).

The future enforcement of the ESSA 2015 regulations is not clear, given an administration that supports less federal oversight over education. In releasing new applications for states to develop their accountability plans for ESSA, U.S. Secretary of Education Betsy deVos said that it would allow states and districts to implement the law "with maximum flexibility" (cited in Klein, 2017).

A Critical Review of the Present

ESSA is only the most recent iteration of a broader change in policy orientation toward the education of language-minoritized students in the United States. In fact, as many have remarked, the word *bilingual*—what Crawford has called "the B-word"—is disappearing; public discourse about bilingualism in education has been increasingly silenced (Crawford, 2004; García, 2006a; Hornberger, 2006; Wiley & Wright, 2004). García (2009a) portrays this silencing of the word *bilingual* within the context of federal educational policy by illustrating some of the key name/title changes that have occurred in legislation and offices in Washington, D.C., since the passage of No Child Left Behind. These changes are shown in Table 3.2.

As shown in the first row of Table 3.2, the replacement of Title VII of the Elementary and Secondary Education Act (the Bilingual Education Act) by Title III (Language Instruction for Limited English Proficient [English Learner for ESSA] and Immigrant Students) is indicative of the shift away

Table 3.2. Silencing of bilingualism

Title VII of Elementary and Secondary Education Act: The Bilingual Education Act		Title III of No Child Left Behind, Public Law 107-110: Language Instruction for Limited English Proficient and Immigrant Students
Office of Bilingual Education and Minority Languages Affairs (OBEMLA)	→	Office of English Language Acquisition, Language Enhancement and Academic Achievement for LEP students (OELA)
National Clearinghouse for Bilingual Education (NCBE)		National Clearinghouse for English Language Acquisition and Language Instruction Educational Programs (NCELA)

from the support of instruction in students' home languages through bilingual education.

But it has not been only the government—whether federal, state, or local—that has carried out this discursive shift. Educators and scholars of bilingualism have also been complicit in this discursive shift by not directly naming "bilingualism," perhaps fearful of more backlash against it. One example of this discursive shift among educators and scholars has been the increased use of the term *dual language* instead of *bilingual*. One speaks about *dual-language programs* instead of *bilingual programs*, about *dual language learners* instead of *bilingual learners*, of *dual-language books* instead of *bilingual books*.

The change, however, is not just discursive; it is real. Zehler and colleagues (2003) established that, although between 1992 and 2002 the number of emergent bilinguals in grades K to 12 grew by 72% nationwide, their enrollment in bilingual programs declined from 37% to 17%. Crawford (2007) estimates that approximately half of emergent bilinguals in California and Arizona who would have been in bilingual classrooms in 2001–2002 were reassigned to all-English programs. And yet, after almost 2 decades of English-only instruction for emergent bilinguals in California and Arizona, the results have been very poor (for California, see Wenworth, Pellegrin, Thompson, & Hakuta, 2010; for Arizona, see Rios-Aguilar, González Canché, & Sabetghadam, 2012).

Despite educational policy that has silenced the growing bilingualism of U.S. language-minoritized students, there are apparent new efforts to revive bilingualism in the United States under different names and for different purposes. Among the most promising measures is the implementation of the Seals of Biliteracy (deliberately sidestepping the term *Seals of Bilingualism*) in many states. These seals are generally awarded at the time of graduation from secondary schools to recognize students who have studied and attained proficiency in more than one language. Significantly, California was the first state to award the Seal of Biliteracy in 2012. By 2017, 27 states and the District of Columbia had approved the Seal of Biliteracy, and 11 states were in the early stages of implementation and two more states were considering it (www.sealofbiliteracy.org).

In a way, the Seal of Biliteracy can extend the ways in which policymakers and educators view the languages with which emergent bilinguals enter classrooms. If they consider these languages as a resource not only to acquire English, but also for emergent bilinguals themselves, their high school graduation, and their future careers, perhaps emergent bilinguals would not be subjected to punitive English-only programs that rob them of the opportunity to be and become truly bilingual and biliterate. The danger, however, is that these awards would just become affirmations of "foreign language" ability for language-majority students. The Seals of Biliteracy are but a step into a multilingual future that has the potential of changing the unequal education that emergent bilinguals are receiving today. It remains to be seen to what extent this first step will overcome the largely monolingual approaches to their learning and achievement.

The global economy is being used by proponents of these Seals of Biliteracy as a reason to bring back bilingualism and bilingual ways of educating. Faced with this movement, the questions for all educators who are working to provide an equitable education to language-minoritized students need to be: Who are these policies for? And how do we ensure that they benefit the most vulnerable—those who are classified as English learners? Many have argued that this push to become multilingual in order to compete "globally" is related to a neoliberal economy. That is, the commodification of multilingualism is tied to the push for privatization and the free flow of capitalism in ways that benefit transnational corporations and economic elites (Flores, 2013). As Valdez, Delavan, and Freire (2014) argue, the economic logic of a neoliberal economy ultimately privileges those with the most access to wealth.

Even in states like California and Massachusetts, which had banned bilingual education, a movement to open up some bilingual space is afoot. Proposition 58, the California Multilingual Education Act, was passed in November 2016, effectively lifting restrictions on bilingual education. Proposition 58 passed by a 73% to 27% margin. In Massachusetts, the state senate passed a bill in July 2017 permitting school districts to reinstate a bilingual education option; in June, the Massachusetts house had passed a similar bill. This interest in reversing language education policy in Massachusetts is supported by a 2009 report compiled by the state showing that only about 20% of students receiving structured English immersion achieved proficiency in English, even after 5 years or more; that proficiency rates in science and mathematics academic content were also very low; and that high school dropout rates for these students were twice that of the state's language-majority students (English Language Learners Sub-Committee of the Massachusetts Board of Elementary and Secondary Education's Committee on the Proficiency Gap, 2009).

The changes in California and Massachusetts point to the greater interest in the United States in teaching languages other than English for economic purposes (see Kelly, 2016). This shows that, as López (2005) has said: "Educational opportunities for minority students exist only when the students' interests and the nation's interests converge" (p. 2016).

Callahan and Gándara (2014) have shown that bilinguals coming of age today are entering a different job and career market, one that has been transformed not only by globalization and the online era, but also by the growth of a multilingual consumer base. Yet, in a country where so many people speak languages other than English, especially Spanish, bilingualism and biliteracy cannot be valued only as an instrument of a neoliberal economy (Flores, 2013; Petrovic, 2005; Ricento, 2005). Bilingualism and biliteracy can only be sustained and developed if it also empowers minoritized speakers and their communities—that is, if bilingualism connects with its social justice and equal education opportunity origins. The success of Seals of Biliteracy, as well as two-way dual-language bilingual programs, can only be measured if indeed these policies encompass and benefit the most vulnerable students—those who have been minoritized as bilinguals and who have seldom been able to use their full linguistic repertoire in schools without fear, shame, or stigma.

PROGRAMS AND POLICIES FOR EMERGENT BILINGUALS: UNDERSTANDING THE SHIFTS

In this chapter, we have laid out the range of educational programs for emergent bilinguals and shown how U.S. language-in-education policies have shifted the program options away from focus on the home language and toward English-only instruction and assessment. We ended by arguing that present policies that seem to embrace bilingualism and biliteracy can only be measured as successful if they also work against the present minoritization of bilinguals in the United States.

In the next six chapters, we uncover the fallacies of present educational policy and practices with regard to emergent bilinguals. We explore what has been learned through research in sociolinguistics and psycholinguistics, education and curriculum, sociology, economics, psychometrics, and assessments about educating emergent bilinguals to achieve high standards. We focus on the questions: *What does the research tell us about how best to educate and assess emergent bilingual students? Are we using accepted theories and evidence in the education of these students?* We provide evidence that the gap between policy and practices and the research is indeed wide. In addition, we offer descriptions of alternative practices that do benefit emergent bilinguals.

STUDY QUESTIONS

1. What are the different types of educational programs for emergent bilinguals? Discuss how they differ in their practices and goals.

2. How are emergent bilinguals being educated in your district? Give specific examples.

3. Discuss how it is possible to encourage students' home language practices in all classrooms regardless of whether there are a few or many who speak a language other than English, whether the group is diverse, or whether the teacher speaks their home language.

4. Discuss the development of educational policies targeting emergent bilinguals in our recent past. Make sure you address the changes in the Bilingual Education Act, as well as *Lau v. Nichols* and *Castañeda v. Pickard*.

5. What have been the recent changes in educational policies with regard to emergent bilinguals? What is the difference between No Child Left Behind (NCLB) and the Every Student Succeeds Act (ESSA)?

6. Discuss the recent shifts in policies toward the education of emergent bilinguals. What have been some promising policies?

7. How do you view the commodification of bilingualism? Do you think it will benefit poor and racialized emergent bilinguals?

CHAPTER 4

Bilingualism and Achievement
Theoretical Constructs and Empirical Evidence

In this chapter, we:

- Review the following theories related to bilingualism:
  - ➢ Cognitive benefits,
  - ➢ Linguistic interdependence and common underlying proficiency,
  - ➢ Developing language for academic purposes,
  - ➢ Literacy and biliteracy,
  - ➢ Dynamic bilingualism, and
  - ➢ Translanguaging; and
- Consider the empirical evidence on the relationship between bilingualism and academic achievement.

So far, we have seen that a growing number of language education programs and policies have failed to recognize language-minoritized students' bilingualism and the role of their home language practices in supporting their learning. In this chapter, we consider the theoretical constructs and empirical findings that support the use of students' home language practices in the classroom. Within this context, we also examine the theories and research on bilingual and bilingual acquisition that speak to the developmental process of acquiring English, as well as additional languages, not just for spoken communication but also for academic work.

THEORETICAL CONSTRUCTS

Over the past 4 decades, researchers have developed frameworks for understanding the relationship between bilingualism and academic achievement. We describe here some of the theoretical frameworks that are useful in considering the equitable education of emergent bilinguals. We describe here some of the theoretical frameworks and associated empirical studies from the fields of anthropology, education, linguistics, and psychology that are useful in considering the equitable education of emergent bilinguals.

Cognitive Benefits

Ever since the seminal article by Peal and Lambert (1962), which found that bilingualism is an important factor in cognitive development, the literature on this topic has been extensive. In their Montreal study, Peal and Lambert (1962) found bilingual 10-year-olds to be "more facile at concept formation, and [to] have greater mental flexibility" than monolingual students (p. 22). Many empirical studies have followed, detailing various aspects of cognitive advantages for bilingual learners (for a review of these, see Baker, 2011; Baker & Wright, 2017; Blanc & Hamers, 1985; Díaz & Klinger, 1991; García, 2009a; Hakuta, 1986). Bilingual speakers constantly select some features from their linguistic repertoire and inhibit others, relying on what psycholinguists call the executive function of the brain. Bialystok and her colleagues, who study how bilingualism affects the mind and brain, have used behavioral and neuroimaging methods to show that bilinguals, because of their constant use of two languages, perform better on executive control tasks than do monolinguals (Barac & Bialystok, 2012; Bialystok, 2011, 2015, 2016; Kroll & Bialystok, 2013). In an article reviewing studies showing the cognitive benefits of bilingualism, Bialystok (2011) concludes that

> research with bilinguals . . . provides clear evidence for the plasticity of cognitive systems in response to experience. One possible explanation in the case of bilinguals is that the executive control circuits needed to manage attention to the two languages become integrated with the linguistic circuits used for language processing, creating a more diffuse, more bilateral, and more efficient network that supports high levels of performance. (p. 233)

It has been found that bilinguals' constant use of their different language practices strengthens the control mechanisms of the brain (the inhibitory control) and changes the associated brain regions (see also Abutalebi et al., 2012; Bialystok, Craik, & Luk, 2012; Green, 2011). In addition, because blood flow (a marker of neuronal activity) is greater in the brain stem of bilinguals in response to sound, this also creates advantages in auditory attention (Krizman, Marian, Shook, Skoe, & Kraus, 2012).

Researchers have found other positive cognitive consequences in being bilingual. Bialystok (2004, 2007, 2016) has pointed out that children's knowledge of two languages results in a more analytic orientation to language itself, a facility that is known as greater *metalinguistic awareness*. Bilingual children also have more than one way to describe the world and thus possess more flexible perceptions and interpretations—that is, more *divergent* or *creative thinking* (Ricciardelli, 1992; Torrance, Gowan, Wu, & Aliotti, 1970). And, bilingual children have more practice in gauging communicative situations, giving them more *communicative sensitivity* (Ben-Zeev, 1977).

Young children's potential for metalinguistic awareness, creative thinking, and communicative sensibility is forcefully documented in Perry Gilmore's (2016) close analysis of two 5-year-old boys who shared no common language but soon fashioned their own language during daily play together on a hillside in Kenya. Gilmore's English-speaking son interacted with his newfound Kenyan friend, a speaker of Samburu and some degree of Swahili. With these linguistic tools, they generated novel forms "never before heard or uttered" (p. 55). They invented what Gilmore called Kisisi, their private language.

The development of *academic proficiency* in two languages has been associated with enhancements in cognitive function. August and Hakuta (1997) conclude: "Bilingualism, far from impeding the child's overall cognitive linguistic development, leads to positive growth in these areas. Programs whose goals are to promote bilingualism should do so without fear of negative consequences" (p. 19).

Bilingualism has also been associated with creativity (Kharkhurin, 2015). Bilingual practices have been shown to strengthen certain cognitive mechanisms, which in turn may increase one's creative potential. Hugo Baetens Beardsmore (2018) points to five characteristics of bilinguals that result in greater creativity: a flexible mind, a problem-solving mind, a metalinguistic mind, a learning mind, and an interpersonal mind. In their study of creativity in Montreal, researchers Stolarick and Florida (2006) quote a respondent from a consulting firm who tells them that whenever he is faced with difficult problems to solve, he forms strategy groups with multilingual staff. The respondent observed:

> being multilingual means you understand the world from different perspectives and are more likely to devise creative and innovative solutions: it's "good for the brain to have to learn how to work and think in [multiple languages]." (p. 1812)

All programs to teach emergent bilinguals are thus enabling learners to capitalize on the cognitive and creative advantages of bilingualism. Because bilingualism develops cognitive capacities and enhances sensory processes, educational programs for emergent bilinguals can be effective if they leverage the home language practices along with English in the learning process.

Linguistic Interdependence and Common Underlying Proficiency

Jim Cummins has been a pioneer in developing theoretical frameworks that help us understand the relationship between a student's home language and the development of an additional language. It might seem counterintuitive to imagine that using the home language at school can support higher levels of English proficiency. However, the benefits of such practices are explained by the concept of *linguistic interdependence,* which means that both languages bolster each other in the student's acquisition of language and knowledge (Cummins 1979, 1981). Cummins (2000) explains linguistic interdependence by stating: "To the extent that instruction in Lx [one language] is effective in promoting proficiency in Lx [that language], transfer of this proficiency to Ly [the additional language] will occur provided there is adequate exposure to Ly" (p. 38). Cummins is not positing here that the child's home language needs to be fully developed before the additional language is introduced, but he argues that "the first language must not be abandoned before it is fully developed, whether the second language is introduced simultaneously or successively, early or late, in that process" (p. 25).

Linguistic interdependence is stronger in the case of languages that share linguistic features (such as, for example, Spanish and English) where students can derive interdependence from similar linguistic factors, as well as familiarity with language and literacy practices and ways of using language. Yet, even in cases where the two languages are not linguistically congruent, such as Chinese and English, Chinese-speaking students learning English will benefit academically if they have developed literacy in Chinese because they will understand, for example, that reading is really about making meaning from print and that writing requires the ability to communicate to an unknown and distant audience. In addition, they will have had practice in decoding, a sense of directionality of print and the mechanics of writing in their own language—all useful metalinguistic understandings that help orient learners to text in another language (Fu, 2003, 2009).

A related theoretical construct called *common underlying proficiency* (Cummins, 1979, 1981) posits that knowledge and abilities acquired in one language are potentially available for the development of another. Researchers have consistently found that there is a cross-linguistic relationship between the student's home and additional language, and proficiency in the home language is related to academic achievement in an additional language (Riches & Genesee, 2006). This is particularly the case for literacy. Lanauze and Snow (1989), for example, found that emergent bilinguals, even those students who were not yet orally proficient in their additional language, exhibited similar complexity and semantic content in their writing in both their home and additional languages.

Language for Academic Purposes[1]

Skutnabb-Kangas and Toukomaa (1976), working with Finnish immigrants in Sweden, proposed that there is a difference between the way in which language is used for academic tasks as opposed to its use in informal spoken and written communication. The *surface fluency* so evident in conversational language or in writing to someone we know intimately is most often supported by cues that elaborate and accompany language—gestures, repetition, intonation, emoticons, and so on. Cummins (1981) has called this use of language, which is supported by meaningful interpersonal and situational cues outside of language itself, *contextualized language*. Contextualized language, supported by paralinguistic[2] and other cues, is used for what Cummins (1981) has called *basic interpersonal communication* (BICS). Contextual support, Cummins (2000) explains, can be *external*, having to do with aspects of the language input itself. Contextual support can also be *internal*, having to do with the shared experiences, interests, and motivations that people communicating may have.

To complete school tasks, and especially assessment tasks, a different set of language abilities is needed. Students in school must be able to use language with little or no extralinguistic support, which is very different from the ways that language is used during everyday informal communication. That is, more *abstract language*, or in Cummins's terms, *decontextualized language*,[3] is needed in order to participate in most classroom discourse, read texts that are sometimes devoid of pictures and other semiotic cues, or interpret texts requiring background knowledge that students do not always have. Students also need this more abstract language in order to write the academic essays that require an unknown audience with whom communication is important, and to participate in the specialized discourse of test-taking such as multiple-choice tests that force students to choose only one answer. Cummins (1979, 1981, 2000) refers to the mastery of these abstract language abilities as cognitive academic language proficiency (CALP) and proposes that it takes 5 to 7 years to develop these skills in an additional language. Meanwhile, students can usually acquire the language of everyday communication in an additional language in just 1 to 3 years. As shown in Table 3.1 in Chapter 3, many educational programs for emergent bilinguals do not afford sufficient time to gain these complex ways of using language.

The finding that it takes 5 to 7 years to develop academic proficiency in an additional language is supported by other empirical research. Hakuta, Goto Butler, and Witt (2000) also have found that it takes 5 years or longer to fully develop academic skills in English. They add: "In districts that are considered the most successful in teaching English to EL students, oral proficiency takes 3 to 5 years to develop and proficiency in English for academic purposes can take 4 to 7 years" (p. 13). High school students are said to need a vocabulary of approximately 50,000 words, and the average student learns 3,000 new words each year (Graves, 2006; Nagy & Anderson, 1984). Thus, in 4 years of high school, emergent bilinguals might have acquired 12,000 to 15,000 words in English, falling short of what they would need in order to engage in English with the complex coursework of high school (Short & Fitzsimmons, 2007). In their review of longitudinal research over 32 years on the efficacy of bilingual instruction, Collier and Thomas (2017) confirm that it takes students at least 6 years with good-quality instruction that includes their home language, and at least 10 years without it, to achieve "on-grade" levels of performance in reading in English.

Although spoken language development for academic tasks is required to make sense of literacy activities, emergent bilinguals develop receptive skills in an additional language, especially those of listening, long before they can use the additional language well to read and, especially, to write. Gándara (1999) reports that by grade 3, listening skills in English may be at 80%, but reading and writing lag behind this number. Spoken language development and reading/writing development are intertwined, but it is important to understand the special demands of reading and writing for academic contexts, especially those that are targeted in state-developed standards.

Literacy and Biliteracy

Brian Street, a key figure in New Literacy Studies, challenges scholars and educators to examine the uses of language for academic purposes as a series of social practices. Rather than thinking of literacy as a monolithic construct made up of a discrete set of skills, he recommends that we consider first, that literacies are multiple, and second, that they are embedded in a web of social relations that maintain asymmetries of power (Street, 1985, 1996, 2003, 2005). He notes that literacy practices can also entail privileging some forms of literacy over others, and reminds us to interrogate "'whose literacies are dominant and whose are marginalized or resistant" (2003, p. 77). In other words, learning to "do language" in schools is not a neutral activity, easily divided into two modes of communication—spoken and written. Rather, learning literacy for academic purposes entails much more: It requires abilities that are increasingly multilingual, complex, and contingent upon wider societal factors beyond the school.

Nancy Hornberger (1990) has defined biliteracy as "any and all instances in which communication occurs in two or more languages in and around writing" (p. 213). Hornberger's (2003) model of the continua of biliteracy framework identifies the major social, linguistic, political, and psychological issues that surround the development of biliteracy as they relate to one another. The interrelated nature of Hornberger's continua supports the potential for positive transfer across literacies. Hornberger (2005) says that "bi/multilinguals' learning is maximized when students are allowed and enabled to draw from across all their existing language skills (in two+ languages), rather than being constrained and inhibited from doing so by monolingual instructional assumptions and practices" (p. 607). The nested nature of Hornberger's (2003) continua also shows how literacy transfer can be promoted or hindered by different contextual factors (Hornberger & Skilton-Sylvester, 2003).

The work of Kathy Escamilla and her colleagues (2014) has changed the conversation around biliteracy. Escamilla argues that biliteracy needs to be developed simultaneously, from the start. Focusing on the many Latinx students who are entering U.S. schools with different levels of proficiency in English *and* the language other than English, Escamilla and colleagues propose that literacy can be squared. This means that by introducing students to reading and writing in two or more languages simultaneously, literacy multiplies itself and its effects. As a result of this vision of biliteracy, alternative conceptualizations about instruction and assessment are being created.

The New London Group (1996) coined the term *multiliteracies* to refer to the increased modes of meaning-making that characterize the production and use of texts today (including not only the linguistic, but also the visual, the audio, and the spatial/gestural); the term also accounts for the increased local linguistic diversity around the world. In advocating for a different type of pedagogy, they argue for one that develops "an epistemology of pluralism that provides access without people having to erase or leave behind different subjectivities" (p. 72). (For more on this, see Chapter 6.)

García, Bartlett, and Kleifgen (2007), building on the frameworks developed by Street, Hornberger, and the New London Group, propose the concept of pluriliteracy practices, which are grounded in an understanding that equity for emergent bilinguals must take into account the power and value relations that exist around the various language practices in the school setting and in society. The notion of pluriliteracies recognizes the more dynamic and fluid uses of literacies in and out of schools in a context of new technologies and increased movements of people, services, and goods in a globalized world. Schools that value the use of pluriliteracy practices—including diverse language practices and scripts—are providing an equitable education for emergent bilinguals; they are enabling students to develop a powerful repertoire of multiliteracies that includes English and/or one or more additional languages for academic purposes.

Dynamic Bilingualism

Wallace Lambert (1974), working in the context of Canadian immersion bilingual education for Anglophone majorities in the 1970s,[4] proposed that bilingualism could be either *subtractive* or *additive.* According to Lambert, language-minoritized students usually experience subtractive bilingualism as a result of schooling in another language. Their home language is subtracted as the school language is learned. (Such is the case in the United States with ESL/English-only programs, as well as programs in transitional bilingual education.) On the other hand, claims Lambert, language-majority students usually experience additive bilingualism as the school language is added to their home language (for a review of additive bilingualism, see Cummins, 2017). These models of bilingualism are represented in Figure 4.1.

Figure 4.1. Subtractive versus additive bilingualism

Subtractive Bilingualism	Additive Bilingualism
L1 + L2 - L1 = L2	L1 + L2 = L1 + L2

Responding to the intensified movements of peoples across national borders and attendant language interaction and change brought about by globalization, it has been proposed that bilingualism is not *linear* but *dynamic* (García, 2009a). This conceptualization of bilingualism goes beyond the notion of two autonomous languages and of additive or subtractive bilingualism, and instead suggests that the language practices of *all* bilinguals are complex and interrelated; they do not emerge in a linear way. Bilingualism does not result in either the balanced wheels of two bicycles (as the additive bilingual model purports) or in a monocycle (as the subtractive bilingual model suggests). Instead, bilingualism is like an all-terrain vehicle with individuals using their different language practices and features to adapt to both the ridges and craters of communication in uneven terrains (see Figure 4.2). Like a banyan tree, bilingualism is complex as it adapts to the soil in which it grows (see García, 2009a).

Dynamic bilingualism refers to the development of different language practices to varying degrees in order to interact with increasingly multilingual communities and bilinguals along all points of the bilingual continuum. In some ways, dynamic bilingualism is related to the concept of plurilingualism as defined by the Council of Europe (2000): the ability to use several languages to varying degrees and for distinct purposes and an educational value that is the basis of linguistic tolerance. Jim Cummins (2017) has proposed the term *active bilingualism* to support the dynamic nature of multilingual practices, while maintaining the idea that bilinguals indeed have two separate languages that can support cross-linguistic transfer. There is a subtle difference between the concept of dynamic bilingualism on the one hand, and on the other hand the concepts of plurilingualism and of active bilingualism. Within a dynamic bilingual perspective, languages are not simply perceived as autonomous and separate systems that people "have," but rather as linguistic and multimodal features of a semiotic meaning-making repertoire from which people select and "do." We will expand on this when we discuss translanguaging below.

Educating for dynamic bilingualism for *all* students builds on the complex and multiple language practices of students and teachers, not simply on standardized conventions of named languages. Unlike additive and subtractive models of bilingualism, a dynamic bilingualism model proposes that we start by leveraging the complex practices of bilingual speakers—that is, that we *put their practices front and center.*

In most bilingual encounters today, the language practices of bilingual users function as those portrayed in the graphic on the left in Figure 4.3. The

Figure 4.2. Types of bilingualism

Subtractive Bilingualism	Additive Bilingualism	Dynamic Bilingualism

dynamism refers to the synchronic interrelatedness of language features and practices taking place in a present interaction with different interlocutors, but also to diachronic intermingling of features and practices as speakers blend together remnants of past experiences with those of the present. This is consonant with Bakhtin's (1981) concept of *heteroglossia*, and his idea that "one's own language is never a single language: in it there are always survivals of the past and a potential for other-languagedness" (p. 66).

Speakers in language-minoritized communities, who have experienced extreme language loss and who attend bilingual schools for purposes of language revitalization, undergo a process of what García (2009a) calls *recursive dynamic bilingualism*. They do not start as simple monolinguals (as is assumed in the subtractive and additive models). Instead, they recover features of their existing ancestral language practices as they develop a bilingualism that continuously reaches back in order to move forward. Their bilingualism cannot be called balanced, as in the two wheels of a bicycle, because their language practices need to adapt to the bilingually complex terrain in which they interact. This is the case, for example, of many Native American communities in the United States where their ancestral language practices have been deeply influenced by contact with English and resulting language loss (see, for example, Wyman, McCarty, & Nicholas, 2013). This is also the case of groups who have lived in the United States for more than three generations and who are revitalizing the language their ancestors brought to the United States as immigrants.[5] This recursive dynamic bilingualism is portrayed in the graphic on the right in Figure 4.3. Although we portray it as a series of arrows that go back and forth, the recursive bilingualism of these minoritized groups is also dynamic, experiencing the same dynamism that the multidirection circular arrows on the left depict. That is, the language practices of language-minoritized groups start out by reaching backward, but in order to go forward they experience the same heteroglossic practices of all bilingual speakers.

Educators meaningfully educate when they draw upon the full linguistic repertoire of all students, including language practices that are multiple and fluid, as we will see below. Any language-in-education approach—be it monolingual or bilingual—that does not acknowledge and build upon the fluid language practices in bilingual communities is *more concerned with controlling language behavior than in educating* (Blackledge & Creese, 2010; Creese & Blackledge, 2010; Cummins, 2007; García, 2009a; García, Flores, & Chu, 2011; García & Wei, 2014; Wei, 2011). Effectively educating emergent bilinguals, even in programs that teach through the medium of English, must include and support the dynamic bilingual practices by which bilinguals construct knowledge and understandings.

This conceptualization of dynamic bilingualism is in keeping with that of others in the 21st century. It builds on and challenges traditional second language acquisition work. In the 20th century, researchers in the field of second language acquisition (SLA) were concerned with the degree to which a language learner's "interlanguage" (Selinker, 1972) conformed to the target language. They often cataloged what is called *fossilization* behavior—that is, "errors" associated with interlanguage. Selinker and Han (2001) list some of these fossilizations: low proficiency, non-target-like performance, backsliding or the reemergence of "deviant" forms, and errors

Figure 4.3. Kinds of dynamic bilingualism

Dynamic Bilingualism	Recursive Dynamic Bilingualism

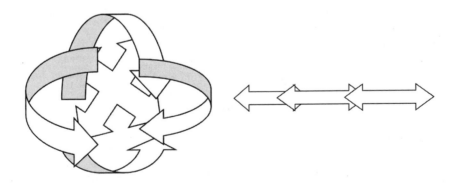

that are impervious to negative evidence. The emphasis on fossilization and "ultimate attainment" in second language acquisition studies have impacted the ways in which some language educators view their learners—as somehow incomplete. In this view, learning an additional language is linear, as if a static and complete set of grammar rules were available for acquisition. However, recent scholarship has increasingly questioned what Ortega (2014) has called "the monolingual bias in SLA." Socioculturally oriented SLA researchers now focus on the meaning-making semiotic resources of speakers, rather than narrowly focusing on language itself (Block, 2014). Additionally, scholarship on language education has increasingly focused on what Conteh and Meier (2014) and May (2015) have called the *multilingual turn*, a recognition that those involved in language education are, or are in the process of becoming, multilingual.

Recent scholarship has also increasingly questioned the idea of a "native speaker" and of "native-like proficiency" (Bonfiglio, 2010; Canagarajah, 1999; Cook, 2008; Doerr, 2009; García, 2009a; Pennycook, 2006; Valdés, 2005). Kramsch (1997) has argued that the concept of native speaker, which had been considered a privilege of birth, is closely linked to social class and education, since the ways of speaking of many poor and working-class native-born citizens are considered suspect and excluded.

In addition, scholars in the field of bilingualism have long argued that bilinguals are not two monolinguals in one (Grosjean, 1985, 1989). Speaking of these bilinguals as first language/second language or L1/L2 users, Guadalupe Valdés (2005) adds:

> L1/L2 users have acquired two knowledge systems that they use in order to carry out their particular communicative needs, needs that may be quite unlike those of monolingual native speakers who use a single language in all communicative interactions. (p. 415)

By proposing the concept of *multicompetence,* Cook (2002) contends that second language users are different from monolingual speakers because their lives and minds are also different; that is, they hold knowledge of two languages in the same mind. Likewise, Herdina and Jessner (2002) have also proposed that speakers of more than one language have dynamically interdependent language systems whose interactions create new structures that are not found in monolingual systems. This view of bilingualism has implications for teaching English to emergent bilinguals. As Larsen-Freeman and Cameron (2008) explain:

> Learning is not the taking in of linguistic forms by learners, but the constant adaptation of their linguistic resources in the service of meaning-making in response to the affordances that emerge in the communicative situation, which is, in turn, affected by learners' adaptability. (p.135)

Emergent bilinguals are developing a complex multicompetence. Educators who are aware of this complexity support home language practices and facilitate the adaptations of these practices as their students make meaning in new social and academic situations.

Translanguaging

Today, research in sociolinguistics and applied linguistics has refocused away from "homogeneity, stability, and boundedness as the starting assumptions" in favor of "mobility, mixing, political dynamics, and historical embedding" as "central concerns in the study of languages, language groups, and communication" (Blommaert & Rampton, 2011, p. 3). These critical poststructuralist approaches (Blommaert, 2010; García, Flores, & Spotti, 2017; Makoni & Pennycook, 2007; Pennycook, 2010) have emphasized not only the very diverse language practices of people in a global world, but also the negative effects that the social construction of *named languages* like English, Spanish, Arabic, Chinese, and so on, have had on language-minoritized populations. In other words, scholars have maintained that named languages have an important social reality, a reality constructed and regulated to serve different nations' political and economic needs. At the same time, these scholars argue that named languages cannot be defined linguistically—that is, based on linguistic features alone, linguists cannot determine whether speakers in, for example, Madrid, Lisbon, Havana, Rio de Janeiro, Barcelona, or Valencia speak the same language or not (see, Otheguy, García, & Reid, 2015).

Translanguaging takes as its starting point, not the named languages of nation-states, but the linguistic system of words, sounds, constructions, and so forth that make up bilingual speakers' vibrant linguistic repertoires, continuously shaped by social interactions. From a societal or political/geographical perspective, bilinguals may be said to have two named languages (for example, English and Spanish or English and Chinese), and bilingual schools are said to teach two named languages. But when seen from the bilingual speaker's own point of view (the *insider's* point of view, and not the *external* nation-state perspective), bilinguals have their own complex linguistic repertoire with features that are *socially* identified as belonging to two or more named languages. Understanding the language practices of bilinguals this way gives us a different starting point for teaching them (Otheguy, García & Reid, 2015; see also García & Kleyn, 2016; García, Johnson, & Seltzer, 2017).

The term *translanguaging* was coined in Welsh (*trawsieithu*) by educator Cen Williams (1994) and translated into English by Colin Baker (2001) to designate a bilingual pedagogy in which one language was used as input and another as output. This meaning of the term *translanguaging* has been extended by many scholars all over the world to legitimize both bilinguals' fluid language practices and the value of leveraging these translanguaging practices in education (see, for example, Blackledge & Creese, 2010; Canagarajah, 2011; Cenoz & Gorter, 2015; Creese & Blackledge, 2010; García 2009a; García & Wei, 2014; Gort, 2018; Hornberger & Link, 2012; Lewis, Jones, & Baker, 2012a, 2012b; Wei, 2011, 2017). Chapter 5 provides examples of translanguaging pedagogy.

García and Wei (2014) posit that the notion of translanguaging has been spurred by "language exchanges among people with different histories, and releases histories and understandings that had been buried within fixed language identities constrained by nation-states" (p. 21). This definition captures, as Mazak and Carroll (2017) have said, "the historical, political, and social embeddedness of language practices and how these practices are and have been intertwined with ideologies" (p. 6).

A theory of translanguaging differs in some ways from the conceptualization of what some scholars and educators term *code-switching*. Code-switching implies a "switch" from one language code to another and rests on the assumption that bilinguals have two separate, bounded language systems. Since Gumperz (1976), the sociolinguistic literature has shown how what some scholars call code-switching points to the agency of speakers (Auer, 2005; Myers-Scotton, 2005) and could have "pedagogic validity" (Arthur & Martin, 2006; Lin, 2013). Jacobson and Faltis (1990) attempted to show how code-switching could be used in bilingual schooling in the United States. But the idea that code-switching could be used constructively in education never had any acceptance. Code-switching was simply considered too much a violation of what was accepted as two separate, autonomous languages.

Translanguaging theory shifts our epistemological understandings, positing that there is no such "switch," because bilingual speakers are selecting or inhibiting (or not) different features in their unitary repertoire based on the given communicative situation. In other words, when called upon to perform using what society calls "English," bilinguals inhibit those features from their repertoire that are associated with Arabic, Chinese, Spanish, Vietnamese, and so on. But when bilinguals are among other bilinguals and in bilingual communities where their language use is not monitored by school authorities or others, they do not always have to exercise such restraint. Translanguaging then becomes the norm, with bilingual speakers having free access to their entire language repertoire in a social context where this language behavior is accepted. Translanguaging thus focuses on the complex language practices of bilinguals in actual communicative settings, and not on the use of language codes whose distinctness is monitored by the standardizing agencies of nation-states such as language academies, grammar books, and, of course, schools.

Li Wei (2011) describes translanguaging spaces as "interactionally created" and emphasizes the performative nature of those spaces. He adds:

For me, translanguaging is both going between different linguistic structures and systems, including different modalities (speaking, writing, signing, listening, reading, remembering) and going beyond them. It includes the full range of linguistic performances of multilingual language users for purposes that transcend the combination of structures, the alternation between systems, the transmission of information and the representation of values, identities and relationships. The act of translanguaging then is transformative in nature; it creates a social space for the multilingual language user by bringing together different dimensions of their personal history, experience and environment, their attitude, belief and ideology, their cognitive and physical capacity into one coordinated and meaningful performance, and making it into a lived experience. I call this space "translanguaging space," a space for the act of translanguaging as well as a space created through translanguaging. (p. 1223)

This creative use of language by bilinguals not only transforms our traditional notions of "named languages" and the ways in which we view the language practices of bilingual students, but also makes room for bilinguals to be themselves rather than "two monolinguals in one" (Grosjean, 1982).

Some scholars have taken up translanguaging, but call for what MacSwan (2017) calls an "integrated multilingual model." MacSwan argues that bilinguals have a single linguistic repertoire, but also two compartmentalized mental grammars that correspond to two named languages. In contrast, Otheguy, García, and Reid (2015); Wei (2017); as well as García and Wei (2014) have argued for a translanguaging perspective that distinguishes between the *internal* mental grammar, the cognitive capacity that people enjoy to develop and use language through and in social interaction, and the *external* named languages of nation-states that make up simply a social norm of linguistic conventions. García and Wei (2014), as well as Otheguy, García, and Reid (2015), posit that *both* the internal cognitive-linguistic perspective, as well as the external socially normed perspective, are equally important in the lives of bilinguals and multilinguals. They argue that in the bilinguals' language system—constructed, of course, in social interaction—there are not two compartments that correspond to named languages. Rather, the linguistic features of a bilingual's mental grammar are disaggregated in a unitary linguistic system that is the speaker's own.

The social construction of named languages is most important and real, and bilinguals have to learn to gauge when to use what features for what situation and with whom, but in the view of García and Wei (2014) and Otheguy, García, and Reid (2015), this is a social selection based on external social norms, not a cognitive-linguistic reality. This is the perspective of translanguaging that we adopt in this book, because it makes a difference as to how we view and teach emergent bilinguals. MacSwan's (2017) version of translanguaging suggests that when emergent bilinguals walk into the classroom, they are _incomplete_, because they still lack a second language system. García and Wei (2014) and Otheguy, García, and Reid (2015) posit that when emergent bilinguals walk into the classroom, they possess a _full_ and unitary linguistic system, a mental grammar made up of features that have been developed in the _social_ context in which they have done language up to now. The pedagogical consequence of the distinction between, on the one hand, the MacSwan version, and on the other that of García and Wei (2014) and Otheguy, García, and Reid (2015) is important. If we adopted MacSwan's view, teachers would be responsible for "adding" a second language to students whom they perceive as lacking it. In the theory of translanguaging adopted by García and Wei (2014) and Otheguy, García, and Reid (2015), teachers create the affordances in the classroom so that students have the social opportunities to acquire new features to incorporate into their own linguistic system and expand it. In this view, ESL teachers see their task as offering interactional affordances so that through the _students' own agency_, and in practice, students take up new features and incorporate them into their unitary linguistic system. Instruction would then focus on providing affordances to emergent bilinguals so that they could use and select these new features according to the social norms of the English classroom. In the case of bilingual instruction, teachers would view their task as offering interactional affordances that would not only enable emergent bilingual students to take up new features, but also to _select the features_ from their unitary linguistic system according to the more complex social norms of a bilingual classroom. As we will see in Chapter 5, sometimes teachers would offer opportunities for students to select and use features of what is seen as one named language or the other in order to develop the students' biliteracy, an important goal of bilingual instruction. Other times, the teacher would offer bilingual students opportunities to engage with their full unitary language repertoire, freeing them from the monolingual social norms of named languages. Always, however, the starting point would be the students' rich unitary language system and a view of the students' linguistic system as capable of adapting to new sociolinguistic situations and able to expand, whether the instruction is monolingual or bilingual, and whether the goal of instruction is monolingualism or bilingualism and biliteracy.

EMPIRICAL EVIDENCE ON THE RELATIONSHIP BETWEEN BILINGUALISM AND ACHIEVEMENT

Around the world there is near consensus among researchers that greater support for emergent bilinguals' home language practices, and academic development using those practices, is "positively related to higher long-term academic attainment" (Ferguson, 2006, p. 48). Because in the United States the notion of bilingual education itself is so politically loaded, research about the question of whether bilingual education or monolingual (English-only) education works best for emergent bilinguals is often contradictory. Nevertheless, and on balance, there is much research support for the positive effects of the use of students' home language practices over English-only education (for a comprehensive review, see Baker & Wright, 2017; see also Baker & Lewis, 2015).

Several large-scale evaluations (e.g., Ramírez, 1992; Thomas & Collier, 2002) have demonstrated that using the home language in instruction benefits language-minority students. For instance, Ramírez (1992) carried out a longitudinal study of 554 kindergarten-to-6th-grade Latinx students in five states (New York, New Jersey, Florida, Texas, and California) who were in English-only structured immersion programs, transitional early-exit programs, and late-exit developmental bilingual programs. (In this study, two-way dual-language bilingual education programs were not evaluated.) The results of this study favored late-exit developmental bilingual programs that use students' home languages for 5 to 6 years. Although there were no differences between programs among students in the 3rd grade, by 6th grade, students in late-exit developmental programs were performing better in mathematics, English language arts, and English reading than students in the other programs.

In 2002, Thomas and Collier published a study of the effectiveness of different types of educational programs for language-minority student achievement. They compared the achievement on nationally standardized tests[6] of students in different kinds of programs, who entered school in kindergarten or 1st grade with little or no proficiency in English, and followed them to the highest grade level reached. They determined that bilingually schooled students outperformed comparable monolingually schooled students in all subjects. Furthermore, they found that the strongest predictor of the students' English language achievement was the amount of formal schooling they had received in the home language. Developmental bilingual education programs (one-way dual language) and two-way bilingual education programs (two-way dual language) were the only kinds of programs that enabled emergent bilinguals to reach the 50th percentile in both languages in all subjects. These bilingual education programs also produced the fewest dropouts. Two types of two-way and developmental bilingual education programs were included in the study: (1) the 50:50 model, meaning that 50% of the instruction is in the child's home language and 50% in the additional language; and (2) the 90:10 model, meaning that *initially* 90% of the instruction is in the child's first language and 10% in the other language, but gradually moves to a 50:50 arrangement. Thomas and Collier (2002) found that the 90:10 type of instruction was more efficient than the 50:50 instructional model in helping students reach grade-level achievement in their additional language.

In 2017, Collier and Thomas summarized the findings of 32 years of research on the effects of bilingual instruction on achievement. Their summary concludes that only high-quality long-term bilingual programs are effective in making bilingual students achieve academically, whereas bilingual students in English-only and transitional bilingual programs of the early-exit type are not successful.

Lindholm-Leary (2001) conducted a comprehensive evaluation of programs serving emergent bilinguals in California. These included English-only programs, transitional bilingual education, and two types of two-way bilingual education (what she called simply dual-language education or DLE—90:10 and 50:50). Like Thomas and Collier (2002), Lindhom-Leary found that students who were in instructional programs in which initially English was used for only 10% to 20% of the time (whether transitional or 90:10 dual language) did as well on English proficiency tests as those in English-only programs or 50:50 two-way dual-language bilingual programs. By grade 6, however, Latinx students in what Lindholm-Leary called "dual-language education" (two-way bilingual education) outperformed transitional bilingual education students. In mathematics, all students in dual-language education outperformed by 10 points those educated only in English.

In their synthesis of the research evidence in the education of emergent bilinguals, Genesee, Lindholm-Leary, Saunders, and Christian (2006) confirmed that students who are in educational programs that provide extended instruction in their home language through late-exit bilingual education programs (developmental/one-way dual-language and two-way bilingual education/dual language) outperform students who receive only short-term instruction through their home language (early-exit transitional bilingual education). They also found that bilingual proficiency and biliteracy were positively related to academic achievement in both languages. Finally, Genesee and colleagues (2006) found that emergent bilinguals in primary school programs providing home language support had acquired the same or superior levels of reading and writing skills as students in English-only programs by the end of elementary school.

Five independent meta-analyses of experimental studies (August & Shanahan, 2006; Greene, 1997; Rolstad, Mahoney, & Glass, 2005; Slavin & Cheung, 2005; Willig, 1985) concluded that learning to read in the child's home language promotes reading achievement in an additional language, an unprecedented level of convergence (Goldenberg, 2008). Likewise, the National Literacy Panel on Language Minority Children and Youth, appointed by the George W. Bush administration, concluded that bilingual education approaches, in which the student's home language is used, are more effective in teaching students to read than are English-only approaches (see August & Shanahan, 2006). Thus, there is firm evidence that learning to read in the student's home language promotes reading achievement in English. In a guide to the research on how to promote academic achievement among English learners, Goldenberg and Coleman (2010) say:

> Primary-language reading instruction is clearly no panacea, just as phonics instruction is no panacea. But relatively speaking, it makes a meaningful contribution to ELLs' reading achievement in *English*. (p. 27; emphasis added)

In 2014, Umansky and Reardon conducted an analysis of reclassification patterns among Latinx emergent bilinguals in schools in California in three different types of programs—sheltered English immersion, transitional bilingual education, and two-way dual-language bilingual (dual-immersion) programs. They found that Latinx emergent bilingual students in two-way dual-language bilingual education (DLBE) programs were reclassified (as fluent bilinguals) more slowly than were students in other programs. However, they also found that, over time, students in DLBE programs had higher overall reclassification rates, and higher English proficiency and academic performance.

Lindholm-Leary and Genesee (2014) synthesize all these studies by concluding:

> Over three decades of research in the U.S. indicates that minority language students in two-way and DBE [developmental bilingual education] programs acquire English speaking, listening, reading and writing skills as well and as quickly as their minority language peers in mainstream programs. (p. 172)

Despite the support for two-way immersion or two-way dual-language bilingual education, we cannot conclude that they are the *only* way to educate language-minoritized students successfully and bilingually. The promise of two-way dual-language bilingual education (DLBE) notwithstanding, not all localities can implement these programs in all languages because many language-majority communities are not eager to have their children schooled with language-minority children. For example, even though two-way DLBE programs are growing in English/Chinese and English/Spanish, other language groups—Haitians, for example—are not benefiting from such programs. Why? Language-majority parents are many times reluctant to have their children learn Haitian Creole, which they consider to be a low-prestige language. Haitian Creole is, however, essential for the meaningful education of Haitian children and youth (Ballenger, 1997; Cerat, 2017; Hudicourt-Barnes, 2003), and thus, it would be important to develop bilingual education programs for the Haitian community.

It is also important to point out that often students are "selected" for participation in two-way DLBE programs on the basis of good scores on screening instruments and parental interviews (see, for example, the case of some schools in New York City in García, Velasco, Menken, & Vogel, forthcoming). Emergent bilinguals who are considered less "gifted" linguistically when they enter kindergarten are assigned to ESL programs or transitional bilingual education programs because room has to be made for English-speaking monolingual students in the DLBE program. Thus, emergent bilingual students in two-way DLBE programs where half of the students are White English-speaking students are often not the same type of students as those in transitional bilingual education or ESL programs.

As August and Hakuta (1997) state in their National Research Council report, any type of program to educate emergent bilinguals can be implemented well or poorly. However, what is evident from the research is that the classroom use of students' home language practices over a longer period of time is crucial for their long-term cognitive growth and academic achievement in English and in the home language. De Jong and Bearse (2011) report a positive correlation between level of bilingualism and academic achievement, as well as between level of bilingualism and level of proficiency in English and the home language. All teachers, both those who are required to deliver instruction in English only and those who do so bilingually, can take a more effective pedagogical path by constructing bilingual instructional spaces, as we will describe in the next chapter.

EDUCATING EMERGENT BILINGUALS: BUILDING ON BILINGUALISM FOR ACADEMIC SUCCESS

Although additive schooling *practices* are important, additive conceptions of bilingualism fail to capture the complexity of bilingual acquisition and development. A linear conception of additive bilingualism does not describe adequately the ever-changing multilingual practices of the 21st century; thus, we choose instead to use the term *dynamic bilingualism*. We make evident that some language-minoritized students who speak languages that are not prevalent in the school community cannot be schooled bilingually, given the ways in which many bilingual education programs have been constructed. It is, of course, easier to build bilingual education programs for large language groups—especially Spanish speakers, the largest and most rapidly growing linguistic minority in the United States. Yet every teacher, even those teaching in spaces that are formally denominated as ESL or English only, can draw on students' linguistic practices.

By way of summary, Table 4.1 shows the types of educational programs described in Chapter 3, alongside linguistic goals, and the kind of bilingualism that they promote according to the understandings that we have proposed in this chapter.

Table 4.1. Types of educational programs and bilingualism

Program	Goal	Bilingualism
Submersion	Monolingualism	Subtractive
ESL pull-out	Monolingualism	Subtractive
ESL push-in	Monolingualism	Subtractive
Structured English immersion	Monolingualism	Subtractive
High-intensity English language training	Monolingualism	Subtractive
Transitional bilingual education	Monolingualism	Subtractive
Developmental bilingual education (one-way DLBE)	Bilingualism	Dynamic & recursive; dynamic
Two-way bilingual education (two-way DLBE or two-way immersion)	Bilingualism	Dynamic
Dynamic bi/plurilingual education	Bilingualism	Dynamic

CHAPTER 5

Language and Bilingualism
Practices

In this chapter, we will:

- Identify three inequitable practices with regard to language use in education:
  - ➢ Insufficient support and development of home language practices,
  - ➢ Isolation of English,
  - ➢ Compartmentalization of English and languages other than English in instruction, and

- Consider four alternative practices:
  - ➢ Heteroglossic bilingual instructional practices,
  - ➢ Translanguaging pedagogy,
  - ➢ Critical multilingual awareness, and
  - ➢ Complex language/literacy use.

Our task in this chapter is twofold: We first identify the inequitable language education practices that educators should avoid. We then describe in detail four alternative language education practices that we advocate.

INEQUITABLE LANGUAGE/LITERACY PRACTICES

Having established that educational policy and practice does not reflect current research on emergent bilinguals and their education, we examine here three inequitable school practices—insufficient support and inadequate development of home language practices in instruction, the isolation of English into a monolingual learning space, and the compartmentalization of languages in ways that devalue students' own fluid bilingual community practices. In the second part of this chapter, we propose alternatives that we believe could address some of the problems in the present practices.

Insufficient Support and Inadequate Development of Home Language Practices

The NCLB and ESSA laws, described in Chapter 3, have generated some attention by scholars and the public to the education of emergent bilinguals. Yet, as we will see in this section, there has been a decrease in the number of students receiving an adequate education, and support is insufficient. We will also see that the participation of emergent bilingual students in educational programs that meet their needs remains inadequate both because of the types of programs offered and the length and level of service rendered.

Decrease in numbers receiving adequate services. As reported in Chapter 3, emergent bilingual students are increasingly educated in English-only programs despite the growth of the emergent bilingual student population. Zehler et al. (2003) summarized the declining conditions in which emergent bilinguals were being educated in 2003 by saying: "Compared to prior years, LEP students are now more likely to receive instructional services provided in English, and less likely to receive extensive ELL services" (p. 35). The situation has not improved in the decades that followed. According to the Office for Civil Rights, in 2011, approximately 9% of students who had been identified as English learners (420,826) were not enrolled in any targeted English language instructional programs.

New York City exemplifies the decline in the use of students' home language practices in education. In 1974, the Aspira Consent Decree mandated transitional bilingual education programs for the city's Latinx students (Reyes, 2006); today, however, fewer than ever emergent bilingual students are in New York City bilingual classrooms. In the school year 2002–2003, 53% of emergent bilinguals in New York City were in ESL programs; by the school year 2007–2008, 69% were instructed in ESL programs, and this number increased to 79.2% by 2013–2014. Likewise, whereas 37% of emergent bilinguals were in transitional bilingual education in 2002, only 21% participated in such programs in 2007–2008 and 15.4% in 2013–2014. In 2002, 2% of emergent bilinguals were in two-way dual-language bilingual programs, whereas only 3.6% were in such programs in 2007–2008 and 4.5% in 2013–2014. Thus, in 2013–2014, less than 20% of the emergent bilingual student population in New York City was in any type of bilingual program (NYCDOE, 2013–2014). Despite the greater interest in two-way dual-language bilingual education among language-majority students, bilingual education programs have been progressively eliminated in New York City (Menken & Solorza, 2013, 2014).

Inadequate educational programs: Program types. English as a Second Language/new language programs have been reshaped in the past 20 years. But pull-out ESL/ENL, where the focus is on English as an isolated language subject, continues to be the most commonly used type (Martínez, 2002), although research has shown that the use of English in content-area instruction, as in push-in programs or in structured English immersion programs, is associated with higher long-term educational attainment (Collier & Thomas, 2017; Thomas & Collier, 1997).

As we have said, even when the emergent bilingual students' home languages are used in bilingual education programs, most programs in the United States are "early-exit" transitional bilingual programs. These programs often have the secondary consequence of tracking emergent bilinguals into remedial programs (Ovando & Collier, 1998). The effect of such policies is that bilingualism and biliteracy for academic purposes does not emerge; instead, the result for these students is academic failure.

All types of bilingual education programs in the United States focus primarily on the development of English and its use for literacy purposes. As we have seen, NCLB (2001) and ESSA (2015) require schools to meet adequate yearly progress targets, which include rapid English literacy development as measured by standardized tests. As a result, many schools do not take the development of academic literacy in the home language seriously, because literacy in the language other than English is rarely assessed. In transitional bilingual education programs, the home language is often used and viewed only as a "bridge" to facilitate the learning of English. In dual-language bilingual programs, where the intent is to use the language other than English at least 50% of the time and facilitate the development of bilingualism and biliteracy, students and teachers also tend to value the development of English literacy much more than that in the other language, given the importance of scores in standardized tests in English. Thus, more time and resources are spent ensuring that students do well in the language that "counts."

Although two-way dual-language bilingual programs might be a step in the right direction for the future possibility of a less monolingual society, as these two-way DLBE programs are presently designed, only 50% of students in them are language-minoritized emergent bilinguals. Thus, these two-way dual-language bilingual programs tend to serve fewer English learners. As we said in Chapter 3, the appeal of these programs is their focus on the commodification of bilingualism for "the global economy" rather than the provision of the bilingual education that language-minoritized students deserve.

In 1997, as two-way dual-language bilingual education programs started to spring up, Guadalupe Valdés issued an important cautionary note about these programs, saying that they move away from providing equal educational opportunity to language-minoritized students to focus on providing language-majority students with the opportunity of becoming bilingual. Although the mainstream media generally offer only positive portrayals of these two-way DLBE programs, many scholars, following Valdés (1999), have begun to raise critical voices, arguing that the primary intent of these programs is the connection to a global economy rather than to educational equity for emergent bilinguals (see, for example, Cervantes-Soon, 2014; Fitts, 2006; Flores, 2016; García, 2009a; Palmer, 2010; Sánchez, García & Solorza, 2017; Valdez et al., 2014; Varghese & Park, 2010). Still others have cautioned that emergent bilingual students are being used as "commodities that can be consumed by White, English-speaking students" (Pimentel, 2011, p. 351). Petrovic (2005) provocatively says:

> Dual immersion programs have the potential of becoming the Epcot Center of foreign language curriculum, providing language majority students an opportunity to view live specimens of the second language. (p. 406)

Utah seems to lead the nation in the development of educational programs that use languages other than English in instruction. In 2008, a "dual-language initiative" created enormous interest in one-way immersion programs for English-speaking students (where 78% of students are presently educated) and two-way programs (where the remainder of students are educated). However, the legislation excluded one-way DLBE programs or developmental bilingual education for language-minoritized students (Valdez et al., 2014). Valdez and her colleagues (2014) document the discursive shift about language education in the print media in Utah from one of equity and heritage to one focused on global human capital.

Inadequate educational programs: Length and levels. Beyond the inadequate types of educational programs in which emergent bilinguals are being educated today, these support services are offered for an inadequate length of time. The failure of the services offered also stems from the fact that they are mostly found at the elementary level.

As we pointed out in Chapter 3, substantial research evidence reports that it takes between 5 and 7 years to develop ways of using English for academic purposes. And yet, in 2015, emergent bilinguals were being reclassified on average after 3 years (Slama, 2014). Thus, according to the research, emergent bilinguals are receiving educational support for about half the time that they will most likely need it. Many states permit emergent bilinguals to remain in special programs for only 1 year (for example, Arizona) or a maximum of 3 years. In fact, ESSA requires states to include in their reports any students who do not attain English proficiency in 5 years or more; ESSA designates those students as long-term English learners.

Although emergent bilinguals at the secondary level arguably have a more difficult task than students at the elementary level, given the complexity of the subject matter they must master to graduate, elementary students are far more likely to have instruction in which the home language is used in any significant way. Because all types of bilingual education programs exist primarily at the elementary school level, there is insufficient development of students' home literacies in middle and high schools. Consequently, most students who attend bilingual elementary programs then go to secondary schools where instruction is exclusively in English.

Middle and high school bilingual programs most often serve recent immigrants, except in the case of students coming from elementary school classrooms who have been unable to pass the English proficiency assessments. These long-term English learners have experienced considerable home language loss, and some have even become monolingual English speakers. Although these students are labeled as English learners, they do not share the characteristics of those for whom instruction is usually planned: They may be fluent speakers of English, although their English for literacy purposes might be inadequate. This low literacy level is often the result of an inconsistent or poor-quality primary educational experience (Menken & Kleyn, 2009; Menken, Kleyn, & Chae, 2012).

Isolation of English

Most education programs for emergent bilinguals in the United States are based on the belief that English is best taught monolingually (Phillipson, 1992). Harmer (1998) summarizes this uninformed yet commonplace advice to ESL teachers by saying that "the need to have them [students] practicing English (rather than their own language) remains paramount" (p. 129).

The emphasis on getting emergent bilinguals to perform as English proficient in assessments means that many teachers forbid the use of students' home languages in their classrooms. They do so with the false belief that if they allow home language use, they will fail as educators to adapt instruction to the English language needs of the students (Cloud, Genesee, & Hamayan, 2000).

Schools in the United States have played a vital role in controlling the language practices of minoritized and racialized students and making them "governable subjects" (Flores, 2013; Foucault, 1979). Named language constructions, such as standard English, have been used as gatekeepers to exclude minoritized students from educational opportunities in which they have rich English input and are allowed entry into meaningful and authentic opportunities to use English. When English is isolated and demands are made that only English be used to learn and to participate in educational opportunities, emergent bilinguals are also excluded from dominant social circles and important occupations (for more on the construction of "English," see Pennycook, 2006, 2007). When students express sophisticated understandings of math, science, and history using language features considered "nonstandard," their knowledge is invalidated because only English is accepted. This further prevents emergent bilinguals from having opportunities to become the mathematicians, scientists, and historians that we so desperately need.

Compartmentalization of English and Languages Other Than English in Instruction

Bilingual education programs have also fallen prey to a monoglossic ideology that treats bilinguals' languages as one autonomous language added to another, instead of understanding these students' dynamic, fluid linguistic practices (García, 2009a). Thus, bilingual schools usually strictly separate the languages. It was Wallace Lambert (1984) who perhaps best expressed this ideology of language separation in his discussion about French immersion programs in Canada in the 1980s:

> No bilingual skills are required of the teacher, who plays the role of a monolingual in the target language . . . and who never switches languages, reviews materials in the other language, or otherwise uses the child's native language in teacher-pupil interactions. In immersion programs, therefore, bilingualism is developed through two separate monolingual instructional routes. (p.13)

This practice of strict language separation and sheltering of languages has prevailed in bilingual education. Jacobson and Faltis (1990) explain the reasons for this practice: "By strictly separating the languages, the teacher avoids, it is argued, cross contamination, thus making it easier for the child to acquire a new linguistic system as he/she internalizes a given lesson" (p. 4).

There are four language allocation strategies traditionally used to separate languages in bilingual education:

- Time-determined, with one language exclusively used half the day, on alternate days, or even alternate weeks;
- Teacher-determined, with two teachers who speak one language exclusively;
- Place-determined, with one room or even building used for one language exclusively; and
- Subject-determined, with one language being exclusively used to teach one subject (García, 2009a).

In bilingual education, language allocation policies are important. But those that adhere to complete language separation—what Cummins (2008) called "the two solitudes"—should be reexamined. Rigid adherence to one language or another without regard to students' own practices and how they make meaning contradicts research findings. Unless these strict language allocation policies become more flexible, they will keep language-minoritized students within a closed circle from which they cannot access opportunities and knowledge.

Bilingual education programs understandably must maintain instructional spaces for one language or another so that students receive adequate input and have opportunities to use the language of instruction. This is especially important for the development of a minoritized or threatened language. But language development (whether in English or in the additional language) cannot occur in isolation from the world. *Minoritized languages need to be protected, but they cannot be isolated.* Students develop new linguistic practices when they learn to use language for meaningful purposes, particularly when they learn something of interest and want to use language to show that understanding.

Heller (1999) has made us aware of the dangers of valuing only what she calls "parallel monolingualisms," practices in which "every variety must conform to certain prescriptive norms" (p. 271). Because languages other than English are not validated publicly in powerful spheres (even when they are spoken in local communities), they are often reified in schools—that is, valued only when they are used according to standardized monolingual conventions and norms. And thus, unless language allocation policies are adhered to judiciously, there is the potential in bilingual education programs of further alienating language-minoritized bilingual students from what is assigned to them as their "first language," "L1," or "mother tongue," because the school language does not resemble their own bilingual practices.

ALTERNATIVE LANGUAGE/LITERACY PRACTICES

Whether teaching exclusively in English or teaching bilingually, effective educators make room in the classroom for emergent bilinguals' leveraging the existing features of their repertoire in order to acquire new ones. How do teachers manage this, given policies that many times run counter to these practices? They can do so, as we will demonstrate here, by negotiating educational policies for the benefit of their students, thus becoming policymakers themselves (Menken & García, 2010). In what follows, we describe educational practices that work for emergent bilinguals given the dynamic nature of bilingualism that we have laid out above. We describe the following four language-focused educational practices that build on theoretical constructs and research evidence that we have been considering:

- Heteroglossic bilingual instructional practices
- Translanguaging pedagogy
- Critical multilingual awareness programs
- Complex language/literacy use

Contradicts
the
Bridge article, No?

Heteroglossic Bilingual Instructional Practices

Language teaching has traditionally excluded the students' home language practices from ESL and bilingual classrooms, whether the approach used has been communicative, immersion, or focused on linguistic structures. In ESL classrooms, many teachers continue to believe that it is best to use what is considered "appropriate English" exclusively. In bilingual classrooms, the separation of languages has been the most accepted practice, with only "appropriate English," but also "appropriate language other than English" accepted during the times allotted to each of the languages.

A meaningful and rigorous education for emergent bilinguals will *always* leverage the home language practices as much as possible. Some ESL/ENL educators may be constrained by program structures that require English-only instruction. Others might be inhibited because the emergent bilinguals in their classrooms speak many languages. Bilingual educators may be confined by strict language allocation policies. But *all* educators—bilingual, ESL, and mainstream—can draw upon the language practices of their bilingual students for a meaningful education. We call them heteroglossic bilingual instructional practices here because they disrupt the monoglossic nature of programs that purport to be in English only or solely in two standard languages with separate articulations. These heteroglossic bilingual instructional practices are grounded on the ways in which emergent bilinguals use language, and not simply on the restrictive ways of using language that schools impose.

Heteo-Glossic

There are many classrooms in the United States where educators are finding ways of leveraging the students' home language practices regardless of program structure or "model" used. As Cummins (2009) says, "bilingual instructional strategies can be incorporated into English-medium classrooms, thereby opening up the pedagogical space in ways that legitimate the intelligence, imagination, and linguistic talents of ELL students" (p. xi). Describing how all teachers can include the students' home language practices in instruction, Cummins (2007) suggests that "[W]hen students' L1 is invoked as a cognitive and linguistic resource through bilingual instructional strategies, it can function as a stepping stone to scaffold more accomplished performance in the L2" (p. 14).

In their discussion about modifications needed to advance literacy instruction for emergent bilinguals, Goldenberg and Coleman (2010) recommend what they call "strategic" uses of the language other than English. In teaching vocabulary, they recommend presenting words in the LOTE before teaching them in English, previewing lessons using texts in the LOTE, providing teachers with translation equivalents of the target words, using cognates, and selecting texts and topics that would be culturally appropriate for their students. In developing emergent bilinguals' reading

each in LOTE

LOTE

comprehension, they recommend previewing English reading texts in the LOTE, teaching metacognitive reading strategies in the students' home language, and pointing out similarities and differences between English and the students' home language.

Wright (2010) refers to what he calls primary language support, a form of scaffolding. Wright identifies several such strategies that use the home language in (1) preview-review, in which teachers preview lessons in the home language, present in English, and review in the home language; (2) giving quick explanations; (3) labeling and displaying words and works; (4) providing resources (dictionaries, books, technology); and (5) accepting all students' contributions to the lesson.

García, Flores, and Chu (2011) have described how two high schools include bilingual instructional practices despite the fact that neither has an official bilingual education program. In one high school where everyone is an emergent bilingual of different language backgrounds, students decide which language they want to use when researching topics and reading and writing about them. Students develop their own strategies for making sense of the academic lesson in English, often using Google Translate and other websites as a resource. As they develop their projects, students teach one another phrases in both English and additional languages. Whenever possible, the teacher interacts with small groups and individual students in the languages they are using. When students are using a language that the teacher does not understand, one of the more advanced emergent bilinguals provides translation.

In an ESL elementary school classroom, Christina Celic (2009) "stretches" her self-contained ESL class by getting students to read and write in languages other than English. Most of her emergent bilinguals are Spanish speaking, but there are also Mandarin speakers and students from Nepal, India, and Bangladesh. Students are paired strategically so that fluent bilingual students work with emergent bilingual students. Celic uses a workshop model of teaching literacy (Calkins, 1994). Calkins's workshop model recommends mini-lessons: short teacher-centered lessons in which teachers model explicit metacognitive strategies used in reading and writing texts (see also Swinney & Velasco, 2011). During the mini-lessons, students "turn-and-talk," which means they practice what the teacher has been modeling with a peer, using all the linguistic and other semiotic resources at their disposal—Spanish, English, language prompts, drawings, gestures. For independent reading, Celic provides leveled reading material for her emergent bilinguals in English and the other language. During the writing workshop, students have the option to write in any language, or to write fully bilingual texts, similar to the bilingual children's books that Celic uses as read-alouds (C. Celic, personal communication, October 31, 2009). Celic also helps emergent bilinguals develop their understanding of new vocabulary in English by making explicit connections between languages. To do that, she asks her students if they know what the word means in their language and, whenever possible, has them add the translation to the "word wall" in their classroom.

In middle schools studied by Danling Fu (2003, 2009), the students use Chinese writing as a stepping-stone to English writing. Teachers allow beginning ESL students to write in Chinese, while incorporating the few words they know in English. Gradually, more English writing emerges. Fu (2009) says:

> Learning to write in English for ELLs who are literate in their native language is actually a process of becoming bilingual writers, rather than merely replacing one language or writing ability with another or mastering two separate language systems. . . . If writing reflects who and what the writers are, then ELLs' native language (voice and expressions) will either visibly appear or be blended with English. (p. 120)

The work of Cummins and other researchers in Canadian classrooms also clearly demonstrates how teachers can use bilingual instructional strategies in English-only classrooms. Cummins (2006) calls for the use of "identity texts," as students use both languages to write about their own immigration and education experiences. Elsewhere, he quotes Madiha, one of the girls involved in a project of producing bilingual identity texts:

> I think it helps my learning to be able to write in both languages because if I'm writing English and Ms. Leoni says you can write Urdu too it helps me think of what the word means because I always think in Urdu. That helps me write better in English. (Cummins, 2009, p. x)

In some classrooms, teachers encourage students to write double-entry journals (see García & Traugh, 2002). In this assignment, students copy fragments of academic texts they are reading in one column, then react to the texts from their own personal perspectives in the second column, contributing both their experiences and their cultural and linguistic understandings to make sense of the texts. The reactions/reflections are written using the students' own language practices. These double-entry journals are then shared with fellow classmates as a way to build multicultural and multilingual understandings of the same text and to generate different understandings from multiple perspectives.

Lucas and Katz (1994) document more bilingual instructional practices that do not require teachers to be bilingual, such as:

- Teachers devising a writing assignment in which students use their home language;
- Students reading or telling stories to one another using their home language and then translating them into English to tell other students;
- Students from same language backgrounds being paired together so that students who are more fluent in English can help those less fluent;

- Students being encouraged to use bilingual dictionaries;
- Students being encouraged to get help at home in their home languages;
- Books being provided in students' home languages; and
- Awards being given for excellence in languages not commonly studied.

Strengthening the relationship between languages is also the approach taken in Beeman and Urrow (2013) in what they identify as "the Bridge," an important strategy in bilingual instruction. Beeman and Urrow explain: "The Bridge is the instructional moment when teachers purposefully bring the two languages together, guiding students to transfer the academic content they have learned in one language to the other language, engage in contrastive analysis of the two languages, and strengthen their knowledge of both languages" (p. v).

The practices described above are ways in which bilingualism is used in all types of educational programs for emergent bilinguals. These heteroglossic bilingual practices are consonant with theoretical and empirical evidence for how home language practices support students' development of language for academic purposes. These bilingual instructional practices serve as important instructional scaffolds.

Translanguaging Pedagogy

A pedagogical approach based on translanguaging theory supports and extends the heteroglossic bilingual instructional practices described above. A translanguaging pedagogy is more than a simple scaffold; it leverages the unitary language repertoire of bilingual speakers. In so doing, it *transforms* practices in schools as well as societal views of such practices.

A translanguaging pedagogy is not simply a series of strategies and scaffolds, but also a philosophy of language and education (García & Wei, 2014) that is centered on a bilingual minoritized community. Translanguaging pedagogy leverages *all* the language practices that bilingual students bring to school. Because emergent bilinguals are always embodying their translanguaging—that is, their unitary language system—educating them cannot be a matter of isolating or compartmentalizing one language from the other, using one language in support of another, or simply promoting "transfer" from one language to another. A translanguaging pedagogy values and supports the translanguaging practices that are the norm in bilingual communities, thus having the potential to transform the contempt with which bilingual fluid language practices are often held by schools and majority society (Canagarajah, 2011).

As we indicated in Chapter 3, translanguaging emerged and has been developed in "the borderlands" (Anzaldúa, 2012) by minoritized bilingual scholars for minoritized bilingual speakers; it was first used to ensure the bilingual development of Welsh speakers (Baker, 2001; Williams, 1994). To educate bilingual minoritized students, translanguaging recognizes and leverages their single language repertoire and unitary identity as bilinguals.

García and Kleyn (2016) summarize the transformative impact on educators who take up translanguaging theory:

> A theory of translanguaging can be transformative for educators. Once educators start looking at language from the point of view of the bilingual learner, and not simply at the named language with its prescribed features, everything changes. Educators then teach in order to discover what, in the child's arsenal of language features, can be enhanced through interactions with others and texts that have different language features. They do not tell students to stop using their own language features or to stop drawing on them for learning. Educators become co-learners (Wei, 2014), instead of simply identifying as teachers who transmit a canon of linguistic knowledge. Equipped with translanguaging theory, educators leverage the students' full language repertoires to teach and assess, enabling a more socially just and equitable education for bilingual students. (p. 17)

García, Johnson, and Seltzer (2017) identify the four purposes of translanguaging pedagogy:

1. Supporting students as they engage with and comprehend complex content and texts;
2. Providing opportunities for students to develop linguistic practices for academic contexts;
3. Making space for students' bilingualism and bilingual ways of knowing; and
4. Supporting students' social–emotional development and bilingual identities.

These four purposes work together to advance social justice and to ensure that bilingual learners are educated for success and not just to conform to monolingual norms. With the help of translanguaging pedagogy, the language practices of minoritized speakers cease to be an excuse to deny access to rich educational experiences and instead are leveraged to educate deeply and justly (García, Seltzer, & Witt, 2018).

Educators who enact translanguaging pedagogies recognize the fluid language use of bilingual communities and its value in learning, although they also recognize the importance of two or more named languages and biliteracy in standard languages. For example, Creese and Blackledge (2010) have explored the relationship between translanguaging practices, identity performance, and language learning and teaching in complementary schools, which support home language learning in Great Britain. From a biliteracy perspective, Hornberger and Link (2012) have argued that "individuals' biliteracy develops along the continua in direct response to contextual demands placed on them" and "biliteracy development is enhanced when they have recourse to all their existing skills" (pp. 244–245).

García, Johnson, and Seltzer (2017) identify three interrelated strands that define a translanguaging pedagogy:

1. The translanguaging stance,
2. The translanguaging design, and
3. The translanguaging shift.

Teachers of minoritized bilingual students must have a *translanguaging stance*—the philosophical, ideological, or belief system that students' various and wide-ranging language practices work together and are a resource for learning. Educators with this stance believe that the classroom space must promote collaboration across language practices, content understandings, peoples, home, and school. A translanguaging stance also includes the belief that, to truly assess what bilingual students know and can do, both in language and content, assessment has to allow students to access all the features of their language repertoire, instead of less than half of them, as most monolingual assessments do.

The *translanguaging design* involves the careful planning of (1) the multilingual resources needed in the classrooms and their use, (2) the grouping of students, (3) the unit/lesson planning that includes not only content and language objectives but also translanguaging objectives, (4) translanguaging pedagogical strategies, and (5) translanguaging assessments (for more on this, see García, Johnson, & Seltzer, 2017).

Finally, the term *translanguaging shifts* refers to the many moment-by-moment decisions that teachers make all the time. It indicates a teacher's flexibility and willingness to change the course of the lesson and assessment, as well as the language use, in response to students' needs.

U.S. scholars have been increasingly providing evidence of how translanguaging enhances understanding of academic content and extends the emergent bilinguals' linguistic repertoire to incorporate features considered "standard" in U.S. schools. This is evident in ESL/ENL classrooms (see Ebe, 2016; Woodley, 2016), in transitional bilingual education classrooms (Collins & Cioè-Peña, 2016; Kleyn, 2016; Sayer, 2013; Seltzer & Collins, 2016), or in dual-language bilingual education classrooms (Espinosa & Herrera, 2016; Gort & Sembiante, 2015; Palmer, Martínez, Mateus, & Henderson, 2014). An issue of the *International Multilingual Research Journal* edited by Gort (2015) and Gort (2018) indicates the growing appeal of translanguaging for purposes of supporting bilingualism and biliteracy, while making the structures and practices in bilingual education classrooms more flexible so that they buttress the meaning-making of students.

Developing translanguaging pedagogical strategies that support the education of emergent bilinguals has been the focus of the work of CUNY-NYSIEB (www.cuny-nysieb.org), a Graduate Center, City University of New York project, funded by the New York State Education Department. The project works with all types of schools and teachers with large numbers of emergent bilinguals to improve their education. It does so by focusing on a vision that rests on dynamic bilingualism and development, and by adopting two nonnegotiable principles—leveraging the students' home language practices as a resource, and developing a multilingual ecology for the school.[1]

Educators who understand the power of translanguaging encourage emergent bilinguals to use their home language practices actively to think, reflect, and extend their semiotic meaning-making repertoire. And educators work with emergent bilinguals to ensure that the new language features they are "adding" or learning become appropriated into a repertoire that students perceive as their own. English cannot be their "second" language. Instead, the new linguistic features of what schools call "English" must become part of bilingual students' "own" complex language system. Students cannot simply perceive and use these new features as if they were part of a new, alien, second language system. A translanguaging pedagogical approach ensures that students become *agentive* users of the linguistic and communicative semiotic sign systems that they have available to mean and learn. By immersing students in opportunities to practice language for authentic and complex operations, students become agentive in *selecting* the most appropriate features to interact with others, while inhibiting other features of their complex unitary repertoire.

A translanguaging pedagogy cannot simply be a "scaffold" to understand English lessons and produce English texts, or to understand instruction in a language other than English. In understanding translanguaging as part of the unitary system of bilingual speakers, educators *transform* ESL/ENL and bilingual education. Adopting translanguaging in ESL/ENL classrooms means that the language practices of *all* students can be used as a resource for learning at all times. In bilingual education, it means that *all* the students' language practices, beyond those that reflect the two standardized languages used as a medium of instruction, can be leveraged. It also means that educators judiciously define the language allocation policy in their bilingual program, but keep the focus on how to use language so that students make meaning of their learning and their worlds (see Sánchez, García, & Solorza, 2017). García and Wei (2014) acknowledge that in today's dynamic world of interaction, "students need practice and engagement in translanguaging, as much as they need practice of standard features used for academic purposes" (pp. 71–72). Emergent bilingual students must be given agency to be creative and critical, "able to co-construct their language expertise, recognize each other as resources, and act on their knowing and doing" (p. 75).

Critical Multilingual Awareness Programs

Emergent bilingual students foreground language practices that differ significantly from the ways in which language is used in school. Additionally, these different language practices are often manifestations of social, racial, political, and economic struggles. Critical multilingual awareness programs build students' understandings of the social, political, racial, and economic struggles surrounding the use of many languages (see Fairclough, 1992, 1999; García, 2017; Kleifgen, 2009; van Dijk, 2008). Shohamy (2006) reminds us that it is important for all students to reflect on ways in which languages are used to exclude and discriminate. In calling for ways to work against raciolinguistic ideologies of language inappropriateness, Flores and Rosa (2015) argue that students need to become more aware of the way that language-majority speakers listen to and perceive the linguistic practices of minoritized speakers as deficient, regardless of how closely they follow supposed rules of appropriateness (see also DeGraff, 2005, 2009).

Critical multilingual awareness programs generate greater understandings of the intersectionality between language, geopolitics, race, socioeconomic status, and gender. They also help students understand how language use in society has been naturalized, falsely claiming that only what are constituted as "standard" features and uses of language are considered legitimate. Foucault (1979) has argued that this process of establishing an idealized norm of conduct and then punishing individuals who deviate from it is a tactic of social control. This naturalization of language constitutes what Foucault (1979) calls "disciplinary power."

When teachers make students aware that named languages are socially constructed, and thus socially changeable, to give voice to others, young people are given agency to redress the historical oppression of certain linguistic groups. As García (2017) has said, this can generate "not only a new order of discourse, but also a new praxis, capable of changing the social order of what it means to 'language' in school" (p. 269).

One useful critical multilingual awareness activity is to have students of different language backgrounds read the same news item published in various languages. Through translating the news into English, the students can analyze how the discourse (and the content) varies across languages and reflect on the reasons for the variation. They also can make recordings and transcriptions of their own rendering of the news in their home languages and reflect on the differences between their language practices and those of the media.

In classrooms with older students, teachers can engage them in becoming critical ethnographers of communities by looking at the ways in which different languages are represented in public spaces—what many call linguistic landscapes—and interpreting why they appear as such (Gorter, Marten, & Van Mensel, 2012; Landry & Bourhis, 1997; Shohamy & Gorter, 2009). Students can take photographs of signs in the community for analysis of similarities or differences across languages and reflect on the variations of use and the different messages that are communicated. Students can also analyze bilingual signs and their fluid language designs. Other students can analyze the hierarchy of power with regard to languages by studying the order in which languages appear in print, the nature of signage, and what all these different social positionings mean.

Ethnographies of language communities that are part of these critical multilingual awareness practices must also include spoken language. Teachers can ask students, for example, to observe and compare language use in different neighborhoods and places, and explore questions, such as: Which languages are selected for use in different neighborhood locales—businesses, government offices, places of worship, parks? Students can be asked to explore language use in an upscale store and in a *bodega* in a Latinx neighborhood, and answer questions such as: Which clients are attended to in service encounters—English speakers or speakers of another language, and what are the social and racial indices of the speakers? What are the language practices of the employees and the clients? How do they differ? Why?

Educators also can engage students in studying the languages represented in newspapers and magazines found in their neighborhood stands and in the media—television, radio, and the internet. How does language choice and use differ and who are the target readers/listeners? Students also can critically analyze how different language groups are represented in film, television, and other media outlets.

To ensure that students also reflect on translanguaging in society, students can generate banks of examples in media and print, as well as spoken language. These examples should identify sources and keep in mind different audiences and interlocutors. These problem sets can be then subjected to further analysis and become the focus of explicit language and literacy instruction.

The best critical multilingual awareness programs are those in which students study their own school: What are the different language practices they hear and see in their school? How do these differ by interlocutor, or task? What is the meaning of this language use? In describing language and literacy practices within the classroom, students can draw from the data they have gathered outside the classroom and in the community. This comparison can serve well to help students anchor language use in particular domains and for specific purposes, and then reflect on its meaning.

As part of a critical multilingual awareness program, educators may also present students with an explicit curriculum on multilingualism in the United States. Educators might engage students in researching the following questions: What are the language practices in different regions of the United States and what are the historical, social, and economic reasons for those differences? Where do bilingual communities live and what are the differences in their schooling? Why do they live there? How did this come about?

Students looking beyond the United States can be engaged in questions such as: What is the sociolinguistic profile of different nation-states? Whose language practices are represented as official or national? Why? How did this come about? Students engage in making links between socioeconomic and other sociodemographic characteristics and the status of named languages within different countries. They also search the internet as they become aware of different scripts used to write different languages and the relationship, in some cases, between scripts and cultural history.

Complex Language/Literacy Use

Educators who understand theories and empirical evidence about bilingualism in education are aware that literacy for academic purposes must be developed through a challenging curriculum combined with explicit, overt instruction. Teachers present complex ideas that develop the students' metacognitive skills—that is, curricular plans that enable learners to successfully approach academic tasks and help them monitor their thinking, thereby creating greater metalinguistic awareness (Walqui, 2006). Effective teachers do not oversimplify the English language or offer remedial instruction. Instead, they offer intensive support, while providing challenging instruction (see Walqui & van Lier, 2010). This is consonant with Cummins's (2000) model of pedagogy, which suggests that "language and content will be acquired most successfully when students are challenged cognitively but provided with the contextual and linguistic supports or scaffolds required for successful task completion" (p. 71).

These supports or scaffolds can also include:

- Contextualization not only through home language support but also through body language, gestures, manipulatives, realia, technology, word walls, and graphic organizers;
- Modeling thorough think-alouds and verbalization of actions and processes of lessons, including asking questions;
- Bridging and schema building by weaving new information into preexisting structures of meaning;
- Thematic planning by which vocabulary and concepts are repeated naturally;
- Multiple entry points, by which some children might use their home language practices, whereas others might be able to conform to the English language of the lesson. Still others might use gestures or drawings.
- Routines in which language is used consistently and predictably. (García, 2009a, p. 331).

Emergent bilinguals also need some overt instruction by which the use of certain meaning-making strategies is made explicit. Genesee and his colleagues (2006) summarize their findings from a major meta-analysis by saying: "The best recommendation to emerge from our review favors instruction that combines interactive and direct approaches" (p. 140). Swinney and Velasco (2011) provide guidance to teachers of emergent bilinguals on how to implement what they call "a curriculum of talk" in order to build language use. They also include structures of balanced literacy that support emergent bilinguals.

Vocabulary is a central area in teaching emergent bilinguals. The consensus among scholars is that vocabulary instruction is important, but that despite the importance of helping students break down words to build meaning (Kieffer & Lesaux, 2007), word study cannot be isolated from its use in narratives, discussions, explanations, and other forms of extended discourse. Words identified in the extended discourse of texts can be identified, studied, posted on word walls, and reused in oral discussion and writing (Carlo et al., 2004). Snow (2017) summarizes:

> Everything we know about vocabulary acquisition suggests strongly that children acquire large vocabularies in the context of responsive interactions about topics of interest to them . . . most reliably when those topics are shared with adults, in *discussions and negotiations about content.* (n.p.; emphasis added)

All disciplines have different linguistic registers, and students must be made aware of such differences (Gibbons, 2002) through actual interactions with the complex texts in which they appear (Wong-Fillmore & Fillmore, n.d.). Emergent bilinguals need support in understanding these "juicy sentences" (Wong-Fillmore & Fillmore, n.d.), a process whereby each day, a teacher selects a sentence or two from the texts students are reading to discuss in conversation. The students and teacher then engage in instructional conversation about the linguistic and discourse features of the sentence, thus setting the context for unpacking the content of a text. Instruction for emergent bilinguals about the explicit features of language needs to be embedded within extended, rich instructional discourses.

All scholars and educators working with emergent bilinguals agree that students must engage with complex texts and complex conversations. Pedagogical strategies must then acknowledge and leverage the students' translanguaging, as they not only scaffold instruction, but transform lives.[2]

EDUCATING EMERGENT BILINGUALS: INCORPORATING MULTILINGUAL PEDAGOGIES

This chapter has presented ways of transforming pedagogies to leverage the dynamic language practices of emergent bilinguals. It has reviewed how to use heteroglossic bilingual instructional practices, how to leverage the students' translanguaging, how to raise their critical consciousness concerning multilingualism, and how to ensure that the complexity of language use is reflected in instruction. The semiotic meaning-making potential of human beings is not limited just to what we call "language." Also important are the extralinguistic resources that human beings learn to use. In the next chapter, we consider how information and communication technology (ICT) expands the semiotic potential of human beings. We also explore how ICT practices can enhance the learning potential of emergent bilinguals.

Study Questions

1. What is the situation today regarding the use of languages other than English in U.S. education? How is it done in your school district?

2. What does language compartmentalization mean? What are some of the ways in which this is done? What are its potentials and drawbacks?

3. How could bilingualism include all students? Describe some ways in which you might be able to do this in your classroom.

4. How might teachers use the home languages of their students for more effective academic instruction? Describe one way in which this might be done regardless of program structure.

5. What are translanguaging pedagogies and how might they be used in classrooms? What is the epistemological difference between bilingual instructional strategies and translanguaging strategies?

6. Describe a critical multilingual awareness activity that you might conduct. Explain why it would be important in your own teaching context.

7. What are some ways in which teachers of emergent bilinguals could help them engage with complex texts?

8. Why is instruction in the decontextualized isolated features of language not appropriate for emergent bilinguals?

CHAPTER 6

Affordances of Technology

In this chapter, we will:

- Provide the theoretical underpinnings of multiliteracies and the "digital turn" in multimodality,
- Highlight the consequences of inequitable access to computers and the internet, and
- Lay out the research evidence for the efficacy of such access for emergent bilinguals.

In earlier chapters, we discussed the importance of building on the linguistic resources that emergent bilingual students bring to school and of choosing appropriate curricular approaches to support their academic growth. Throughout, we have signaled examples of applying digital technologies to classroom instruction for these purposes. In this chapter, we bring these technologies to the fore, as our world is increasingly networked and communication increasingly digital in our working, playing, and learning lives (Castells, 2007; Cummins, Brown, & Sayers, 2007; Kleifgen & Kinzer, 2009; Leu, Kinzer, Coiro, Castek, & Henry, 2013). We draw together threads of increased human mobility across national borders, new digital technologies that connect speakers of different languages, and the enhancement of multimodal resources that can assist learning in a bilingual classroom. As in the other chapters, we first provide the theoretical underpinnings for technology use, including *multiliteracies*, a term we introduced in Chapter 4, and the associated approach known as *multimodality*. Next, we point out some consequences of inequitable access to digital resources in a society permeated by new information and communication technologies (ICTs). Finally, we discuss the research evidence for the benefits of such access for emergent bilinguals.

The need to provide innovative instruction for all students, especially emergent bilinguals, has never been greater. We will show that digital technologies enhance learning and achievement and, in addition, that using these tools requires new literacy skills (Kinzer, 2010), which these students are also entitled to learn. Our argument is grounded in the theoretical and empirical underpinnings discussed next.

THEORETICAL UNDERPINNINGS

In the mid-1990s, a group of international scholars known as the New London Group (1996; see also Cope & Kalantzis, 2000) wrote a manifesto—a "pedagogy of multiliteracies"—calling on educators to recognize and respond to the intertwining of two phenomena: the increased linguistic diversity of learners populating our classrooms and the proliferation of new resources for learning owing to the rise of digital technologies. Their call rings true even today, as more of our students come to school with different language practices and bring their diverse assumptions about the world into the classroom. Our tools for learning today are providing greater access to other forms or modes of communication, such as sound, image, and video, which can be deployed conjointly with the spoken and written modes during the learning process. The central argument that the New London Group made over 20 years ago still stands: All students should benefit from a pedagogy designed to provide a future of full participation in their working, civic, and private lives.

One of the authors of this manifesto, Gunther Kress, has written extensively about the concept of multimodality, which seeks to explain how people communicate, not only through language, but also through the other aforementioned communicative modes (Kress, 2003, 2010). His work on multimodality is grounded in the social-semiotic theory of M. A. K. Halliday (1978, 1993). Before we discuss the link between multimodality and digital technologies, let us examine the idea behind social semiotics in a little more detail. Basically, semiotics is the study of signs used as elements of "making meaning," to use Halliday's phrase, in communication. Signs can take the form of words, gestures, images, sounds, and so on. Briefly, social semiotics takes the position that people draw on available signs within a particular context to make meaning. In terms of linguistic signs (spoken or written), rather than thinking of language as a "thing" made up of rule-governed forms, Halliday's approach underscores the importance of the "meaning potential" in any given communicative context because people draw on socially situated options—what he terms *semiotic resources* or *modes*—for communicating. (Notice how his approach resonates with our own shift away from focusing on *language* as a noun to *language practices*, or *languaging* as a verb, an action.) Studies on multimodality by Kress and others expand Halliday's historical focus on the spoken and written modes by identifying and examining more closely the nonlinguistic modes that people draw on in different communicative contexts. These scholars have contributed detailed analyses of the functions of these other modes; examples include Kress and van Leeuwen's (1996) focus on images and van Leeuwen's (1999, 2011) work on film, music/sound, and color. These deep-dive studies of individual modes have shifted to the exploration of how the different modes are *combined* to make meaning, bringing forward a multimodal approach to analysis (e.g., Jewitt, 2009; Kress, 2010; Kress & van Leeuwen, 2001; O'Halloran, 2008).

Researchers have written extensively about the importance of multi-modality in education (e.g., Bezemer & Kress, 2016; Jewitt, 2002; Jewitt & Kress, 2003; Kleifgen, 2006; Kress, Jewitt, Ogborn, & Tsatsarelis, 2001; Lemke, 1998). In some ways, this is not a new idea: Classrooms themselves are multimodal spaces filled with textbooks, worksheets, talk, body posture, and gestures; classroom walls are adorned with posters, diagrams, images, texts, and illustrations that serve to guide student learning or to display student work; teachers design and use these resources in different ways, which can in turn affect student learning differentially, as is richly illustrated in a study of high school English classrooms in the United Kingdom (Kress, Jewitt, Bourne, Franks, Hardcastle, Jones, & Reid, 2005). A multimodal social-semiotic theory of communication helps educators think about the interrelationships among all the modes that may be brought to bear during any given learning situation.

In terms of technology, which is our focus in this chapter, students using computers and the internet are making meaning with vast and growing numbers of semiotic resources that reach beyond the boundaries of the classroom: still and moving images, sounds and music, colors, and spoken and written language(s). Students who are engaging with one another and exploring the multimodal resources available on the computer screens before them are participating in complex forms of communication to learn. In Kress's (2003) words, they are learning with "ensembles" of modes that may differ and change depending on the context of the learning activity (p. 70). Each mode within a given ensemble contributes to the whole of meaning-making, or shall we say, to the learning of something new. As we will see, this complexity is further heightened/enhanced when the spoken and written modes that are part of these ensembles entail the use of more than one language; emergent bilinguals can exploit this complexity by using their home language practices online to scaffold their learning.

Central to this theoretical approach is human agency. People who are interacting and learning together bring diverse languages, cultures, and understandings into this complex digital environment. Kress (2010) states:

> In a social-semiotic account of meaning, individuals, with their social histories, socially shaped, located in social environments, using socially made, culturally available resources, are *agentive* and generative in sign-making and communication. (p. 54; emphasis added)

Using a multimodal social-semiotic approach to learning, educators can facilitate optimal ways to use the wide-ranging modes, including multiple language modes, that are available on the internet and other ICTs to build new knowledge (Bezemer & Kress, 2016; Jewitt & Kress, 2003).

But what happens when emergent bilinguals have little or no access to ICTs in their schools or homes? We outline some consequences next.

INEQUITABLE ACCESS TO DIGITAL TECHNOLOGIES

There is little doubt that to function in contemporary society, one must have digital competence, the ability to use and evaluate digital technologies for communication, learning, employment, and everyday life (Llomaki, Paavola, Lakkala, & Kantosalo, 2016). The Organisation for Economic Co-Operation and Development (OECD, 2005) has identified skilled technology use inside and outside the workplace as one of the key competencies that graduating students need to participate fully in society. Fortunately, the good news is that, in recent years, internet access, which is needed in order to gain digital competence, has increased for many students. Yet, for many others, the doors to digital competence are still closed. The most recent data show that, whereas by the beginning of this decade, 68.2% of American households had adopted broadband internet connections, there were still 38 million households without connectivity to the internet (NTIA, 2011).

Among the indicators of educational access (along with school funding, books, and highly qualified teachers and curricula) is computer use. Yet, poor and minoritized students have less access to computer technologies than do White affluent students (Darling-Hammond, 2010). National studies show that, for students attending schools in low-income districts, as many emergent bilinguals do, technology is inadequate (Gray, Thomas, & Lewis, 2010). The same is true of students' access outside of school; they are less likely to have computers at home or to own smartphones (Madden, Lenhart, Duggan, Cortesi, & Gasser, 2013). Teachers also report different realities about which technologies are available in their schools: Those teaching in low-income environments have fewer technology resources and their students own fewer devices such as tablets and smartphones than those teaching high-income students in wealthy schools, thus affecting the teachers' ability to plan for technology use in their instruction (Purcell, Heaps, Buchanan, & Friedrich, 2013). According to a Pew Research Center survey conducted in English and Spanish (Zickuhr, 2012), demographic factors such as educational attainment (graduation rates) and level of household income are factors related to internet use, and those who responded to the Pew survey in Spanish reported that they were less likely to use the internet than those responding in English. Of those who reported not using the internet, many said that they did not own a computer, could not afford the broadband connection, or were not able to get access to technology. A later Pew report on digital technology use (Poushter, 2016) found that people around the world, including the United States, who have lower incomes and less education, are less likely to gain access to the internet or to own smartphones than those with higher incomes and more education. Thus, although ICT use has skyrocketed in developing and developed nations alike since 2013, the digital divide remains. State education departments, recognizing the need to incorporate digital technologies into curricula for emergent bilinguals, are revising standards to include the effective use of these tools (e.g., California Department of Education, 2012; Connecticut State Department of Education, 2015).

We have seen how differential access to ICTs exacerbates the problem of educational inequities for underserved students, many of whom are emergent bilinguals. With proactive help from policymakers and educators, emergent bilingual students, too, can benefit from appropriate uses of technology for learning. We now turn to empirical studies showing examples of ways in which these digital tools, when used judiciously and targeted to these students' needs, can promote educational attainment.

HOW DIGITAL TECHNOLOGIES CAN BENEFIT EMERGENT BILINGUALS

The research is clear. New digital technologies, if made available and when used thoughtfully, can enhance student learning. The emphasis on multi-modalities in educating emergent bilinguals is very much attuned to our conceptualization of translanguaging (see Chapters 4 and 5), which is, as we have said, an agentive process by which students select and suppress the features of their unitary language system. A verbal repertoire forms part of a broader communicative repertoire (Rymes, 2014) that includes gestures, facial expressions, eye movements, posture, and so on. Sometimes, certain modes in this larger communicative repertoire are more prevalent than at other times; for example, the deaf community capitalizes on this aspect of communication in order to make meaning. Emergent bilinguals select those features from their complex linguistic repertoire that have the greatest chance of communicating an appropriate message to a single interlocutor or an audience. To do so, these students increasingly enjoy access to an expanded multimodal system facilitated by technology to find appropriate modes—linguistic, visual, and others—to communicate their message.

Human beings make meaning through many representational and communicational resources. These include those within each of them (e.g., the linguistic features of their repertoire), those that they embody (e.g., their gestures, their posture), as well as those outside of themselves, which, through use, become part of their bodily memory (e.g., computer technology). The fact that technology has transformed the ways in which we use multiple modes to communicate and learn means that students' *full-semiotic repertoire*, including multimodalities, has to be taken into account in teaching and learning, especially to engage in disciplinary practices (Grapin, forthcoming).

Empirical research has demonstrated the positive outcomes of implementing these technologies in classrooms and beyond. ICTs as learning tools offer a variety of affordances: *accessibility, retrievability, interactivity* (Kleifgen, Kinzer, Hoffman, Gorski, Kim, Lira, & Ronan, 2014), and *creativity*. Although these affordances are tightly intertwined, and they overlap to produce a positive effect on learning, we separate them in our discussion for illustrative purposes.

Accessibility

Students need access to information so that they can become both consumers and producers of knowledge. The internet is a potential virtual library holding a massive and growing global archive of information for students to explore without the limitations of distance or time. With the internet, learning becomes ubiquitous. As Leu and his colleagues (2013) put it, the internet "has become this generation's defining technology for literacy in our global community" (p. 1159). This virtual library provides ready-to-hand multimodal content—video and sound recordings, maps, graphs, photographs, and of course, texts. Web-based texts themselves are almost entirely embedded with other semiotic resources and/or hyperlinks that take students to additional related content.

In schools where low-income students receive one-to-one access to computers and the internet, it has been found that these students take advantage of using the technology at school because their access elsewhere is limited; their increased access has resulted in achievement gains (Darling-Hammond, Zielezinski, & Goldman, 2014). A 2-year longitudinal study by Grimes and Warschauer (2008), where low-income students in three diverse schools participated in a laptop program, found that the students in laptop classrooms showed positive test scores beginning in the second year of the program, and that they used laptops at school and home to write. Results showed that they were inclined to write and revise more, using multiple modes and a wide variety of genres, including research projects.

Students with access to mobile devices have the added benefit of ubiquitous use. Kukulska-Hulme and Wible (2008) provide examples of users learning "in the wild" with mobile phones in a range of settings, such as the transmission of video, audio, and images by undergraduates doing geology fieldwork; the building of a learning experience with photos, text, and voice in a museum; collaboration among students in class with students taking a tour in the outdoors; and student creation and sharing of learning games with mobile phones.

The current research on multimodality and learning has appropriately paid increased attention to the nonlinguistic modes, which in the past had been neglected; this new focus, however, has often resulted in less attention being paid to the rich potential of the variety of linguistic modes that are accessible online. Many languages and language varieties live on the internet. Access to home language practices for inclusion in a multi-modal ensemble has been until recently an understudied learning resource (for an exception, see Kleifgen's [1991] early study of Haitian students using an electronic bulletin board for young people to write emails in their home language along with English, thereby strengthening their bi-literacy skills). We argue that emergent bilinguals can draw on this home language resource using today's internet to strengthen their academic English practices. For example, they improve their understanding of a text written in English by searching online for a version that has been translated into their home language; alternatively, they themselves may use an internet tool such as Google Translate to secure a Spanish version of the English document. In this way, students are able to read about topics in, say, science, history, or language arts, which can aid their understanding of what is being studied in class. Teachers, too, can use the internet to provide home language versions of subject-matter content to support student learning. As has been pointed out throughout this book, research shows that learning subject-matter content using home language practices while adding English practices to the repertoire facilitates academic achievement. In short, combining access to home language practices with other modes available online, students can go through this content-learning process efficiently and at the same time develop their bilingual language use.

The benefit of gaining access to the home language in a multimodal context was shown in a study by Kleifgen, Lira, and Ronan (2014), which was part of a larger web-based intervention project called STEPS to Literacy, funded by a federal grant to support emergent bilingual adolescents' learning. The project took place in three schools in the New York City area over a 4-year period.[1] Kleifgen and her colleagues studied a bilingual science classroom of Spanish-speaking immigrants, who were just beginning to learn English; the public middle school provided subject-matter instruction in Spanish while the students were also receiving instruction in ESL classes. For the STEPS to Literacy intervention project, students used a web-based research and writing system to study complex concepts about evolution. The system contained a library of historical and scientific resources related to evolution, including bilingual texts, maps, labeled diagrams, images, and videos. Students could select from an extensive number of documents to study the key concepts in Spanish as well as English. For example, students had online access to a description of fossils in both languages [*Los fósiles proporcionan un registro de organismos que vivieron en el pasado . . .* / Fossils provide a record of organisms that lived in the past . . .].

Videos included in the digital library were used as "anchors" (Bransford, Sherwood, Hasselbring, Kinzer, & Williams, 1990) to introduce new instructional units. If the videos were recorded in English, Spanish subtitles were provided, as seen in Figure 6.1 below, a screenshot from an animated music video of Darwin's voyage to the Galápagos Islands (Borlase & Haines, n.d.).

Figure 6.1. Mr. Darwin's music video with subtitles in Spanish

el señor Darwin recibió

The system's collection of digital images and diagrams was gathered from the internet, scanned from science texts, or designed by the STEPS team and school partners; these were often accompanied by captions in Spanish to provide a mutually elaborating ensemble of information for understanding. This ensemble is seen in Figure 6.2, taken from a middle school science textbook and showing that, by studying fossils, scientists have traced the hypothesized evolution of the camel.

Over the course of six instructional sessions, students used the system's pop-up function to open a notepad and one or more resources on the screen to examine them and take notes. They used the accumulated notes to develop an essay in response to a writing prompt. Records of their notes and essay drafts showed that they drew on ensembles of images, videos, and texts in both Spanish and English as they gained content knowledge about evolution and put their ideas into writing. Students were able to construct an argument supported by evidence and examples, thus developing foundations for academic literacy.

Retrievability

Closely related to the accessibility of content on the internet is the notion of retrievability of that same content. Using the internet, emergent bilingual students can easily return to materials multiple times to examine them for deeper understanding. In the study described above, Kleifgen et al. (2014)

Figure 6.2. A camel's changing characteristics over time

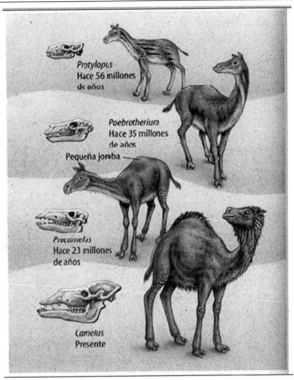

also analyzed log files, which captured students' digital behaviors in the web-based system, including which items in the library they chose to open and how often they returned to any given item. The authors found that the students returned often to the multimodal curricular resources and that some resources were viewed repeatedly, a signal that students deemed them important enough to review in order to gain information for note-taking and writing.

Similarly, Ronan (2014, 2017) studied student behaviors using the same STEPS web-based system in a different school. She describes how four students in a social studies class accessed a variety of multimodal resources, many of them more than once, to learn about and take notes on the Civil Rights Movement. The STEPS digital library held 31 resources associated with this instructional unit. In her analysis of students' choices about which kinds of resources they selected from among these digitized materials—texts, video and audio recordings, photographs, maps—Ronan considered the overall counts recorded in the log files indicating how often they clicked on the resources for a pop-up view on the computer screen. In addition, she analyzed the corresponding transcripts of students' talk, writing, gestures, and their interactions with the online space to determine precisely how the students incorporated a given multimodal resource into their talk and notes. Each of the four students, who represented different English language proficiency levels, took distinct paths to initial examination and subsequent retrieval of the online materials based on their interests and language choices. Ronan's (2017) work, showing students' agency as they varied in online selection and retrieval of bilingual and multimodal materials, provides a strong argument that "unlike traditional textbooks that impose a sequential structure upon a reader, open-ended digital spaces . . . allow students to direct their own learning" (p. 102).

Other integrated online environments that focus on language learners' writing allow students to review their developing essays as well as their teachers' feedback. For example, David Wible and his colleagues (Wible, Kuo, Chien, Liu, & Tsao, 2001; Wible, Kuo, Tsao, Liu, & Lin, 2003) describe the retrievability of archived essays and comments in a writing platform called IWiLL (Intelligent Web-based interactive Language Learning). Students using this system were able to retrieve and review their collection of compositions, conduct pinpoint searches of their persistent writing difficulties, and search for their teachers' comments to find patterns of difficulty; teachers also could search and retrieve students' writing and provide targeted instruction in frequent problem areas, such as word choice, sentence fragments, subject-verb agreement, and so on.

In sum, with digital technologies, students can construct, retrieve, and review texts in one or more languages as a way to comparatively analyze the material, thus attaining a clearer understanding of concepts and improving their written language production.

Interactivity

We approach the examination of the affordance of interactivity by focusing on two aspects: student interactions with digital tools and interactions among students while using the tools.

Interacting with digital tools. Studies have shown that underserved students benefit academically from highly interactive activities on computer-based tools. This was one of the key findings in a literature review conducted by Zielezinski and Darling-Hammond (2016); their review of more than 50 studies confirms that, when students are given the opportunity to collect and analyze data online or to engage with multiple resources such as simulations and video instruction modules to gain understanding of concepts, their learning is enhanced. One of the studies cited in their review (Bos, 2007) shows that an experimental group of 96 low-achieving high school students' mathematical achievement improved significantly when they studied quadratic equations using the Texas Instruments InterActive software lessons to manipulate interactive graphs and tables; this software was assessed as high in cognitive and mathematical fidelity (Bos, 2009). The struggling students' achievement scores were greater than those of the student control group who studied the same material in conventional classes consisting of lecture, notes, and drill and practice.

Cope and Kalantzis (2013) describe a robust web-based writing platform, Scholar, developed at the University of Illinois and designed for 4th-grade level and above. They show how this digital space affords learning transformations or "openings" such as ubiquitous access to the system from any device in or out of school, student knowledge production using multiple modes, and collaboration with and feedback from teachers and peers. They also stress that the system occasions another pedagogical opening: "differentiated" learning, which is based on individual students' developing understandings and requirements. This feature is particularly important for low-income students, including many minoritized emergent bilinguals, who may not have had equitable educational opportunities in school or internet connectivity at home; with the *Scholar* learning environment in their classrooms, they can work at their own pace, receive individualized teacher support, and find their own writing voices.

Although the positive effect of well-designed interactive tools for minoritized students has been shown in the studies reported above, the students' home language was not taken into account as another valuable resource. This next study highlights the students' language practices as a key element in their interactions with digital media to learn complex concepts in the areas of science, technology, engineering, and mathematics (STEM). The work of MIT's Michel DeGraff (2013) and his colleagues demonstrates that putting into students' hands powerful interactive software translated into Haitian Creole (Kreyòl) for engaging in scientific experiments has the potential to positively impact learning in the entire country of Haiti. The MIT-Haiti Initiative has been working since 2010, first, to translate and design digital tools alongside nondigital materials for active learning in mathematics, physics, biology, and biochemistry in the home language, and, second, to conduct workshops for teachers of high school and university students on ways to use these tools and materials effectively in their classrooms (DeGraff, 2016; Miller, 2016). Examples of the highly interactive science software include StarGenetics, which simulates genetics experiments with yeast, fruit flies, and Mendel's peas; PhET, which simulates physics experiments in density, electromagnets, and gas properties; and Mathlets, for learning about differential equations and complex arithmetic (MIT-Haiti Initiative, n.d.). Supporting teachers in their adoption of a discovery approach to learning and their comfort with digital tools in the classroom has been crucial to the success of this work. This ambitious project is built on a framework that accounts for the learner's language and the school's capacity to deliver high-quality instruction using digital tools for learning complex concepts in the STEM areas. Integrating the home language practices of

Haitians with technology and a proven instructional approach has resulted in positive attitudinal changes in pedagogy for participating teachers and students in Haiti.

It is essential to underscore the fact that not all software claiming to be interactive is associated with positive academic outcomes. Studies have shown that, when "programmed instruction" such as drill and practice activities for rote learning are the only digital options offered to students from low SES backgrounds, their test scores are negatively affected (Warschauer & Matuchniak, 2010; Wenglinsky, 2005). Well-designed interactive programs for complex learning must also be available to "allow students to see and explore concepts from different angles using a variety of representations" (Darling-Hammond, Zielezinski, & Goldman, 2014, p. 7).

Interactions among learners with and through technology. Interactivity includes, not only an individual's interaction with engaging software, but also students' conjoint meaning-making and design. More research is demonstrating the educational value of students' collaborative interactions while using technology. For example, Ronan's (2014) study of students in a social studies class documents the collaboration among learners as they participated in a classroom activity while engaging with web-based multimodal materials to accomplish an online writing task. Multimodal transcripts were constructed and analyzed to illustrate student-pair interactions as they shared a common space on the computer screen. During this activity, the students conjointly examined online visual and textual resources, used gesture along with talk in two languages, and along the way applied these resources to construct a written note. The analysis uncovered the process of transformation of a student's writing while engaging with different modalities for examination, discussion, and note-taking. Ronan's (2014) findings help us "(understand) writing as a multimodal/multilingual, *socially interactive* practice" (p. 247; emphasis added).

Besides collaboration among users as they are working in pairs or small groups on web-based activities, another setting in which technology enhances interactivity is through users' collaborations that occur almost entirely online. For example, online collaborative inquiry that leads to culminating projects can take place between classrooms located in different regions of the world. An instructional approach known as project-based learning (PBL), said to originate in the work of John Dewey, has been adopted by classroom teachers to engage students in collaborative investigations around authentic problems and develop projects or presentations to address them (Thomas, 2000). Research shows that, when the PBL approach is integrated into digital environments that are thoughtfully designed and with teachers who receive professional development and support for using these alternative spaces for learning, emergent bilinguals can thrive academically (Condliffe, Visher, Banger, Drohojowska, & Saco, 2016).

Teachers have reported that using collaborative online PBL enhances their instructional strategies for English learners. In a collective case study, Foulger and Jimenez-Silva (2007) describe how 14 classroom teachers received technology training and sustained support from a professional developer to implement project-based activities that involved writing. One of the teachers joined a global learning group called the International Education and Resource Network (iEARN)[2] so that her class could participate in an online exchange with students in a school outside the United States. In selecting iEARN, the teacher had the benefit of a robust digital learning space with a long history of teacher-led interchanges. iEARN began in 1988 with a telecommunications project between teachers and students in New York State and Moscow and soon expanded in 1990 to nine countries. Since then, more than 120 countries have been involved in more than 100 international collaborative projects online in English and in 18 other languages. Its online platform allows teachers to connect with other teachers and their students around the world to interact with one another and to collaborate on meaningful projects and make contributions to local and/or global communities.

After joining the iEARN learning space, the teacher selected the Teddy Bear Project and paired her class in the United States with a school in Australia. Each class sent a teddy bear to its partner school; the bear was to keep a diary, sending descriptions of its adventures as a guest in the host school and host families. The U.S. teacher and students prepared their classroom for the Australian bear's arrival and read books on koalas. In the teacher's words:

> Koala Lou joined us in our daily classroom activities. . . . Students took Koala Lou home to visit their homes and families. Her overnight backpack included pajamas, a book, a camera (to take pictures with the families), and a journal so that students could include their adventures with Koala Lou in her journal. Messages to Australia continued over this time. (Foulger & Jimenez-Silva, 2007, p. 116)

In this way, students in the school receiving the journals submitted by the partner school's students (through the visiting teddy bear) learned about another culture and way of life, and both student groups strengthened their writing with the knowledge that a real audience was reading their journal entries.

In a more recent online project involving U.S. and Middle East and North African (MENA) classrooms, analyses have been carried out of the online social interactions among teachers in iEARN's development workshops as well as the follow-up interactions between their students, who are collaborating on projects across languages and cultures. The progress reports have shown that participants, through their online interactions, have gained ground in intercultural understanding, learned about different life worlds, and developed their communicative and technology skills in the on-line space (Kleifgen, 2017a, b).

Creativity

To examine the notion of creativity as an affordance, we turn again to the work of Gunther Kress, who first introduced the concept of *design* for edu-cation in the early 1990s. For Kress, design implies that both teachers and learners exercise agency and freedom to become creative in their academic work. He argues for a pedagogy of creativity, agency, and change in the curriculum. He states: "Curriculum is a design for the future" because such a curriculum has the potential to shape individuals' positive participation in society (Kress, 2000a, p. 161; see also Kress, 1995, 2000b). Design is also a way to demonstrate individual learners' agency, interests, and freedom to become creative in their academic pursuits "through the design of messages with the resources available to them in specific situations" (Kress, 2010, p. 23; see also Kress, 2003). In using the term *messages*, Kress is referring to "making" or "producing" new forms of content in today's digital age by assembling the meaning-making resources available to students in many modes. More than ever, learning is about drawing on multimodal resources to design something new.

Creativity occasioned by the support of technology is a process of de-sign in environments that can range from the design of the smallest fragment of text to the construction of more extended multimodal discourse. We learn how a short note begins to be created in Ronan's (2015) work. She carried out a fine-grained analysis of two emergent bilinguals examining a multimodal resource in the STEPS digital library in order to take notes on the system's digital notepads. During a class lesson on segregation in the United States, the two students collaboratively discuss and come to an inter-pretation of a historical photograph from the segregationist South showing a park sign barring People of Color from entry (Figure 6.3).

Both students begin to take their own notes describing the photograph. At one point during their discussion and note-taking, one student asks her classmate in Spanish what she should write next. He suggests a reason for the discriminatory order: "*Porque ¿ellos son differentes razas?*" [Because they are different races?]. She transforms the message written in English on the image along with her classmate's suggestion in spoken Spanish into a new written note in her developing English:

> white people only (negros and Mexican) out. i think the white people not like that peoples of Mexican and negrous because they different countrys and different color of skin.

Figure 6.3. Image of a park sign in the segregationist South, barring People of Color from entry

The student, in this unfolding creative process of interaction with a peer and drawing on and reinterpreting multiple modes—including a multimodal image and spoken and written language in Spanish and English—has transformed those resources and begun her design of a new text in written English.

Studies give evidence that, when struggling students are challenged to engage in their own content creation using new media, they are more likely to do well on competency tests. In one such study, at-risk students who were designing projects in technology-rich classrooms, compared with students who were on level but not using these tools, outperformed their peers in state-mandated exams (Maninger, 2006). Maninger's research on 9th-grade English classrooms provides illustrations of teachers guiding students as they produced blogs about the literature they were studying, used online software to compose assigned papers, and created multimodal webpages for their projects.

Other studies show the benefits when underserved students of color are presented with the opportunity to engage in creative digital storytelling. Hull and Nelson (2005) examine one young man's multimodal composition, an ensemble of modes—language, image, and music—to tell an autobiographical story called "Lyfe-N-Rhyme." The author developed his digital story at a community technology center in an urban setting where many youths have little or no access to digital tools at school or at home. The researchers' detailed analysis of a digital artifact focuses on how the semiotic relationships across the modes progressively elaborate one another and eventually create a new form of meaning where the whole is greater than the sum of its parts.

Nevertheless, as Iedema (2003) points out, studies of "finished" designs like these demonstrate "the complexity of texts or representations as they are, and less frequently how it is that such constructs [are elaborated]" (p. 30; see also Kleifgen, 2013).

Whereas Hull and Nelson's (2005) "Lyfe-N-Rhyme" analysis is a case study of a finished product, the work by Angay-Crowder, Choi, and Yi (2013) offers a play-by-play description of how teachers can open up opportunities for their emergent bilinguals' creative storytelling. They provide a blueprint of lessons grounded in the New London Group's theory of pedagogy and lay out in detail the process by which 12 middle school students, all children of immigrants, were instructed in the basics of digital storytelling and in strategies for constructing a story. Ten of the students came from Spanish-speaking homes, one spoke limited Bengali, and one spoke Tagalog. They were encouraged to consult with one another and with adults in their communities to verify their narratives as well as to explore their multiple languages and literacies in the process of applying both linguistic and other semiotic modes to their stories. The students were also taught how to use the storytelling software, and they were guided in how to assess and select the different modes in order for their stories to have greater effect. The study demonstrates the importance of providing specific guidance and encouragement to English learners to unleash their creativity throughout the process.

Marshall and Toohey (2010) conducted research in a Canadian elementary school where Punjabi-Sikh 4th- and 5th-grade students participated in a multimedia intergenerational stories project. The students took home MP3 players and recorded interviews with their grandparents in Punjabi, Malay, and Hindi about what it was like growing up in India. The students translated these spoken interviews into written English and produced the text on computers, leaving space for their illustrations. They then decided to translate their written work into the grandparents' home language (with the help of the grandparents or other adults who were literate in the language) so that they would have bilingual texts. Finally, they recorded their readings of the stories in English and Punjabi; the recordings were put on compact discs to accompany the books. In short, the students used multiple modes over time, both online and off, to complete their creative work.

Increasingly, learning is about drawing on multimodal resources to design something new, as these studies illustrating the affordances of creativity have shown. Although most of the examples we have given describe digital storytelling, other spaces on the internet are being used by young people for creative work. In a Pew internet Survey, over half of the adolescents surveyed report that they have created web content (Lenhart & Madden, 2005). Young people are also exploring wikis, video production, games, social media, and virtual worlds on the internet. And they are self-publishing zines with original or copied texts and images used in new ways. All of these digital spaces make use of multimodal resources.[3]

Taken together, the affordances for learning that new digital technologies can provide—accessibility, retrievability, interactivity, and creativity—demonstrate the potential that these new learning environments have for the equitable education of emergent bilinguals.

RESOURCING EMERGENT BILINGUALS' CLASSROOMS

We have argued that emergent bilinguals can benefit academically from high-quality digital tools and from teachers who have preparation, commitment, and experience in using these tools in their schools and classrooms. We know theoretically and empirically that new media technologies are good for emergent bilinguals. So, what can we do to make this happen? Here, we refer again to the four affordances described in this chapter to address this question.

First, students need *access* to digital tools in their schools. Schools require the necessary infrastructure—servers, storage, and bandwidth—for fast and reliable connectivity and to avoid the frustration of breakdowns. We know that one-to-one *access*, one device per student, is beneficial for emergent bilinguals. This is especially the case if they do not have *access* to computers or other devices at home; they need more opportunities at school to *retrieve* online materials for study, note-taking, review, and the production of new knowledge artifacts.

Second, web-based and other software materials that are well-designed and *interactive* must be made available to students. Software designed for rote learning should not be the only menu of options for emergent bilinguals; technologies designed for complex and collaborative learning-in-*interaction* must be part of the digital curriculum.

Third, teachers are students' best advocates in obtaining sustained and efficacious *access* to digital technologies. Students will learn appropriate and *creative* uses of new media with the guidance of teachers who are well prepared to integrate technology into their teaching. This means that teachers must be given the opportunity to explore the scholarship on multimodality and to experiment with implementation of multimodal learning using digital resources so that they can support students' *creative* designs.

In short, ICTs for learning must be intelligently designed and tested, schools must be supplied with adequate technical infrastructure, and educators must be given the professional preparation and ongoing support to be students' guides in these alternative learning spaces.

Multimodalities cannot be solely considered scaffolds for language development, but also must be seen as an essential part of emergent bilingual students' meaning-making resources at their disposal (Grapin, forthcoming; Kleifgen & Kinzer, 2009). Foregrounding multimodalities can transform educators' conceptions of how to leverage the students' meaning-making potential beyond just accessing what is traditionally conceived as language. But unlike the linguistic repertoire that resides *within* the student (although sometimes it is inaccessible because teachers do not allow students to use it), the multimodal repertoire lies *outside* the body. It is possible to embody multimodalities so as to access them creatively and naturally, but educators must make these available, as well as accessible, as affordances for learning (for examples, see Ronan, 2015, 2017; Vogel, Ascenzi-Moreno, & García, 2017).

EDUCATING EMERGENT BILINGUALS:
THE IMPORTANT ROLE OF TECHNOLOGY

In this chapter, we have addressed the important role technology has in the education of emergent bilinguals. Many studies like those reported in this chapter, which are based on multiliteracies pedagogy and the more recent thinking in social semiotics about multimodality, offer ideas for classroom instruction with technology that is engaging and meaningful for emergent bilingual students. The four affordances we discussed can serve as guidelines as teachers and other adults in students' lives select motivating and educative digital materials and activities for students. Other excellent resources that suggest sensible technology implementation are becoming available: Teachers can benefit from ideas in Cecilia Magadán's (2015) volume (written in Spanish), which offers theoretically based, empirically demonstrated, and pedagogically effective ways of integrating technology into the classroom. Bruce, Bishop, and Budhathoki's (2014) work describes examples from a wide variety of settings that show how students use new media to support other people in their communities.

We conclude this chapter by calling upon leaders and school administrators to properly resource schools, classrooms, and communities with technologies for optimal learning in our increasingly diverse, digitized, and globalized world. But we also call upon educators to consider multimodalities as part of students' meaning-making capacity, and not as a simple scaffold. That is, we call for a transformation of the *incomplete ways* in which schools often view emergent bilinguals' meaning-making semiotic repertoire. Schools often consider only what emergent bilinguals are *missing*—English—instead of all the language features and practices that make up their existing language repertoire. When they leverage them, they often do so only as scaffold. Likewise, when schools consider multimodalities, they sometimes think of them as a way to support the "language" that students don't have—again, what they are *missing*. For example, students are allowed to draw only when they can't write, or act only when they can't speak, or use technology only to contextualize tasks with images. But if we take a translanguaging view, we see *all of it—all* linguistic features and *all* multimodalities—as *essential* affordances making up the students' meaning-making repertoire, transforming the capacity to learn of all students.

Educators of emergent bilinguals need to remain "wide awake," as Maxine Greene (1995) tells us, as to why some students are given the opportunity to use all their meaning-making resources and others aren't. And educators must remain vigilant about the reasons why emergent bilinguals are often given inequitable curricular opportunities and resources, the subject of the next chapter.

STUDY QUESTIONS

1. Discuss the concepts of multiliteracies, initiated by the New London Group; multimodality, as defined and elaborated by Gunther Kress; and social semiotics, the foundational theory proposed by M. A. K. Halliday.

2. What are some of the inequities that low-income and minoritized students face with regard to where and when they can use digital technologies?

3. Describe the four affordances offered by ICTs and give examples from the research of how they support emergent bilinguals' learning.

4. Select one or two of the practices described in the research and discuss how they illustrate more than one affordance for learning. For example, how might one technology implementation demonstrate both accessibility and retrievability? Interactivity and creativity? Other combinations?

CHAPTER 7

Curriculum and Other Practices

When we narrow the program so that there is only a limited array of areas in which assessment occurs and performance is honored, youngsters whose aptitudes and interests lie elsewhere are going to be marginalized in our schools. The more we diversify those opportunities, the more equity we are going to have because we're going to provide wider opportunities for youngsters to find what it is they are good at.

—Elliot Eisner, 2001

In this chapter, we will:

- Review theoretical constructs that support curricular opportunities and practices for emergent bilinguals:
  - ➢ Orientation of social justice and linguistic human rights,
  - ➢ Curriculum that is challenging and creative, and
  - ➢ Pedagogy that is transformative and collaborative;
- Identify inequalities in curricular opportunities and resources:
  - ➢ Inequitable curricular opportunities: lack of early childhood programs, remedial education and tracking, special education placements, exclusion from gifted and AP classes;
  - ➢ Inequitable resources: inadequate instructional materials, school facilities, and funding; and
  - ➢ Inequitable access to high-quality educators; and
- Consider some alternative practices:
  - ➢ A challenging inclusive curriculum that starts early, and
  - ➢ Preparing caring, creative, and qualified teachers.

In this chapter, we focus on curricular opportunities and practices affecting the education of emergent bilinguals. Gándara and Contreras (2009) say: "The problem of English learners' underachievement . . . is more likely related to the quality of education that these students receive, regardless of the language of instruction" (p. 145). We consider here the *quality* of the education that emergent bilingual students are receiving, beyond the issue of language or multimodality of instruction; in doing so, we continue to give attention to the central question in this book: *What does research tell us about how best to educate and assess emergent bilingual students? Are we using accepted theories and evidence in the education of these students?* Just as we observed a gap in Chapters 4, 5, and 6 between language education theory and practice, we note in this chapter a gap between accepted theoretical foundations for curriculum and practices and the classroom realities for many emergent bilinguals. We conclude the chapter by laying out alternative practices that can do much to accelerate the academic achievement of these students.

THEORETICAL CURRICULAR AND PEDAGOGICAL CONSTRUCTS

In this section, we identify three theoretical constructs that promote equity in curriculum and practice for emergent bilinguals—an orientation of social justice and linguistic human rights, a curriculum that is challenging and creative, and a pedagogy that is transformative and collaborative.

Social Justice and Linguistic Human Rights

Social justice in education is derived from the work by the American philosopher John Rawls in *A Theory of Justice* (1971). Applied to education, the concept of social justice refers to the appropriate distribution of benefits and burdens among groups, based on the principles of human rights and equality. Social justice theories demand that we analyze discriminatory structures and practices within institutions such as schools; these theories also require that part of educating youth includes engaging them in taking action to remedy social wrongs (Adams et al., 2013; Anyon, 1997, 2005; Ayers, Hunt, & Quinn, 1998; Cammarota & Fine, 2008; Cochran-Smith, 2004; Tuck & Yang, 2013). This analysis of structures and practices is especially important in the teaching of emergent bilinguals. As we have seen in Chapter 2, most emergent bilinguals are poor, and many are students of color. Many emergent bilinguals, although not all, are immigrants who are feeling dislocation and separation from both their countries of origin and sometimes families they have left behind. In addition, as we have also seen, more than half of the foreign-born immigrant students in the United States are undocumented (Jensen, 2001; Suárez-Orozco et al., 2008), thus intensifying feelings of dislocation and not belonging. Others are indigenous, having experienced subjugation and oppression in their own lands. All these students have the right to an education that includes a rich and rigorous curriculum.

The idea of teaching for social justice has roots in U.S. social history of democracy and oppression. Consistent with defending the basic human rights and freedoms guaranteed under the Bill of Rights of the U.S. Constitution, educating for social justice also requires that teachers and students act in the construction of a socially just world. This was the case, for example, of the Freedom School movement of the 1960s, when Black students in the segregated South participated in programs that not only engaged them in a rigorous academic curriculum but also in a citizenship curriculum, enabling them to understand their rights and their role in bringing about change (Hale, 2011; Morrell, 2008). Movements to teach for social justice have been inspired by the work of the Brazilian scholar Paolo Freire. In his *Pedagogy of the Oppressed* (1970), Freire urges educators to engage students in a dialectal praxis so that they can act upon the world in order to transform it.

Rights to education are at the core of these social justice efforts. In this regard, UNESCO (1960) has been most influential. In the UNESCO Convention against Discrimination in Education (adopted December 14, 1960; entered into force May 22, 1962), Article 1 reads:

> For the purposes of this Convention, the term "discrimination" includes any distinction, exclusion, limitation or preference which, being based on race, colour, sex, language, religion, political or other opinion, national or social origin, economic condition or birth, has the purpose or effect of nullifying or impairing equality or treatment in education. . . .

The focus on social justice and human rights, coupled with the rise of critical theory on the role that language has played in asymmetrical power relations (see García, Flores & Spotti, 2017), has led to increasing calls for linguistic human rights (Skutnabb-Kangas, 2000, 2006; Skutnabb-Kangas & Phillipson, 1994, 2017). Skutnabb-Kangas and Phillipson (1994) identify two categories of linguistic human rights that are important to consider in educating emergent bilinguals:

- Individual rights, including the right to identify with one's own language and to use it both in and out of school, and the right to learn the official language of the state; and
- Community rights, including the right of minoritized groups to establish and maintain schools and other educational institutions and to control their curricula.

Taking these categories into account, we can argue that in the United States, linguistic human rights are not fully observed. For example, although many languages other than English are spoken, the use of these languages in everyday situations is sometimes considered suspect (Lippi-Green, 1997). Most of these languages are excluded from schools; in high schools, classes to learn and develop languages other than English may be offered, but these usually only include Spanish, French, German, and more recently Chinese (Center for Applied Linguistics, 2009). As for minoritized groups' linguistic rights, although these groups have the right to establish their own complementary schools where their languages and cultures are taught after school and on weekends, they do not receive state funding (García, Zakharia, & Otcu, 2013; Peyton, Ranard, & McGinnis, 2001). One of the questions for educators, then, is how to extend these language rights to all students in the curriculum. Social justice and linguistic human rights are the philosophical values that motivate a challenging and creative curriculum for emergent bilinguals.

Curriculum That Is Challenging and Creative

Research on teaching and learning indicates that all students need to be given opportunities to participate in challenging academic work that promotes deep disciplinary knowledge and encourages higher-order thinking skills. Goldenberg (2008) summarizes:

> As a general rule, all students tend to benefit from clear goals and learning objectives; meaningful, challenging, and motivating contexts; a curriculum rich with content; well-designed, clearly structured, and appropriately paced instruction; active engagement and participation; opportunities to practice, apply, and transfer new learning; feedback on correct and incorrect responses; periodic review and practice; frequent assessments to gauge progress, with re-teaching as needed; and opportunities to interact with other students in motivating and appropriately structured contexts. (p. 17)

And yet, as Gibbons (2009) points out, "the development of curriculum distinguished by intellectual quality and the development of higher-order thinking has in reality rarely been a major focus of program planning for EL learners" (p. 2).

Many have called attention to the importance of maintaining high expectations for emergent bilinguals and of providing them with challenging academic work (Carrasquillo & Rodriguez, 2002; Walqui, 2006). As with all students, emergent bilinguals require practice in complex thinking; they deserve teachers who engage them in combining ideas to synthesize, generalize, explain, hypothesize, or arrive at some conclusion or interpretation (Walqui, García, & Hamburger, 2004). Speaking about the importance of an action-based perspective of language for emergent bilinguals, van Lier and Walqui (2012) explain:

> Language is an inseparable part of all human action, intimately connected to all other forms of action, physical, social and symbolic. Language is thus an

expression of agency, embodied and embedded in the environment. . . . In a classroom context, an action-based perspective means that ELs engage in meaningful activities (projects, presentations, investigations) that engage their interest and that encourage language growth through perception, interaction, planning, research, discussion, and co-construction of academic products of various kinds. During such action-based work, language development occurs when it is carefully scaffolded by the teacher, as well as by the students working together. (n.p.)

Gibbons (2009) advances seven intellectual practices for emergent bilinguals:

1. Students engage with the key ideas and concepts of the discipline in ways that reflect how "experts" in the field think and reason.
2. Students transform what they have learned into a different form for use in a new context or for a different audience.
3. Students make links between concrete knowledge and abstract theoretical knowledge.
4. Students engage in substantive conversation.
5. Students make connections between the spoken and written language of the subject and other discipline-related ways of making meaning.
6. Students take a critical stance toward knowledge and information.
7. Students use metalanguage in the context of learning about other things.

Alongside challenge and rigor, it is important to provide students, especially emergent bilinguals, with a creative curriculum that provides space for them to experiment and innovate (Greene, 1995). There is not a more creative and innovative human activity than learning how to make meaning through another language, linking bilingualism and creativity (Ward, Smith, & Vaid, 1997).

Therefore, responsive schools will not only provide emergent bilinguals with a challenging and rich curriculum, but also with a creative one. By having teams of multicultural and multilingual students, who work collaboratively as equals using all their linguistic and cultural resources to address educational challenges presented to them, schools can foster the creative conceptual expansion of all students. To do so, schools must have teachers who can deliver a transformative/intercultural pedagogy, the subject of our next section.

Pedagogies That Are Transformative and Collaborative

Many scholars, working to redress the educational inequities affecting minoritized students, have advocated several practices, all with the potential to transform society. We have already referred to the potential of translanguaging as part of that transformation.

Cummins (2000) calls for a "transformative/intercultural pedagogy" (p. 45) to be used with language-minority students where the students' language practices and cognitive abilities are included in the learning process and where students' identities are affirmed. Cummins defines this transformative pedagogy as "interactions between educators and students that attempt to foster collaborative relations of power in the classroom" (p. 253). In addition, he notes that such an approach "recognizes that the process of identity negotiation is fundamental to educational success for all students, and furthermore that this process is directly determined by the micro-interactions between individual educators and students" (p. 253). Cummins's transformative pedagogy not only authorizes language-minority students to engage in collaborative critical inquiry, but also, by affirming their cultural practices, recognizes their knowledge and identities.

Focusing on teaching by building on the ethnolinguistic identities of language-minority students, other scholars have also advocated a culturally relevant pedagogy for minority students (Gay, 2002; Ladson-Billings, 1994, 1995; Valdés, 1996; Villegas & Lucas, 2002). Paris and Alim (2014) have gone beyond the "relevant" aspects to propose what they call a "culturally sustaining pedagogy" (CSP). They explain the difference:

> CSP seeks to perpetuate and foster—to sustain—linguistic, literate and cultural pluralism as part of the democratic project of schooling and as a needed response to demographic and social change. CSP, then, links a focus on sustaining pluralism through education to challenges of social justice and change. (p. 88)

Culturally sustaining pedagogy not only seeks to promote equality across communities, but also ensure access and opportunity by demanding that outcomes not only be centered on "[W]hite, middle-class, monolingual and monocultural norms of educational achievement" (Paris & Alim, 2014, p. 95). Besides aligning classroom experiences with the students' cultural and linguistic practices, culturally sustaining pedagogies attempt to counteract inequitable power relations in society and empower minority students to use their own repertoire of practices (Freire, 1970; Giroux, 1988).

Research on teaching and learning has also validated the importance of pedagogy that builds on collaborative social practices in which students try out ideas and actions and, thus, socially construct their learning (Vygotsky, 1978). Lave and Wenger (1991) describe learning within a given social group as a process of participation that moves gradually from being "legitimately peripheral" to being fully engaged in what they call a *community of practice*: "a set of relations among persons, activity and world, over time and in relation with other tangential and overlapping communities of practice" (p. 98). This social view of learning and pedagogy takes the position that emergent bilinguals do not come to "possess" or "have" English; rather, they learn by "doing" and "using" practices and features associated with English repeatedly over the course of a lifetime in communities of practice. As van Lier (2000) explains:

> The ecologist will say that knowledge of language for a human is like knowledge of the jungle for an animal. The animal does not have the jungle; it knows how to use the jungle and how to live in it. Perhaps we can say by analogy that we do not have or possess language, but that we learn to use it and to live in it. (p. 253)

A collaborative pedagogy relies, then, on a great deal of practice of talk, or what Tharp, Estrada, Dalton, and Yamauchi (2000) call *instructional conversation* or what Padrón and Waxman (1999) call *teaching through conversation.* We know, for example, that high-quality literacy instruction for emergent bilinguals must include "efforts to increase the scope and sophistication of these students' oral language proficiency" (August & Shanahan, 2006, p. 448). That is, a focus on reading and writing alone is insufficient to develop emergent bilinguals' abilities to use and live in English.

To build this community of practice, groups of students need to be engaged in *cooperative learning* (Kagan, 1986; Kagan & McGroarty, 1993). The National Literacy Panel review found that having students work cooperatively on group tasks increases the literacy comprehension of emergent bilinguals (August & Shanahan, 2006).

For this transformative/intercultural and collaborative pedagogy to be delivered, highly prepared teachers and school leaders are needed. For example, value-added assessment studies in Tennessee have shown that students who have high-quality teachers over a period of 3 years achieve, on average, 50 percentile points more on standardized tests than those who have low-quality teachers (Sanders & Rivers, 1996). Furthermore, teachers with less teaching experience produce smaller gains in their students compared with more experienced teachers (Murnane & Phillips, 1981). Studies have shown that teacher preparation and certification are the strongest correlates of student achievement in reading and mathematics (Darling-Hammond, 1999), and many others have affirmed that teacher quality matters (Rice, 2003; Wenglinsky, 2000).

Despite research that shows the importance of having curricular programs that emphasize social justice and that are academically challenging and creative, and pedagogy that is transformative and intercultural, emergent bilinguals are often excluded from meaningful educational programs and rigorous instruction. Their teachers are also often poorly prepared. We discuss these inequitable curricular and pedagogical practices before proposing what can be done about it.

INEQUITABLE CURRICULAR OPPORTUNITIES AND RESOURCES

Curricular, pedagogical, and educator-quality issues result in inequities in the education of emergent bilinguals. And because high-quality instruction does not happen without adequate resources, funding is needed to provide high-quality education for emergent bilinguals.

Inequitable Curricular Opportunities

It all starts early. When emergent bilinguals enter kindergarten, they are already disadvantaged. According to the Early Childhood Longitudinal Study (ECLS), about half of kindergartners who speak English at home but no more than 17% of kindergartners who speak a language other than English at home, perform above the 50th percentile in California (Gándara, Rumberger, Maxwell-Jolly, & Callahan, 2003). This disparity has to do with the fact that emergent bilingual kindergartners cannot understand English well enough to be assessed in English. From the very beginning, then, these children are often placed in remedial education.

It has been shown that early childhood education programs can help narrow gaps in preparation for elementary school, especially among poor children (Haskins & Rouse, 2005; Takanishi, 2004, in Capps et al., 2005). Additionally, researchers have demonstrated the benefits of early childhood education programs that contribute positively to children's health, emotional adjustment, and cognitive functioning (E. Garcia & Gonzalez, 2006; Karoly & Bigelow, 2005). For example, in a study of the effects of a preschool program on poor children in Ypsilanti, Michigan, a control group received no preschool services. At the age of 40, those who had attended preschool had not only increased earnings, but also decreased reliance on public assistance and had lower rates of criminal activity and substance abuse (Nores, Belfield, Barnett, & Schweinhart, 2005). A study in North Carolina obtained similar results—the group that had attended preschool had higher IQs, increased levels of high school graduation and college attendance, as well as decreased rates of grade retention and rates of special education classification than a control group that did not attend preschool (Barnett & Masse, 2007).

The benefit of preschool education for Latinx emergent bilinguals has also been demonstrated (Ackerman & Tazi, 2015). Gormley Jr. (2008), for example, showed that Latinx emergent bilinguals in a prekindergarten program did better in all aspects of the Woodcock-Johnson Test and the Woodcock-Muñoz Battery—assessing letter-word identification, spelling, and answers to applied problem items. Tazi (2014) has likewise shown the value of bilingual education programs for these young students. Very young Latinx children who participated in bilingual instruction were evaluated by their teachers as more socially competent, more interested and prepared for early academic skills such as literacy and numeracy, and more ready for school. When allowed to use their entire language repertoire, Latinx kindergartners schooled bilingually also showed greater use of language and facility in expressing their ideas.

And yet, emergent bilinguals are less likely than their monolingual counterparts to be enrolled in early childhood programs (Espinosa, 2013b). Furthermore, we know that the best form of early childhood education for emergent bilinguals would be one that builds on the linguistic and cultural strengths they bring from home, and such programs are extremely rare (Garcia & Gonzalez, 2006).

Overall, states have done little to support emergent bilinguals in preschool. Illinois in 2010 and Texas in 2012 became the first states to mandate the use of home language practices to educate emergent bilinguals in prekindergarten. The passage of the ESSA (2015) marks the first time in the reauthorization of the Elementary and Secondary Education Act that some attention has been paid to early childhood education. It includes provisions to strengthen early childhood funding, especially for children of low- and moderate-income families. It remains to be seen whether these programs will support the bilingual practices of very young children.

Remedial education and tracking. Because emergent bilinguals are seen only as English learners from whom little is expected, their schooling often consists of remedial programs where the emphasis is on drill and remediation (De Cohen et al., 2005). As a result, the learning of emergent bilinguals is frequently about compensating for their limited English language skills (Harklau, 1994; Olsen, 1997). They are often given multiple periods of classes in ESL instead of meaningful content, a product of the emphasis on developing English. This is exacerbated in the high-intensity English language training provided in states such as Arizona, where students spend many hours studying decontextualized language structures. Other times, in order to focus on English acquisition at the expense of other content-related learning, emergent bilinguals are often taken from their regular classes for "pull-out ESL," creating further inequities (Anstrom, 1997; Fleischman & Hopstock, 1993). Furthermore, although it is widely accepted that a balanced approach to literacy that incorporates more time to discuss, create, read and write, alongside some explicit instruction in the structure of English, is central to literacy development (Birch, 2002; Calkins, 1994; Honig, 1996), many emergent bilinguals are taught to read through heavily phonics-based approaches instead of more balanced ones.

For academic courses other than English, emergent bilinguals are also regularly tracked into courses that do not provide them with challenging content (Callahan, 2003, 2005; Oakes, 1990). In some cases, they are given shortened-day schedules when the extra time blocks are filled with physical education or art classes rather than core subject content courses (García, 1999). In fact, many times, their learning of content-area academics is delayed until they have acquired English proficiency (Minicucci & Olsen, 1992). Alternatively, when newcomers are taught subject matter exclusively through English, instruction often takes on a slower pace and less content is covered (Minicucci & Olsen, 1992). In California, only 41% of teachers reported being able to cover the same material with emergent bilinguals as with all students (Gándara et al., 2003).

In a study of secondary schools in California, less than one-fourth of the schools surveyed offered the full range of content courses for emergent bilinguals (Minicucci & Olsen, 1992). This results in an inferior education, because by the time the emergent bilinguals develop their full proficiency in English, they have not taken the appropriate high-level courses compared with their grade-level English-speaking counterparts, and thus they score lower on college admission tests (Mehan, Datnow, Bratton, Tellez, Friedlander, & Ngo, 1992; Pennock-Román, 1994). In a major test case on the viability of curriculum tracking as an educational practice, *Hobson v. Hansen* (1967), the Washington, D.C., Superior Court noted that 6th-grade students who are taught a grade 3 curriculum are likely to end the year with a 3rd-grade education (Gándara et al., 2003).

According to data from the U.S. Department of Education and the Office for Civil Rights, in 2016 emergent bilinguals were not being challenged in high school. The proportion of emergent bilinguals in advanced math and science classes and enrolled in one Advanced Placement (AP) class was less than 5% in 2016, as shown in Table 7.1.

Furthermore, fewer than 3% of students designated as gifted and talented in 2016 were emergent bilinguals (U.S. Department of Education and Office for Civil Rights, 2016).

Special education. Emergent bilinguals are also overrepresented in some categories of special education, particularly in specific learning disabilities and language and speech impairment classes, and most especially at the secondary level (Artiles, Rueda, Salazar, & Higareda, 2002). Emergent bilinguals who are in bilingual programs are less likely to be in special education than those students who are in English-only programs (Artiles et al., 2002). Gándara et al. (2003) have shown that emergent bilinguals who have low proficiency scores in both English and their home language are even more vulnerable. They are 1.5 times more likely at the elementary level, and twice as likely at the secondary level, to be diagnosed as speech impaired and learning disabled.

The overrepresentation of emergent bilinguals in the learning disability category (57% in this category versus 53% in this category among the rest of the student population) and in the speech/language category (24% in this category versus 19% among the rest of the population) suggests that many

Table 7.1. Emergent bilinguals and advanced math and science and AP

Subject	% of students in schools that offer course	% of students enrolled in course
Algebra II	5%	4%
Calculus	5%	1%
Physics	5%	4%
AP (one course)	5%	2%

Source: U.S. Department of Education and Office for Civil Rights, 2016

educators may have difficulty distinguishing students with disabilities from those who are still learning English (Yates & Ortiz, 1998). Many emergent bilinguals in special education have been classified erroneously as having a speech/language disability (Zehler et al., 2003). This error comes as a result of the shortage of special educators who are trained to understand issues of bilingualism and development of an additional language (Ortiz, 2001).

According to Zehler et al. (2003), approximately 9% of the total population of emergent bilinguals in public schools had been placed in special education classes in 2001–2002.[1] Of these, 61% were male, indicating an overrepresentation of male emergent bilinguals with disabilities, since only 51% of all emergent bilinguals were male (Zehler et al., 2003). Most emergent bilinguals in special education programs were at the elementary level (50.5%), followed by middle school (22.8%), and then high school (18.6%) (Hopstock & Stephenson, 2003b).[2]

Latinx students represented 80% of the total special education emergent bilingual population, indicating that they are slightly overrepresented in special education programs compared to English learners overall (Zehler et al., 2003). This could relate to cultural biases against Latinx students. However, it may also have to do with the abundance of assessment instruments in Spanish, compared to other languages, which makes it possible to diagnose these students. There are also more Spanish-English bilingual special education teachers and school psychologists, meaning that more programs for Spanish speakers may be available.

Exclusion from gifted programs and Advanced Placement. The other side of the coin for emergent bilinguals when it comes to access to the most challenging educational programs is their underrepresentation in gifted and talented programs and Advanced Placement courses. In 2016, fewer than 3% of students who were designated gifted and talented in 2013–2014 were emergent bilinguals (U.S. Department of Education and Office for Civil Rights, 2016). In 2013–2014, emergent bilinguals represented only 2% of students enrolled in one Advanced Placement course (U.S. Department of Education and Office for Civil Rights, 2016).

Although other data on participation by emergent bilinguals in college preparatory courses are not available, these students' placement in remedial literacy and mathematics courses and lower-level core academic courses is well documented (Gándara et al., 2003; Parrish et al., 2002). Yet the data suggest that because of emergent bilinguals' performance on invalid standardized tests, they are too often judged unfit for mainstream college-preparatory classes (Koelsch, n.d.).

Inequitable Resources

As has become quite evident throughout this book, emergent bilingual students have not received their due in terms of equitable resources for academic achievement in American classrooms. Here, we cast further light on the lack of curricular materials and technology, poor school facilities, limited educational funding, and inequitable access to well-prepared teachers.

Instructional materials. Oakes and Saunders (2002) have argued that there is a clear link between appropriate materials and curriculum and student academic outcome. Emergent bilinguals need developmentally appropriate materials to learn English, but they also need appropriate content materials in their home languages. However, more often than not, emergent bilinguals do not have appropriate resources. Only 25% of teachers surveyed in an American Institute for Research (AIR) study reported that they used a different textbook for emergent bilinguals than their English proficient students; and only 46% reported using any supplementary materials for them (Parrish et al., 2002). More than one-quarter of the teachers in California reported not having appropriate reading material in English, and almost two-thirds of those with high percentages of emergent bilinguals in their classes had few instructional materials in Spanish or other languages (Gándara et al., 2003). Teachers with high percentages of emergent bilinguals also reported more frequently that their textbooks and instructional materials were meager, and that they and their students had less access to technology (Gándara et al., 2003; see also Chapter 6).

Although federal regulations require states to have English language proficiency standards that are aligned with the state academic content standards, the alignment of instruction for emergent bilinguals with state standards is much poorer than for English proficient students (Gutiérrez et al., 2002; Hopstock & Stephenson, 2003b). There are also few instructional materials to support this alignment (Hopstock & Stephenson, 2003b).

School facilities. Emergent bilinguals attend the most impoverished and underresourced schools, which is clearly related to their growing isolation and segregation within the public educational system (Orfield, 2001). Research has shown that classrooms for emergent bilinguals are often located on the periphery of, in the basement of, or outside of the school building (Olsen, 1997). Emergent bilinguals also go to schools in buildings that are often not clean or safe. For example, in a survey of 1,017 California teachers conducted in 2002 by the Lou Harris polling group, close to half of the teachers in schools with high numbers of emergent bilinguals reported that their schools had unclean bathrooms and that they had seen evidence of mice, compared to 26% of teachers in schools with few, if any, English learners (Gándara et al., 2003).

In 2006, a report concluded that new school buildings were needed across the country, and that minoritized students, in particular, were attending schools with decrepit facilities (BEST, 2006). Despite unprecedented spending and growth in school construction since then, resources for school construction have not been equally available in all school districts. For example, between 1995 and 2004, school districts with high levels of minority student enrollment invested only $5,172 per student in school construction, while school districts with predominantly White student enrollment spent the most ($7,102 per student) (BEST, 2006). In addition, high-minority school districts used the money to fund basic repairs, such as new roofs and asbestos removal, whereas schools in wealthier districts funded science labs and performing arts studios.

Inequitable funding. One of the most important equity issues surrounding the education of emergent bilinguals has to do with the ways in which programs are funded. Today, funding for education programs for emergent bilinguals comes mostly from local and state sources.[3] In fact, the federal education funding on average represents about 11% of what local school districts spend overall (Sánchez, 2017).

Until 2002, Title VII of the Elementary and Secondary Education Act had provided funding for projects and services for emergent bilingual students at the state, district, and school levels on a competitive basis—that is, they were *discretionary grants* that states and districts applied for and used to fund schools and programs serving emergent bilinguals.

In contrast, under Title III of No Child Left Behind, and continuing under ESSA, there are *formula grants that the federal government awards directly to the states*. Under No Child Left Behind, these federal grants to the states were determined by two factors that are weighted differently in the formula:

1. The number of English language learners (80% of the formula), and
2. The population of recently immigrated children and youth[4] (relative to national counts of these populations) (20% of the formula).

The expectation under ESSA was that Title III funding would be increased. But actual funding depends on appropriation from Congress, and under the 115th Congress that met after January 2017, it is not clear whether this promise will be fulfilled.

Under No Child Left Behind, Title III funds only reached approximately 80% of the 5 million ELLs nationwide (Office of English Language Acquisition, 2006). The Great City Schools report found that the average Title III subsidy of $109 per student was insufficient to meet the educational needs of emergent bilinguals (Council of the Great City Schools, 2004).

Because Title III grants are deemed insufficient to provide adequate funding for emergent bilinguals, 46 states provided additional funding to school districts in 2015. But even across these states, emergent bilinguals are not funded equitably or in the same way. For example, Maryland assigns a weight of 99% for each emergent bilingual student, meaning that school districts get an additional 99% of the base amount of what they get for general education students, whereas Kentucky uses a weight of 9.6% for each emergent bilingual student (Millard, 2015). So, on paper, it is much better to be an emergent bilingual in Maryland than in Kentucky.

Per-pupil funding figures assume that schools target funds to those emergent bilinguals who need services and distribute funding somewhat evenly among them. In reality, however, the money allocated for each school is given directly to the principal in one lump sum, and the principal decides what to do with it. Little information exists on how these funds are allocated at the school level.

Striving for transparency is a central part of seeking equitable funding. Since 1991, when the press for higher standards and more accountability became more intense, courts, state legislatures, and education advocacy organizations have requested "costing out" studies[5] in order to obtain more information on how to fund students, including emergent bilingual students, equitably. Such research helps inform the legal movement to seek adequate funding for groups deemed in need of additional resources, including emergent bilinguals (AIR, 2004; Rebell, 2007, 2009).

Most studies have shown that it costs more to educate emergent bilinguals than it does to educate English speakers (Baker, Green, & Markham, 2004; Parrish, 1994), although a few studies have argued otherwise (AIR, 2004). Still, estimates of these additional costs per emergent bilingual student vary greatly and range from 5% more to 200% more than the cost of educating mainstream students (Baker, Green, & Markham, 2004; J. Crawford, personal communication, March 17, 2007). In other words, there is great variation in this literature on the cost of a meaningful education for these students. Jiménez-Castellanos and Topper (2012) conclude that all methods agree that current funding levels are insufficient. Despite the differences, some consensus on the cost of providing high-quality education to emergent bilinguals is beginning to emerge.

Overall, it has been established that emergent bilinguals require additional personnel at rates of approximately 20 students with one full-time teacher and one or more instructional aide per teacher. This leads to an additional cost (above a regular program) of $2,403 to $3,822 per pupil at the elementary level and $2,851 to $4,937 per pupil at the secondary level, depending on the per-pupil cost and teachers' salaries in a given state and district in optimally sized schools (Baker et al., 2004). These additional costs of educating emergent bilinguals can also vary by district size, concentration of students, and the type of instructional program offered.

Parrish (1994) found that the most expensive educational programs for emergent bilinguals are pull-out ESL programs. In 1994, ESL programs cost $2,687 per pupil, even more than two-way bilingual education (dual-language bilingual) programs, which cost $2,675 per pupil. In the same year, the least expensive educational programs were transitional bilingual education programs, with early-exit programs estimated to be the least expensive at $1,881 per pupil and late exit at $1,976 per pupil. Structured English Immersion or Sheltered English programs follow, costing approximately $2,050 per pupil.[6] So, ironically, the least effective pull-out ESL programs seem to be the costliest.

Clearly, there is a need for additional funding to provide emergent bilinguals with the educational services they require, and deserve. However, before anyone can establish precisely how much more is needed for their education, it is necessary to carefully examine the local context in which these emergent bilinguals are being educated and the goals for their education.

Inequitable access to high-quality educators. Teacher and principal quality are two of the most important factors in determining school effectiveness and, ultimately, student achievement (Blase & Blase, 2001; Clewell & Campbell, 2004). But few school leaders and not enough teachers are well versed in issues surrounding bilingualism. Additionally, there is high turnover among both administrators and teachers of language-minoritized students. Thus, it is even more difficult to find high-quality teachers and school leaders for emergent bilingual students than it is for students in general. In 2016, 32 states reported having shortages of teachers who could work with emergent bilinguals (Sánchez, 2017).

Although principals and teachers at schools with large numbers of English learners are more likely to be Latinx or Asians, these principals and teachers also tend to be less experienced and have fewer credentials than those at schools with few or no emergent bilingual students (De Cohen et al., 2005). Forty percent of Asian teachers and 45% of Latinx teachers nationwide teach in schools with high levels of emergent bilinguals (De Cohen et al., 2005). These Latinx and Asian teachers are more likely to be bilingual and knowledgeable of the students' cultures, thus enabling the support of the students' languages and identities. And yet, teachers in schools with high numbers of emergent bilinguals have fewer credentials on average than teachers at schools with few or no emergent bilinguals (De Cohen et al.,

2005). Although only slightly more than 50% of teachers in schools with high levels of emergent bilinguals have full certification, almost 80% of teachers in other schools do.

In California, the least experienced teachers are placed disproportionately in schools that have the greatest number of minority students (Esch & Shields, 2002; Esch et al., 2005; Gándara, Maxwell-Jolly, & Driscoll, 2005). In 2002, 25% of teachers of emergent bilinguals in California were not fully certified, compared to 14% statewide (Rumberger, 2002). Schools with high concentrations of emergent bilinguals have more difficulties filling teaching vacancies; they are more likely to hire unqualified teachers (De Cohen et al., 2005).

The U.S. Government Accountability Office (GAO) report of 2009 also shows that states have much difficulty in finding qualified personnel to teach emergent bilinguals. Only 11% of the teachers of emergent bilinguals are certified in bilingual education, whereas 18% are certified in ESL. And although being bilingual is an important asset for teachers of emergent bilinguals, only 15% are fluent in a LOTE (Crawford & Krashen, 2007).

Beyond teacher certification in specialized areas, most teachers in the United States have not had any preparation on how to teach emergent bilinguals. Nationwide, less than 20% of teacher education programs required at least one course focused on English learners and bilingualism, and less than a third exposed their students to any fieldwork experience with emergent bilinguals (U.S. Government Accountability Office, 2009). Although 42% of teachers surveyed in a 2003 report of the U.S. DOE National Center for Education Statistics indicated that they had emergent bilinguals in their classrooms, only 13% of these teachers had received more than 8 hours of professional development related to emergent bilinguals.

The inadequate preparation of teachers on issues affecting language-minority students negatively impacts their ability to teach these students. It has been found that teachers who are certified in ESL or bilingual academic development, as well as those who have fluency in a LOTE, have more positive attitudes toward the bilingualism of the students and their own teaching (Lee & Oxelson, 2006).

According to Gándara, Maxwell-Jolly, and Driscoll (2005), there is not only a shortage of qualified teachers, but also of school professionals to assist emergent bilinguals. Bilingual speech pathologists are sorely needed, and guidance counselors with bilingual skills are also in short supply. In California, less than 8% of the school psychologists are bilingual and capable of conducting an assessment in the home language of an emergent bilingual.

From the foregoing discussion, it is evident that emergent bilinguals have to contend with much more than language inequities. With regard to Latinx students, Gándara and Contreras (2009) say:

Although Latinos have suffered many of the same inequities as blacks and other minority groups in schooling—inadequate and overcrowded facilities, under-prepared teachers, inappropriate curriculum and textbooks, and segregated schools—the civil rights focus in education for Latinos has been primarily the issue of language. (p. 121)

The fact that 80% of emergent bilinguals are Latinx students means that more attention has been paid to the inequities of language use instead of the inadequacies of the educational opportunity they have been given. And yet, to offer equitable curricular opportunities to emergent bilinguals would require a fundamental change in the ways in which we view the students' languages other than English, and in particular, Spanish, as well as their dynamic bilingualism.

ALTERNATIVE CURRICULAR PRACTICES AND PREPARING CARING EDUCATORS

A Challenging Inclusive Curriculum That Starts Early

Emergent bilinguals are fully capable of developing ways of using English for academic purposes if given the same socioeducational opportunities as wealthy White children. "The same," however, does not always mean integrated educational programs in which emergent bilinguals could be overlooked, or worse, discriminated against. An equitable curriculum and pedagogy for emergent bilinguals must adapt to their needs. A challenging inclusive curriculum for emergent bilinguals must be ecologically adaptive, as students' bilingualism and biliteracy emerge.

In early childhood, emergent bilinguals must be given the opportunity to engage with caring adults who not only speak their home languages and understand their linguistic and cultural practices, but also can guide their bilingual development by providing opportunities for them to practice listening to and speaking English, as well as their home language. The beginnings of communication around print must include children's home language practices, the ways in which they use language to make meaning from print. Chumak-Horbatsch (2012) provides a plethora of recommendations for linguistically appropriate practice with young immigrant children.

Although it may be necessary to provide a separate instructional space away from English-only students to develop an emergent bilingual's literacy, care must be taken to also provide integrated spaces where emergent bilinguals can interact with other children who speak English at home. This can happen during the time for snack or lunch, play, nap, music, art, dance, or any of the range of activities in which very young children are involved. These integrated spaces must function not only as catalysts of English language acquisition for emergent bilinguals, but also of acquisition of other linguistic and cultural norms for English monolingual young children.

It is of primary importance that culturally and linguistically relevant early childhood programs with bilingual instruction be created for very young emergent bilinguals (Garcia & Jensen, 2009; Tazi, 2014). And it is crucial that this preschool education be state funded and provided for free to all 3- and 4-year-olds. An investment in bilingual preschools for all emergent bilinguals would correspond strongly with improved language development by the time the children reach elementary school.

In Chapter 5, we discussed alternative practices that foster the development of English academic literacy through complex language use. Much has been said about the ways in which a challenging academic curriculum can be delivered to emergent bilinguals while also developing their spoken language use in academic contexts and their academic literacies (Celic, 2009; Chamot & O'Malley, 1994; Echevarría, Vogt, & Short, 2004; Freeman & Freeman, 2008; Gibbons, 2002, 2009). But in order to provide inclusive educational spaces and curricular opportunities for emergent bilinguals throughout schooling, while maintaining opportunities for emergent bilinguals to develop their bilingualism and biliteracy, home language cannot be considered suspect. An inclusive and equitable society would provide the means by which emergent bilinguals are assessed for gifted-and-talented programs in the language they know best. In turn, these gifted-and-talented programs would then include these different ways of using language and make the development of bilingualism and biliteracy a goal for all the children. As we have seen, bilingualism and biliteracy are important for improved cognitive functioning and creative performance. Thus, gifted-and-talented programs would include emergent bilinguals, and at the same time would make spaces where bilingualism and biliteracy would be a goal for all.

Likewise, if all students' language practices were given their rightful place in the U.S. curriculum as important tools for sociocognitive and academic development, more advanced classes and Advanced Placement classes would be taught through languages other than English. Recent New York State policy that mandates translation of some math, science, and social studies graduation exams into five languages—Spanish, Chinese, Korean, Russian, and Haitian Creole—has resulted in a more challenging high school curriculum for emergent bilinguals because students who were previously relegated to ESL, music, art, and physical education classes are now included in content classes taught in these languages. Many high schools are also now teaching AP classes in LOTEs. In one high school we know, for example, AP Biology is taught in Spanish for Latinx emergent bilinguals. Although the students read the advanced biology text in English, they discuss and do experiments and scientific work in Spanish. In another high school, the teacher makes the advanced biology text available in both English and Spanish; students work collaboratively in small groups and are encouraged to use all their meaning-making resources to make sense of the text. In this classroom, the bilingual students' translanguaging is leveraged so that all can participate in advanced classes, even those taught in English. Students are given responsibility to use all their communicative resources to research and learn advanced content.

Finally, with deeper understandings of bilingualism, educators may be less inclined to immediately recommend special education placement for those students who have not yet developed academic English practices. Educators would know that the development of bilingualism and biliteracy takes practice over a lifetime, and that using English for academic purposes to perform school tasks comes with time and practice. With this knowledge, educators would ensure that students receive high-quality education throughout an educational program that supports their linguistic and cultural differences.

Preparing Caring, Creative, and Qualified Educators

Perhaps no other area is so crucial to the improvement of education of emergent bilinguals as the preparation of educators for emergent bilinguals—school leaders, teachers, and school professionals such as school psychologists, guidance counselors, therapists, and paraprofessionals. All school leaders today need to become experts in bilingualism and language learners (Reyes, 2006). Not just specialized bilingual and ESL teachers but also "mainstream" teachers have to understand issues of bilingualism in education and how to include emergent bilinguals in a high-quality and challenging education (Lucas & Grinberg, 2008).

With the intensified migrations of peoples and convergences of languages and cultures in today's globalized world, there cannot be language teachers on the one hand and content teachers on the other (Téllez & Waxman, 2006). All language teachers must have some expertise in the content area, whereas all content teachers must have some expertise in language. To achieve this, teacher education programs would have to change significantly, making a commitment to include courses on bilingualism and language development in all curricula, and ensuring that their prospective teachers have clinical experiences with emergent bilinguals (Grant & Wong, 2003).

Teacher apprenticeship models have sprung up where prospective teachers team up with experienced teachers for a year of teaching, while pursuing university courses in partnership with the school district. One such model is that being pursued by the Internationals Network for Public Schools in New York City. Prospective teachers have a yearlong teaching apprenticeship in high-performing International high schools. After completing the program, apprentices receive New York State certification in TESOL and an innovative master's degree in TESOL from Long Island University. The program is designed around the tenet that, like students, teachers learn best when they apply the theories and content of teaching in an authentic learning context and develop teaching abilities by practicing alongside an experienced teacher.

Teachers who provide emergent bilinguals with a challenging and creative curriculum are those who are committed to the development of language-minoritized communities, both socially and academically. A way to capitalize on this commitment would be to attract prospective teachers from the language communities themselves (Clewell & Villegas, 2001). Gándara and Contreras (2009) remind us that there has never been a true effort to recruit these teachers and prepare them to the highest standards.

The engagement of the community is crucial not only to ensure that there is a supply of committed and qualified caring and creative teachers, but also to provide an equitable education to students themselves. This will be the subject of Chapter 8.

EDUCATING EMERGENT BILINGUALS:
EMBRACING CHALLENGE AND CARE

It is evident that providing an equitable education to emergent bilinguals is not only an issue of language. And yet, unless the students' home language practices are accepted in schools and not considered suspect, there will continue to be ways of excluding emergent bilinguals from the equal educational opportunities that they deserve. Given the ways in which schools are structured, only a language rights orientation based on principles of social justice will ensure that emergent bilinguals are given equitable curricular opportunities and be included in advanced courses and gifted-and-talented programs. But language rights have to be balanced with socioeducational rights, which insist that emergent bilinguals have equitable resources, equitable funding, and equitable access to high-quality teachers. Social justice for emergent bilinguals includes providing them with a challenging inclusive and linguistically and culturally relevant curriculum that empowers them to counteract the linguistic and social oppression in which they often live.

STUDY QUESTIONS

1. What is social justice? How is social justice related to language rights? What do you think about language rights?

2. What are the characteristics of a challenging and creative curriculum for emergent bilinguals? Describe inequities in curricula that emergent bilingual students face.

3. How would you define transformative pedagogy? What are the differences in conceptualization between culturally relevant pedagogy and culturally sustaining pedagogy? In what ways are culturally relevant and sustaining pedagogies transformative?

4. Why are emergent bilinguals often classified as special education students? Why are they often excluded from advanced courses and gifted-and-talented programs? How could this exclusion be remedied?

5. Discuss how instructional resources are often inadequate for emergent bilinguals. What would be necessary to alleviate this situation?

6. What is the situation regarding funding of high-quality educational programs for emergent bilinguals? What do "costing out" studies say?

7. Why are many educators inadequately prepared to serve emergent bilinguals? What would be a way of attracting and preparing caring, creative, and qualified teachers of emergent bilinguals?

8. Discuss ways in which an inclusive and just curriculum for emergent bilinguals could be accomplished.

CHAPTER 8

Family and Community Engagement

This chapter addresses the roles of families and communities in the education of emergent bilinguals. The chapter focuses on:

- Theoretical constructs and empirical evidence for family and community engagement:
  - ➤ Research on parental and family engagement, and
  - ➤ The funds of knowledge construct;
- Inequitable practices:
  - ➤ Stigmatization of language-minoritized families and communities,
  - ➤ Exclusion of home language practices, and
  - ➤ One-size-fits-all parental and family education programs; and
- Alternative approaches:
  - ➤ Parent and family engagement as a shared responsibility,
  - ➤ Broadening the view of parental and family engagement, and
  - ➤ Community organizing.

Both popular belief and research over the years have supported the value of parental and family[1] engagement in their children's schooling, maintaining that several caring adults (school personnel and family members), working together, can accelerate students' learning. It is "the mantra of every educational reform program" (Gonzalez, 2005, p. 42), including NCLB (2001) and the current ESSA (2015) legislation, which, as we noted in Chapter 3, promotes "language instruction educational programs for the parents, families, and communities of English learners" (Section 3102, 129 STAT. 1954). In this chapter, we examine what the research tells us regarding the benefits of parental and family engagement overall and discuss specific benefits for families with emergent bilingual children. We take a critical look at what actually happens to many of these families and children when they reach the schoolhouse door—the discrimination and marginalization they experience. We argue for the implementation of alternative approaches—more promising ways in which families, schools, and communities can come together on a more equal footing to support an equitable education for emergent bilinguals.

RESEARCH AND THEORIES
ON PARENTAL AND COMMUNITY INVOLVEMENT

Involvement or Engagement?

Historically, the role of parents and communities in relationship to schools has been characterized in the research literature as one of "involvement" (Jeynes, 2011). Joyce Epstein, the originator of a widely cited model of parental involvement (e.g., Epstein, 1987; Epstein & Dauber, 1991), now suggests that, rather than the term *parental involvement*, the phrase "school, family, and community partnerships" is more appropriate because it describes the shared responsibility that the concerned parties should have for students' education (Epstein & Sheldon, 2006). Other researchers and educators also have moved away from the concept of involvement, which, they say implies a partial, subservient role that parents and families have in their own children's education in general and in the workings of the school in particular.

More recently, *engagement* is the term being used to conceptualize the relationship among parents, families, communities, and schools. This preference for the term *engagement* was advanced by Shirley (1997) in the context of a community's role in organizing school reform. In introducing the term, Shirley makes a distinction between "*accommodationist* forms of parental *involvement* and *transformational* forms of parental *engagement*" (1997, p. 73; emphasis in original). Goodall and Montgomery (2014), who focus on the family's relationship to the school, outline a continuum between parents' involvement with their children's schools and parents' engagement with their learning. The latter, they say, implies parents' commitment and their exercise of agency in choice and action. In the remainder of this chapter, we use the designation *engagement* except when the studies discussed specifically describe their work in terms of involvement. We show how, when *engagement* becomes more than a word and translates into action, parents, communities, and schools can work as partners to educate emergent bilinguals.

Studies

Research has shown that parents' engagement in their sons' and daughters' education leads to better attendance, higher achievement, improved attitudes about learning, and higher graduation rates. These benefits of parental and family engagement have been demonstrated for children in their early years of schooling (Caspe, Lopez, & Wolos, 2007; Weiss, Caspe, & Lopez, 2006) as well as for adolescents from middle school to high school (Eccles & Harold, 1993), although the parental role diminishes during these later years, partially because of adolescents' desire for more autonomy (Kreider,

Caspe, Kennedy, & Weiss, 2007). According to Kreider and her colleagues, three family involvement processes leading to students' school success include (1) parenting attitudes and practices in the home, (2) formal and informal home–school connections, and (3) parental responsibility for their children's academic growth.[2]

In addition, and of particular importance for this chapter, studies show that children from minoritized and low-income families gain the most from parent engagement (Epstein, 1990; Henderson, 1987; Henderson & Berla, 1994; Henderson & Mapp, 2002; Hidalgo, Siu, & Epstein, 2004; Jordan, Orozco, & Averett, 2001). A meta-analysis conducted by Jeynes (2005) of 41 studies on urban elementary schools demonstrates a significant relationship between parental involvement and academic achievement; this relationship holds for Whites and minoritized groups as well as for both boys and girls. Jeynes (2007) found positive effects for secondary school students, as well, in his meta-analysis of 52 such studies. More recently, Jeynes (2012), in a meta-analysis of 51 studies of school-based parental involvement programs, found a significant relationship between these programs and academic achievement.

Psychology researchers have found what they describe as three overarching "determinants" of parental involvement. The first is parents' beliefs regarding the support roles they have in their children's education; the second is the extent to which they believe that they possess the knowledge and tools they need as educators of their children; the third relates to their perceptions regarding the schools' (or their children's) willingness to have them participate (see Hoover-Dempsey & Sandler, 1997).

Researchers who focus on social theory examine sociocultural and socioeconomic factors of parent involvement. These scholars point out that parents who possess certain kinds of social and cultural capital—social connections, relationships, and shared understandings that provide support and access to institutional resources (Bourdieu, 1985; Portes, 1998)—are successful in helping their children do well academically.[3] Becoming involved in their children's schooling requires that parents understand how the school system functions, what curricular choices are available for their children, and whether they are aware of counseling and advice for accelerated learning and other college-preparatory options. Studies show that many language-minoritized parents do not have access to these understandings (Gándara & Contreras, 2009), yet they do have uniformly high aspirations for their children (Delgado-Gaitán, 1990, 1992; Steinberg, 1996). Parents embrace the "opportunity narrative," a belief that with their sacrifices and hard work, their children can get ahead because school represents an opportunity for success (Bartlett, 2007).

Let us examine one such study on families' educative practices at home. Concha Delgado-Gaitán (1992) showed in an early study still cited today that school *does* matter to Mexican American parents. In her close ethnographic observation and interviews of six families, Delgado-Gaitán examined family social interaction in the home, where parents, within the broader context of their local community institutions, transmit their beliefs, values, and experiences to their children. She describes three categories of parental support for their children's education. The first she calls the physical environment, which addresses the economic and social resources in the home and surrounding community, such as arranging study spaces and materials in close-knit quarters at home and consulting people they know in the church and workplace about their children's schooling. The second category includes emotional and motivational climates within the home, such as encouraging their children to study so that they improve the weekly evaluations they bring home from school and ultimately grow up to be well educated. The third category includes the interpersonal interactions among family members around literacy in the home. Delgado-Gaitán found that these interactions, particularly families' approaches to homework activities, varied across the families and illustrated their incomplete knowledge about school literacy practices and expectations. She summarizes parents' dedication to their children's school success this way:

> Parents share a great deal with their children in the areas of aspirations, motivations, physical resources, and face-to-face interactions, which organize the total learning environment. (Delgado-Gaitán, 1992, p. 512)

Mexican American parents' aspirations for their children are a critical factor in their academic achievement. But more is needed on the part of the school. Delgado-Gaitán (1992) concludes that schools need to "open lines of communication with families and whole communities in a systematic way in order to facilitate the families' access to necessary academic and social resources" (p. 513).

The Funds of Knowledge Construct

Delgado-Gaitán's (1992) findings were further expanded in later research on ethnolinguistic-minority parents and families. A group of anthropologists from the University of Arizona have developed a program of research, spanning nearly 3 decades, on "funds of knowledge" for schooling (e.g., Esteban-Guitart & Moll, 2014; González, Moll, & Amanti, 2005; Greenberg, 1989, 1990; Moll, Amanti, Neff, & González, 1992; Moll & Greenberg, 1990). "Funds of knowledge" is a construct that refers to different strategies and ways of knowing needed for a household to function effectively. It is based on the notion that everyday practices, including linguistic practices, are sites of knowledge construction and that these resources can be brought into the classroom.

We all know that education begins in the home, and because children in U.S. schools come from diverse linguistic and cultural backgrounds, family educational practices can take on distinctive characteristics. In other words, emergent bilinguals' families possess endogenous knowledge and skills that are often overlooked by educators who too often ignore John Dewey's (1938) much earlier call to arrange teaching to take into account children's prior experiences. By exploring their students' family and community practices, teachers can become learners when they reach out to families and communities to understand students' existing knowledge repertoires (McIntyre, Rosebery, & González, 2001). Research has demonstrated variation in ways of knowing—that is, funds of knowledge—among families from different backgrounds, including a number of classic works. Philips's (1983) work on the Warm Springs Reservation in Oregon showed that children learn participation structures at home that are different from the participation structures in the school, resulting in White teachers' misinterpreting the children's turn-taking behaviors and other ways of speaking. Heath (1983) demonstrated how practices in the home sometimes clash with school practices, in her research describing the home–school relationship of three communities in the Piedmont Carolinas: Maintown (representative of the middle class) and Trackton and Roadville, representing working-class Black and White mill communities, respectively. Literacy activities in the working-class communities differ from the literacy taught in schools, which represent middle-class "ways with words." Heath argues that literacy is practiced in all three communities in situations with rich mixtures of orality and literacy, but that teachers often fail to recognize and build upon the literacy practices of some communities, particularly those most marginalized in the larger society.

Other studies have shown how teachers can learn about communication patterns in the home, which can be adapted for improved learning opportunities in the classroom. For example, Rosebery, Warren, and Conant (1992) found that speakers of Haitian Creole use certain discursive practices that are culturally congruent with the discourse of argumentation in science, thus demonstrating how the home language can be a resource rather than an impediment for learning, as is often assumed. Case studies of other work on home language and culture in science classrooms have shown similar findings (e.g., Hudicourt-Barnes, 2003; Rosebery & Warren, 2008). In a similar vein, Au (1993) described efforts to meet the needs of native Hawaiian children, with particular attention to children's reading development, demonstrating that these students' reading improves when the participation structure of reading lessons maintains a close fit with the discourse of talk-story, part of the Hawaiian storytelling practice (see also Au, 2005). These and similar studies show that, working with parents, school personnel can effectively draw on family and community linguistic and other knowledge to guide students toward educational attainment.

We have described just a few examples from an extensive body of research on the educational applications of the funds of knowledge concept. Rodriguez (2013) has written a review of studies between 1992 and 2011. Llopart and Esteban-Guitart (2016) have published a review of studies between 2011 and 2015. The robust literature on this approach shows its durability and value as a resource for strengthening school–community relationships.

The idea behind identifying funds of knowledge that can be used in the classroom is to create a more inclusive learning environment and thereby foster academic achievement for all students. The question becomes: Who decides which of the varied funds of knowledge circulating in students' homes and communities will be applied to the standard academic curriculum?

"Who" Decides "Which" Funds of Knowledge?

We examine the application of funds of knowledge in the classroom by returning briefly to Marshall and Toohey's (2010) research on Punjabi-Sikh 4th- and 5th-grade children's multimedia project on intergenerational stories. The project empowered the Punjabi students to raise questions regarding the absence of their home languages from the school. Taking the initiative to incorporate their home languages into their illustrated storybooks led them to question why, in their French-English dual-language school, Punjabi was not also included even though 73% of the children in the school were Punjabi speakers.

The authors point out that the stories the children heard and retold included more "difficult" funds of knowledge such as grandparents' traumatic memories of life in India—encounters with snakes, lightning strikes, beatings, and war. These depictions of struggle became a source of concern; the teacher was ambivalent about what would be appropriate to include in storybooks being created for the school. In the end, stories were published with the difficult family funds of knowledge intact. The authors conclude their research by emphasizing the need to recognize and support families' and students' agency in applying their funds of knowledge in the classroom. Marshall and Toohey (2010) state, "We speculate that such knowledge might become the impetus . . . for productive dialogues among community members, children, and teachers about how these matters might become resources for children and teachers and community" (p. 237). Pitt and Britzman (2003) also raise the question from a psychoanalytic perspective about how "difficult" knowledge might be used as a resource rather than a prohibition in schools, families, and communities. They say that such knowledge can be a source of dialogue and critical examination of what students' life experiences might bring to their learning experience in the classroom.

In a similar vein, Zipin's (2009) research draws attention to difficult knowledge by discussing what he calls the "darker" aspects of students' life worlds—crime, alcohol, drugs, bullying. In a challenge to the earlier scholarly work on funds of knowledge that circumvented difficult topics such as these, he argues that dark funds of knowledge are too often avoided in schools and should be included in the curriculum. He describes the process by which one teacher helped her students address problems of bullying and harassment through clay animation stories. This required a great deal of effort on the part of both teacher and students to take on activities that interrupt "usual institutional denial mechanisms that sustain boundaries between dark knowledge and school curriculum" (Zipin, 2009, p. 321).

Zipin, Sellar, and Hattam (2012) also call attention to the difficulty of defining funds of knowledge in today's world of migration and border crossings. These movements give rise to localities that are culturally and linguistically diverse, fluid, often poor, and without funds of knowledge in common. The site for Zipin and his colleagues' study was in the northern suburbs of Adelaide, Australia, where the population included Anglo and Indigenous people along with migrants and refugees from Vietnam, Cambodia, Bosnia, Sudan, and Somalia. Schools were receiving students who spoke different home languages and varied in English proficiency. The researchers argue that in diverse environments like these, local schools need to rethink their curriculum. The focus should be on working with families and students to reimagine "new possibilities for *becoming community*" (2012, p. 185; emphasis in the original). This new thinking compels schools to recognize the agency of learners, who can imagine recontextualizing work beyond existing funds of knowledge toward a more just future.

INEQUITIES IN SCHOOL AND FAMILY/COMMUNITY RELATIONS

Stigmatization of Language-Minoritized Families and Communities

Despite the promise of family, community, and school collaboration indicated in research findings, the parents of emergent bilinguals, who in many cases have limited formal schooling themselves and may not communicate proficiently in English, continue to be stigmatized and considered incapable educational partners (Chappell & Faltis, 2013; Ramirez, 2003). They are thought to have substandard language skills, lack of education, "inferior" family organizational structures and values, and "lack of interest" in their children's education. This deficit view is also applied to their children—even by researchers (e.g., Dunn, 1987). Families' home language practices are devalued, and family members' "accented" English may become a marker of difference and exclusion (Lippi-Green, 1997) especially if families are newcomers to the United States (Wiley & Lukes, 1996). Thus, not only do parents feel marginalized (Warriner, 2009), but their children also often experience a sense of failure during school and may feel unwelcome or even excluded from extracurricular activities (Gándara, O'Hara, & Gutiérrez, 2004).

Yet, the research demonstrates that, in fact, it is the schools that are deficient—schools with the least funding and limited resources as well as teachers who have not been prepared to work with families for whom English is not their first language and to engage effectively with the parents (Gibson, Gándara, & Koyama, 2004). As Valenzuela (1999) noted, schooling is too often a subtractive process, which ignores students' ways of knowing and speaking; opportunities for building on these resources are lost, and schooling eventually becomes complicit in producing failure (see also Varenne & McDermott, 1998). Some schools are less apt to reach out to parents of color who speak a language other than English in spite of the positive effect such connections can have (Gándara & Contreras, 2009; Henderson & Berla, 1994). Teachers themselves admit that their weakest skills are in the area of making effective connections with parents from diverse ethnolinguistic backgrounds (Gándara, Maxwell-Jolly, & Driscoll, 2005). Gándara and her colleagues (2005) tell us that teachers they interviewed reported "their district's failure to devote resources to the training of teachers, aides, and other personnel to communicate with parents and/ or to provide teachers the time to make useful contact with families" (p. 7). Gándara and Contreras (2009) give reasons why hiring qualified teachers from the students' own communities would be important:

> Such teachers not only better understand the challenges that students face and the resources that exist in those communities; they are also more likely to speak the language of the students and be able to communicate with them and their parents. Moreover, teachers who come from the same community in which they work are more likely to stay in the job over time, developing valuable experience and expertise that has been shown to enhance the achievement of their students. (p. 148)

Work is still needed to encourage teacher positive engagement with parents (Maxwell-Jolly & Gándara, 2012). We argue that the schools have to revise their valuation of these parents' educative role and redouble their efforts to engage with parents and communities in order to help pave the way for greater educational equity for emergent bilinguals.

Exclusion of the Most Significant Resource: Home Language Practices

Many educators still consider family practices to be barriers to student achievement. The practice that most often comes under attack is the home language. There is a kind of "exceptionalist" belief (DeGraff, 2005), a deficit view of home language practices as an inadequate vehicle for education.

DeGraff (2009) presents a critical examination of this deficit view of the home language using the example of school and community attitudes toward his native Haitian Creole; he shows the fallacy of this belief and its social cost for Haitian American children's education. In his article, DeGraff describes comments that readers once sent to the *Miami Herald* about the Haitian Creole language: "Creole is not even a language. It is slave lingo. . . . Why on earth are we spending public funds to teach kids in school the language of peasants?" (cited in DeGraff, 2009, p. 124). Such comments are not only demeaning, but also racist and classist. Contrary to these false beliefs, DeGraff demonstrates through detailed comparative analysis of Creole, English, and French language structures that Haitian American students' home language is a powerful linguistic resource.

A great deal of research shows the value of home language practices as an educative tool. Sadly, immigrant parents are often exhorted to "speak English at home," in the mistaken belief that this will improve their children's English at school. This advice, though well intentioned, encourages inconsistent, and often weak, "linguistic input" from parents who themselves may speak little or no English and, above all, devalues the home language (Gándara & Contreras, 2009). As we have argued in earlier chapters, the erasure of the home language through English-only school practices reinforces the deficit view that families and their children need to be linguistically "fixed" or "repaired" before they can succeed academically in the United States.

One-Size-Fits-All Parent Education Programs

There is, of course, the question of what parental engagement with the schools means. The "involvement" view has generally been defined in terms of parental presence at school or parents' assistance with students' academic work, for example. In general, it is the school that decides how parents can become involved with their children's education, which, according to Seeley (1993), is a "delegation" model.

One mainstream approach has been to develop "parent education" or "family literacy" programs. Parent education programs have been initiated to show parents how they can become involved in their children's education. The programs offer services such as providing information about the U.S. educational system; demonstrating ways to interact with teachers, school administrators, and other staff; and offering ways to help children at home—for example, by reading to them, talking with them, and encouraging them in their studies (Chrispeels & Gonz, 2004; Chrispeels & Rivero, 2001).

Although parent education programs are valuable, some focus almost exclusively on what parents do not know: Many of these programs have taken the "let us fix them" approach, assuming that parents lack the requisite motivations and skills to support their children's education. We have already shown the fallacies in any deficit model that claims there is one best way for parents to be involved in their children's education, and other scholars have concurred with this criticism (Auerbach, 1995; Taylor, 1997); Johnson (2009) provides a critique of any unitary "best practices" approach in parent education programs that do not account for diversity in families' ways of educating their children. In the section that follows, we provide alternative routes to family engagement in children's education.

ALTERNATIVE APPROACHES
TO PARENT AND COMMUNITY ENGAGEMENT

Counteracting Stigmatization Through Parent and Community Engagement

Ways of approaching parent and community engagement have evolved to create a more equal partnership between families/communities and the schools. In recommending alternative approaches, we discuss efforts to ameliorate the chasm between parents of emergent bilinguals, their communities, and school personnel. We begin by signaling more culturally sensitive programs to support parents as educators and then discuss how families and communities, often in concert, have asserted more agency in calling for educational policies and practices that take into account their children's linguistic and cultural resources for learning.

Since 1983, scholars in the Harvard Family Research Project (http://www.hfrp.org/) have sponsored a number of initiatives, and have provided tips, research reports, and policy briefs on family engagement in children's education. Their overarching approach is to demonstrate that family engagement is a shared responsibility among parents, the school, and the community.

The Family, School, and Community National Working Group (Weiss & Lopez, 2009) has developed an expanded definition of family engagement that entails three principles, which we cite here:

- First, family engagement is a shared responsibility in which schools and other community agencies and organizations are committed to reaching out to engage families in meaningful ways and in which families are committed to actively supporting their children's learning and development.
- Second, family engagement is continuous across a child's life and entails enduring commitment but changing parent roles as children mature into young adulthood.
- Third, effective family engagement cuts across and reinforces learning in the multiple settings where children learn—at home, in prekindergarten programs, in school, in after school programs, in

faith-based institutions, and in the community. (Weiss & Lopez, 2009, para. 6)

These more sensitive approaches to parent education programs also acknowledge that schools must move beyond a unidirectional undertaking: Schools must learn from families, too, and come to understandings about how student learning occurs at home and in the community. A more useful way to benefit emergent bilinguals' success is to develop bidirectional school-community education programs.

As Rosenberg, Lopez, and Westmoreland (2009) argue, family engagement is a responsibility that must be shared by schools, parents, and communities. That is why the "funds of knowledge" program of research we introduced earlier, which was initiated by Luis Moll and his associates, is so important (e.g., Browning-Aiken, 2005; González, Moll, & Amanti, 2005; López, 2001; Mercado, 2005a, 2005b; Moll et al., 1992; Tenery, 2005). This research has focused on teachers' visits to the homes of families of Latinx students to learn about a variety of abilities that the families possess, such as carpentry, mechanics, music, knowledge about health and nutrition, household and ranch management, and extensive language and literacy practices. López (2001) describes parents' efforts at teaching their children the value of hard work, a value that is transferable into academic life. Other researchers have documented children's first exposures to print, known as local literacies: Bible reading, reading and writing family letters, record-keeping, and following recipes (Delgado-Gaitán & Trueba, 1991; Mercado, 2005b).

Mercado (2005a) describes funds of knowledge in two New York Puerto Rican homes as developing in three areas: intellectual, social, and emotional resources. The families draw on both Spanish and English literacy to address their needs in health, nutrition, and legal matters, and for spiritual development. As Mercado (2005a) says, the funds of knowledge approach "is an approach that begins with the study of households rather than the study of pedagogy . . . and transforms relationships between and among families, students, and teachers" (p. 251). Browning-Aiken (2005) and Tenery (2005) both describe how social networks are formed with extended family, friends, and the wider community. In short, parents of emergent bilinguals have a great deal to teach teachers about knowledge and skills that originate in their households that can, and should, be translated into academic success in schools.

Broadening the View of Family and Community Engagement

A broader definition of parental engagement, which takes into account family and community practices, is that provided by Pérez Carreón, Drake, and Calabrese Barton (2005), who developed the concept of *ecologies of parental engagement* to refer to the participation of parents in a child's schooling in a manner that goes beyond the physical space of the school and is rooted in the understanding of a family's cultural practices. This approach takes into account the different styles of action taken by parents of diverse ethnolinguistic backgrounds. The authors offer the examples of Celia, a mother who engages with the teacher as a helper inside the classroom, and Pablo, an undocumented immigrant father, who engages with a network of neighbors and his son's teacher outside the classroom to question what is happening in school.

Two seminal studies of families' styles of action, published in the 1990s and still read today, deserve examination here. Ana Celia Zentella's (1997, 2005) research in New York and Guadalupe Valdés's (1996) research in California provide evidence that parents of various Spanish-speaking backgrounds are involved in their children's education in a variety of ways, including rich linguistic exposure to storytelling and print in the native language at home. Zentella (1997) explores the lives and rich, varied language patterns of working-class Puerto Rican families with a focus on five girls, whom she follows from childhood until they become young adults. Her observations of family language practices lead her to emphasize the importance of teachers building on students' home language for learning—including vernacular varieties—to support students' self-worth and identity and to help children see connections with the standard variety, in this case, standard Spanish. For Zentella (2005), becoming bilingual—maintaining the home language and developing strong English language and literacy competencies—gives students a chance at economic advancement. She states that parental goals for their children also include becoming *bien educado* (well educated), a term that encompasses moral values and respect along with having book knowledge.

Valdés (1996) describes first-generation Mexican parents' beliefs about their role in their children's schooling. For these parents, teachers were to be entrusted with the children's academic skills. Mothers and fathers, who did not feel that they had the academic preparation to help with these skills, focused instead on giving advice, instilling respect, and fostering moral values (see also Suárez-Orozco & Suárez-Orozco, 2001). Valdés makes a strong argument in this research that school officials' and teachers' response to these parental beliefs has been that the parents are disinterested in the children's education. As we have seen in the research reported throughout this chapter, this notion is far from the truth; parents want to learn how to help their children at home (Epstein, 1990), yet they have in some cases felt disregarded and left powerless in their attempts to be engaged with the school (Pérez Carreón, Drake, & Calabrese Barton, 2005).

More recently, researchers have observed additional forms of parental actions on behalf of their children, including those of immigrant parents, such as searching out a dialogic approach with school personnel (Olivos, 2006; Olivos, Jiménez-Castellanos, & Ochoa, 2011) or approaching outside groups "such as employers, church authorities, or staff of nonprofit organizations about their rights as parents" (Poza, Brooks, & Valdés, 2014, p. 132).

Bilingual families often demand that their children be bilingually educated, with school authorities often telling them that their bilingual children do not qualify for the programs that are available because they already speak English. In some cities, bilingual families and communities are spearheading what Jaumont (2017) has called "a bilingual revolution," demanding that bilingual programs be accessible for their children. Many times, these bilingual families struggle with educational authorities that have constructed two-way dual-language bilingual programs with strict definitions of who belongs in such programs. The bilingual families involved in such efforts provide the clearest evidence of the type of parental engagement we should be encouraging. At the same time, all American bilingual families need to take responsibility to ensure that bilingual education programs are available for all, including those who need them most—emergent bilinguals who are developing English.

Community Organizing

Research shows that parents of emergent bilinguals are beginning to question the existing power relations in the home–school relationship. Some parents have begun to form grassroots organizations to address their schools about concerns they have regarding their children's education. According to a survey of 66 community-organizing groups by Mediratta, Fruchter, and Lewis (2002), 50 of these groups have been in existence since 1994. Though research on these groups' impact has been limited, we know about some of their efforts. Gold, Simon, and Brown (2002) interviewed 19 community-organizing groups and conducted a case study of five of them. The authors learned that members of the community make an impact on the quality of schools by, among other things, insisting on school–community connections and developing parents' leadership skills.

Delgado-Gaitán (2001) studied Comité de Padres Latinos/Committee of Latinx Parents (COPLA), where parents learned to make sense of the school system, build leadership, and become their children's advocates. Delgado-Gaitán (2001) explained: "Shaped by the lesson of their own pain, [the] parents placed their children's needs center stage, giving rise to and sustaining their activism in the community" (p. 8).

Community organizations like these are beginning to require more equitable and responsive actions by the public education system. Community-based organizations (CBOs) with strong connections to marginalized families and communities can add leverage to families' pursuit of more active roles in engaging with schools (Shirley, 1997). For example, a case study approach was used to examine three CBOs in Chicago, Illinois; Los Angeles, California; and Newark, New Jersey, which were working to engage parents more fully in schools (Warren, Hong, Leung Rubin, & Uy, 2009). The three core elements that they found across these diverse urban settings included a focus on building relationships among parents as well as between parents and the school, the development of parent leaders who collaborate with schools in setting agendas, and a mutual exchange of relational power. The authors conclude by stating that not only parents, but also schools, can benefit from the expertise of CBOs to develop a partnership with parents in the education of children and youth.

An example of a successful partnership with community-based organizations is the Padres Comprometidos program of the National Council of La Raza that has been implemented in more than 30 sites in more than 10 states (Arias, 2015). The home language and cultural practices of Latinx parents are seen as assets in the curriculum designed by Padres Comprometidos. In addition to working with families, the program also works with school personnel so that a relationship between families and school personnel is built and strengthened, with all equal partners.

EDUCATING EMERGENT BILINGUALS: RE-CREATING THE SCHOOL-FAMILY-COMMUNITY CONNECTIONS

We can learn a great deal from research about appropriate school-family-community linkages. In addition, we have to recognize that parents are invested in their emergent bilingual children's learning and want them to excel. Further, we should recognize that the education of emergent bilingual students is a partnership with parents and the community. Schools can investigate the funds of knowledge that their students' families and communities hold and then build on them. The most important resource that families possess is their home language and cultural practices, which should be celebrated as a source of knowledge. Teachers also need support: They must be provided with the tools they need to communicate better with these families. Assistance should be given to families to understand the workings of the school system, to build social networks, to seek out school and community services that support their educational efforts, and to proactively initiate alternative agendas for school change. In short, the literature we report here suggests that there needs to be a balance of power with school personnel, parents, and community working to achieve closer mutual engagement for the education of emergent bilinguals.

STUDY QUESTIONS

1. Distinguish between the concepts of family/community involvement and engagement. Why does this matter?

2. Describe what research tells us regarding the benefits of family and community engagement for emergent bilingual children's success in school.

3. What are "funds of knowledge?" Give some examples of these from the research; describe how the research has broadened to include difficult or dark funds of knowledge in the curriculum.

4. In what ways are families of emergent bilinguals sometimes stigmatized?

5. What are the problems and promises of parent education programs?

6. In what ways are parents showing leadership on behalf of their children's education?

7. Describe what would be a promising program to develop partnerships between families of emergent bilinguals and schools.

CHAPTER 9

Assessments

In this chapter, we will:

- Review theoretical constructs that are important for the fair assessment of emergent bilinguals, specifically:
  - ➤ The power of assessments,
  - ➤ The difference between language proficiency and content proficiency,
  - ➤ The discrepancy between general language performances and language-specific performance,
  - ➤ The validity and reliability of the tests for emergent bilinguals,
  - ➤ The fit of the assessment to the population, and
  - ➤ The match of the language of the test to the language practices of the students;
- Identify inadequacies in assessment practices that arise from:
  - ➤ Assessing prematurely and intensely,
  - ➤ Establishing arbitrary proficiencies, and
  - ➤ Ignoring those who need the most help; and
- Consider some alternative practices, including:
  - ➤ Observing closely,
  - ➤ Assessing dynamically,
  - ➤ Enabling testing accommodations,
  - ➤ Disentangling language and content,
  - ➤ Assessing in students' home languages, using translations and transadaptations,
  - ➤ Assessing bilingually, and
  - ➤ Translanguaging in assessment.

One of the key equity issues surrounding the education of emergent bilinguals concerns the ways in which these students are assessed according to national mandates and state accountability systems. Our central question in this chapter is: *Given what we know theoretically and research-wise about assessment of emergent bilinguals, are these students being assessed according to accepted theories and research evidence about language and bilingualism?* The answer to this question, as we will demonstrate here, is an emphatic *no*. It has been widely demonstrated that as a result of inadequate high-stakes tests, emergent bilinguals experience more remedial instruction, greater probability of assignment to lower curriculum tracks, higher dropout rates, poorer graduation rates, and disproportionate referrals to special education classes (Artiles, 1998; Artiles & Ortiz, 2002; Cummins, 1984).

Because the English learner subgroup by definition cannot possibly meet the proficiency targets in these high-stakes tests, *all* programs serving emergent bilinguals are often questioned, including those that are conducted exclusively in English. As Menken (2008) argues, mandating high-stakes tests in English for all has acted as language policy, accelerating students' immersion in English without the advantage of home language support. Valenzuela (2005) maintains that high-stakes testing in Texas has been the most detrimental policy for Latinos and emergent bilinguals and recommends that there be local control over assessment.

We agree with the assertion that all students have to be *included* in every assessment. But there are equity concerns regarding how assessments are currently being conducted and how the data they generate are being used. These equity issues have to do with misunderstandings of theoretical constructs for assessment that disproportionately impact emergent bilinguals. These include (1) the power of assessments, (2) the difference between language proficiency and content proficiency, (3) the discrepancy between general language performance and language-specific performance, (4) the validity and reliability of the tests for emergent bilinguals, (5) the fit of the assessment to the population, and (6) the match of the language of the test to the language practices of the students. This chapter first considers these theoretical constructs, and then identifies the shortcomings of some ill-considered practices that surround assessment of emergent bilinguals. As in other chapters, we note that there is a gap between accepted theories regarding assessment for these students and the testing that takes place. We end the chapter by proposing alternative assessment policies and practices that are more effective for these students based on theory and research evidence.

THEORETICAL CONSTRUCTS IN ASSESSMENT

The Power of Assessments

As Foucault (1979) has indicated, assessment can be a way to exercise power and control (see also Shohamy, 2001). Foucault (1979) explains:

The examination combines the technique of an observing hierarchy and those of normalizing judgment. It is a normalizing gaze, a surveillance that makes it possible to quantify, classify and punish. It establishes over individuals a visibility through which one differentiates and judges them. (p. 18)

Since Alfred Binet developed his intelligence testing methods in the early 20th century, tests have been used to label and classify students, often with grave consequences. For example, the Stanford-Binet test developed by Lewis Terman was used to "prove" that "[Indians, Mexicans, and Blacks] should be segregated in special classes . . ." (Terman, cited in Oakes, 1985, p. 36). The history of assessment has been entangled from the very beginning with racism and linguistic discrimination (Wiley, 1996). Testing is used more often as a vehicle for allocating educational and employment benefits, rather than as a means for informing teaching and developing learning. Thus, educators have to be extremely mindful of the power of tests and how they can be dangerous and discriminatory if used inappropriately.

Language Proficiency and Content Proficiency

Every assessment is an assessment of language (AERA, APA, & NCME, 2014). Thus, assessment for emergent bilinguals, who are still learning the language in which the test is administered, is not valid unless language is disentangled from content. As we have noted, English proficiency for interpersonal communication is not the same as the more complex proficiency required for academic achievement in English. Gottlieb (2006, 2016) describes how *academic language proficiency* is usually assessed by evaluating the comprehension and use of specialized vocabulary and language patterns in the spoken and written modes, the linguistic complexity of these modes, and the appropriate use of the sound system (phonology), grammatical structure (syntax), and meaning (semantics) of the language. *Content proficiency* refers to whether the student has actually acquired knowledge of the subject matter. When assessment uses only English to test emergent bilinguals' content knowledge, both language and content proficiency are entangled.

The Discrepancy Between General Linguistic Performance and Language-Specific Performance

It is also important to keep in mind two dimensions of language performances that we call *general linguistic performance* and *language-specific performance* (García, Johnson, & Seltzer, 2017). General linguistic performance has to do with the ability of students to deploy *any of the features in their language repertoire* to accomplish language and content-specific tasks. Language-specific performance refers to the ability to deploy *only the features considered standard and that correspond to the specific language demanded of the task* (García, Johnson, & Seltzer, 2017).

All speakers use features of their language system that go beyond those sanctioned in schools to perform academic tasks. In part, schools teach students to use language for tasks that are different from those they perform outside of school. In schools, for example, students are given practice in making sense of complex texts they have read or listened to; using language to make convincing arguments, especially in writing; discussing a math problem or theorem; and so on. As we have seen, emergent bilinguals come into schools with very different schooling experiences. Some newcomers arrive in U.S. schools with strong prior education. They know how to use language to perform school tasks, although perhaps they may not have the features of English demanded in a U.S. school. Let us illustrate with two hypothetical cases. Jeehyae, newly arrived from Korea, can use Korean to do all the things that the language arts standards require. In reading, and in Korean, Jeehyae can provide text evidence of key ideas, make inferences and identify main ideas and relationships in complex texts, recognize the text's craft and structure (its chronology, comparison and contrast, identify cause and effect), and associate knowledge and ideas from multiple sources and texts. In writing, and in Korean, Jeehyae can produce text types for various purposes, such as opinion, informative, explanatory, and narrative pieces. But, of course, if in an assessment Jeehyae were asked to show that she can perform these tasks using English features exclusively, she would do very poorly.

Jeehyae's linguistic performance is different from that of Moussa, a student recently arrived from Guinea in Africa whose home language practices he identifies as Fulani, but who has been schooled in French in a poor rural school. Moussa's school did not provide him with the opportunities to use Fulani or French to perform the linguistically complex academic tasks valued in U.S. schools. His school focused on developing Moussa's standard French, through mechanical drills and tasks aimed to "erase" his Fulani. When Moussa entered his U.S. school, he was assessed in English only. As a result, his lack of experience using language for academic purposes was masked by his poor English-only performance.

By not differentiating between general linguistic performance and language-specific performance, assessments run the risk of obviating the important difference between Jeehyae, a student able to use language to perform academic tasks (even if that language is Korean), and Moussa, whose poor language performance is not simply a matter of English language acquisition, but of learning how to use language for academic tasks. Both students' language-specific performances in English language assessments are poor. However, Jeehyae can use Korean to perform academic tasks, whereas Moussa cannot perform academic tasks in French, nor can he do so in Fulani. Assessments that do not differentiate between general linguistic performance and language-specific performance mask an important difference among emergent bilinguals that has important consequences for their education. These entanglements then have important consequences for test validity.

Validity and Reliability for Emergent Bilinguals

In order for test results to be equitable, emergent bilinguals must be included in the design and piloting of the instrument so that the *norming* of the test is not biased—that is, the test must have both validity and reliability for bilingual students (Abedi, 2004; Abedi & Lord, 2001).

Reliability refers to the capacity of the test or of individual test items to measure a construct consistently over time. Research by Abedi (2004); Abedi, Hofstetter, and Lord (2004); and Martiniello (2008) demonstrates that large-scale exams have differential reliability for students whose English language abilities do not match those of the test. Martiniello (2008) shows that emergent bilingual students and monolingual students with the same ability perform differently on particular math test items because of unfamiliar vocabulary and complex syntactic structures.

Chatterji (2003) defines *validity* as having to do with "the *meaningfulness* of an assessment's results given the particular constructs being tapped, purposes for which the assessment is used and the populations for whom the assessment is intended" (p. 56). Given the fact that language and content are confounded in tests, there are concerns over the validity of standardized assessments for emergent bilinguals because a test may not measure what it intends. Furthermore, tests may have little *content validity* for these students because the performance of emergent bilinguals does not reveal much about their learning (Lachat, 1999). Worse still is the *consequential validity* of these tests for emergent bilinguals—the aftereffects and social consequences. Emergent bilinguals often pay a price with regard to how they are taught as a result of these tests, ending up misdirected into remedial educational programs and special education (Cronbach, 1989; Messick, 1989).

Because tests are constructed for White, middle-class, monolingual populations, they always contain a built-in content bias. Tests do not always include activities or concepts from the worlds of minoritized students (Mercer, 1989). Nor do they take into account the multilingual competencies of bilingual children (Shohamy, 2011). These tests designed for monolingual students reflect neither the cultural practices nor the language practices with which emergent bilingual students are familiar.

Fit of Tests to Population

Criterion-referenced assessments, in which each exam is compared to a specific body of knowledge, are distinct from *norm-referenced assessments*, in which each exam is measured against the scores of other students. But criterion-referenced assessments are still not appropriate for testing emergent bilinguals. In criterion-referenced assessments, students are graded according to whether they have met a defined criterion or standard, which determines what students should know and be able to do in various subject areas. But emergent bilinguals, by definition, generally cannot meet the standard of English language proficiency; thus, they are often judged not to be competent with regard to subject knowledge.

Furthermore, because language and subject content are entangled, studies have found that there is a discrepancy between test assessments scores and student performance in the classroom. Katz, Low, Stack, and Tsang (2004) studied Spanish-speaking and Chinese-speaking emergent bilinguals in San Francisco and concluded: "Test data suggested that ELL students underperformed academically compared to EO (English-only) students, but ELL students turned out to be high achievers in the classroom context" (p. 56).

It has been shown that *performance-based assessments*, tests that ask students to produce a product such as a portfolio or perform an action, are better for bilingual students because they provide a wider range of opportunities to show what they know and are able to do in both language and content areas (Abedi, 2010; Estrin & Nelson-Barber, 1995; Gottlieb, 2016, 2017; Navarrete & Gustke, 1996). Genishi and Borrego Brainard (1995) say that performance-based assessment "can be oral, written, 'performative,' as in dance, or visual/artistic" (p. 54). Goh (2004) recommends any alternative technique that can determine what a given student really knows or can do—performances, hands-on activities, and portfolios of student work—arguing that assessment must include multiple modalities. Because student problem-solving skills may be documented in different ways, performance-based multimodal assessments are less language dependent than are traditional tests, enabling teachers to better distinguish between language proficiency and content proficiency. So, although performance-based assessments tax teachers' time, they are more appropriate precisely because they require teachers' attention to the details in students' performance.

Let us reiterate the major caveat about performance assessments: Because their interpretation relies on the judgment of those scoring the tests (Lachat, 1999), it is crucial that individuals knowledgeable about the linguistic and cultural practices of emergent bilinguals participate in the development of rubrics for scoring student work. In this way, scorers may be able to disentangle academic performance on the assessment from language proficiency.

Matching the Language of the Test to Language Practices

The language practices of both emergent and proficient bilingual students are very different from those of monolingual students. Thus, a test constructed for monolinguals cannot match the language use of bilingual individuals who draw from a language system with many more linguistic features. Bachman (2001) refers to the distinction between the language of the test and actual language practices:

> That there must be a relationship between the language used on tests and that used in "real life" cannot be denied, since if there is no such relationship, our language tests become mere shadows, sterile procedures that may tell us nothing about the very ability we wish to measure. (p. 356)

Valdés and Figueroa (1994) point to the difficulties of testing emergent bilingual students with instruments that have been normed for monolinguals:

> When a bilingual individual confronts a monolingual test, developed by monolingual individuals, and standardized and normed on a monolingual population, both the test taker and the test are asked to do something that they cannot. The bilingual test taker cannot perform like a monolingual. The monolingual test cannot "measure" in the other language. (p. 87)

Clearly, monolingually constructed and administered tests cannot validly measure the complex language practices of bilingual students.

INEQUITABLE ASSESSMENT PRACTICES

Emergent bilinguals continue to be assessed prematurely with high-stakes instruments that confound academic language and content and that do not align with their language practices. In fact, much educational time is taken up testing with invalid instruments. And despite the fact that theory and research support the use of performance-based assessments as more valid for these students, they are rarely used as high-stakes tests.

Assessing Prematurely and Intensely

Researchers contend that the high-stakes testing of American school population mandated by NCLB (2001) and continued by ESSA (2015) has had a negative effect on all students (Nichols & Berliner, 2007). Much time and energy is being spent testing, although there is no evidence that the testing is improving the education of emergent bilinguals. Although teachers are assessing students with more performance-based assessments, they often deem the scores on high-stakes standardized tests to be more important, because schools and teachers are held accountable for the performance of students on such tests (Amrein & Berliner, 2002).

The intensity of testing means that less time is being spent in challenging and creative teaching or teaching subject matter that is not tested. The phenomenon known as washback, the process by which testing and formal assessments drive the curriculum, has been well documented, especially in the literature on language teaching (Cheng, Watanabe, & Curtis 2004; Shohamy, Donitsa-Schmidt, & Ferman, 1996). A study by the Center on Education Policy (CEP) found that since 2002, 62% of districts reported they had increased the time for reading and required schools to spend a specific amount of time teaching reading, while 53% of districts had also done so for math (CEP, 2005). In contrast, less time is being spent teaching science, social studies, and the arts. Crucially, the reading and math curriculum narrowly follows the exigencies of the tests.

The CEP (2016) surveyed teachers on a number of issues, assessment being one of them. Eighty-one percent of teachers responding believed that students spend too much time taking state-mandated tests. In high-poverty schools, one-third of teachers said they spend more than 1 month per school year preparing students for mandated exams. However, an overwhelming majority of teachers (86%) believed in formative teacher-made assessments. For state-mandated tests, less than a third of teachers surveyed wanted to eliminate them, but more than half (60%) wanted to reduce their frequency or length.

In 2015, the Council of the Great City Schools estimated that the average student in large city school systems will take approximately 112 mandatory standardized tests between prekindergarten and high school. Each year, students spend an average of 20 to 25 hours taking these tests. A 2015 national PDK/Gallup poll (PDK International, 2015) reported that two-thirds of public school parents agree that there is too much emphasis on standardized testing. This has fueled the parental movement to "opt out" of mandated standardized testing. Although ESSA (2015) has continued to require testing, it also made funds available to states to audit their testing systems and eliminate unnecessary assessments (U.S. Department of Education, 2016).

Establishing Arbitrary Proficiencies

Assessment of emergent bilinguals is done particularly to determine whether or not they are proficient in English. But different states measure English proficiency differently, using tests that have diverging views of what the construct of proficiency entails. Thus, emergent bilinguals may be deemed to be proficient in one state and not in another.

Establishing these arbitrary language proficiencies also stems from a misunderstanding of language development and bilingualism. Proficiency assessments pay attention only to the stage in which English is being learned, as if that process could be completed, while ignoring the translanguaging that bilinguals carry with them. The point of proficiency at which time the student is declared to be "proficient in English" is established arbitrarily. Gándara and Contreras (2009) note that it is a false dichotomy to say that "One is either proficient or not; one is either an English learner or a fluent English speaker" (p. 124), and they argue that this false dichotomy is imposed because of external funding and other pressures to sort students. These assessments consider proficiency only from a monolingual English language point of view, and the emergent bilingual student is considered nothing more than an English learner.

In contrast, speakers "do language;" they "language" actively; they use diverse language features, practices, and modalities. We have argued that the bilingual continuum is not a straight linear process, but rather is one that flows unevenly as students' language practices adapt to the changing social and academic contexts and interlocutors that they encounter. The dynamic relationship between the linguistic features that they draw on means that, although students can be placed along a bilingual continuum both in terms of development of what is considered the home language and English, there is no end point by which students leave one category and enter into another because they are always translanguaging. Bilingual proficiency is dynamic. Like a river current, what García, Johnson, and Seltzer (2017) have called the translanguaging *corriente*, it is always flowing, and always adapting to the communicative terrain in which it is being performed. Emergent bilinguals are somewhere along the starting point of the bilingual continuum, and developmental progress along that continuum is contingent on their opportunities for doing language. However, because bilinguals are constantly selecting appropriate features from their language repertoire for very different tasks, we cannot say that they have ever finished "having" one language or the other.

The federal requirement of ESSA that students meet adequate yearly progress (AYP) standards in state exams drives the construction of categories of proficiency that have little to do with students' real learning and development. Assessments are then used to categorize students arbitrarily, instead of to develop deep understandings and teacher knowledge about students and their learning.

Ignoring Those Who Need the Most Help

Finally, the emphasis of No Child Left Behind and ESSA on ensuring that all students are proficient in English means that it has become common for schools to spend enormous time and energy with those who are close to moving up a proficiency level, those whom many call "the bubble kids" (Booher-Jennings, 2006). As a result, students at the bottom are getting very little help. Students at the top are also not being challenged academically and intellectually, because their positive scores will not make a difference to the schools' AYP measures.

ALTERNATIVE ASSESSMENT PRACTICES

Observing Closely

The best way to assess emergent bilinguals is for teachers to observe and listen to their students and record these observations systematically over long periods of time. Of course, to "re-view" emergent bilinguals in the close ways described by Carini (2000a, p. 56), the observer must be familiar with the linguistic and cultural practices of the student. Carini (2000b) differentiates between assessing what students learned, made, or did, and "paying close attention to how a child goes about learning or making something" (p. 9). Carini (2000b) continues: "[I]t is when a teacher can see this process, *the child in motion*, the child engaged in activities meaningful to her, that it is possible for the teacher to gain the insights needed to adjust her or his own approaches to the child accordingly" (p. 9). Thus, for Carini, observing closely refers to understanding the *process of learning*, not just assessing a product. These ongoing descriptive reviews of children (Carini, 2000a, 2000b; Traugh, 2000) can develop a multidimensional portrait of bilingual learners. Rather than labeling emergent bilinguals as "limited," "at risk," or "deficient," these kinds of assessments provide avenues for understanding the capacities and strengths of emergent bilinguals. Observing closely allows the teacher/assessor to obtain valid, reliable information about the dynamics of the process of learning that then informs the teaching in a cyclical relationship.

Assessing Dynamically and with Performance Assessments

Dynamic assessment rests on the work of Vygotsky on the interactive nature of cognitive development. Its goal is to "determine the 'size' of the ZPD [zone of proximal development]" (Gutiérrez-Clellen & Peña, 2001, p. 212) and to transform students' abilities through dialogic collaboration between learners and the assessor-teacher (Poehner, 2007). Dynamic assessment and instruction mutually elaborate each other. Dynamic assessment is thus mostly formative; it simultaneously supports emergent bilinguals in the learning of language and content (Alvarez, Ananda, Walqui, Sato, & Rabinowitz, 2014; Bailey & Heritage, 2014; Heritage, Walqui, & Linquanti, 2015).

Georgia García and P. David Pearson (1994), in a review of formal and alternative assessment, support the notion that emergent bilinguals be given performance-based assessments that are dynamic, in the sense that they should reveal what the student can do with or without the help of the teacher. In this way, teachers are able to evaluate the kind of support that students require in order to comprehend and complete tasks. For García and Pearson, these dynamic assessments can be conducted in English, the home language, or in both languages. Through dynamic assessments that are administered bilingually, teachers may assess their students' interpretations of material and vocabulary from diverse cultural and linguistic perspectives and then use that knowledge to create further opportunities for students to learn what is appropriate. For example, through bilingual dynamic assessments, bilingual students can demonstrate their literacy understandings using their home and school language practices, and teachers can then assist them in developing academic literacy in the additional language (see also García, Johnson, & Seltzer, 2017).

Gottlieb (2017) provides a succinct guide to assessing multilingual learners using performance assessments. She gives the following characteristics of a performance assessment:

- Represents students' identities, languages, and cultures
- Consists of authentic tasks with real-life application, ideally that take on social action
- Requires hands-on student engagement, preferably in collaboration with peers
- Exemplifies original student work that includes multiple modalities
- Is built from features of universal design for learning
- Connects to students' lives, interests, and experiences
- Offers evidence for learning based on standards-referenced criteria for success

Portfolio assessment is an important part of these performance assessments. In portfolios, emergent bilinguals can collect artifacts of their learning and reflect on what they have learned collaboratively with one another, their teacher, and their families.

Gottlieb (2017) points to other tools that can be used in performance assessments: anecdotal notes taken by the teacher, student self-assessment, peer assessment, reading response logs, read-alouds, using translanguaging, and multiple modalities. All of these are valid gauges of emergent bilingual students' academic progress, taking into account the difference between language and content proficiencies, and general linguistic performances and language-specific performances.

Enabling Testing Accommodations

One way to improve the validity of monolingual standardized assessments is to provide students with test accommodations. Many educational authorities provide accommodations for emergent bilingual students being tested in English. As a result of the accountability-system changes associated with NCLB and continued under ESSA, emergent bilinguals must be provided with appropriate accommodations. ESSA (2015) states that such accommodations should include, "to the extent practicable, assessments in the language and form most likely to yield accurate information on what those students know and can do" (p. 129, Stat. 1826).

State accommodation policies vary substantially (Rivera & Collum, 2006). Rivera and Stansfield (2001) organize the different accommodations into five categories:

1. *Presentation:* permits repetition, explanation, simplification, test translations into students' native languages, or test administration by a bilingual specialist
2. *Response:* allows a student to dictate his/her answers, and to respond in his/her native language or display knowledge using alternative forms of representation
3. *Setting:* includes individual or small-group administration of the test, or administration in a separate location or multiple testing sessions
4. *Timing/scheduling:* allows for additional time to complete the test or extra breaks during administration
5. *Reinforcement:* allows for the use of dictionaries and glossaries

Abedi and Lord (2001) show how *linguistic modification*, the paraphrasing of test items so that they are less complex, has resulted in significant differences in math performance among emergent bilinguals in the United States. In fact, additional research has shown that *the only accommodation that narrows the gap between emergent bilinguals and other students is linguistic modification of questions that have excessive language demands* (Abedi & Lord, 2001; Abedi et al., 2004). Test accommodations, other than linguistic modifications, seem to make little difference in the scores of emergent bilinguals.

Disentangling Language and Content

Although disentangling language and content for assessment is difficult, some alternatives have been proposed. Shepard (1996) has argued that a fair assessment framework for emergent bilinguals should integrate the two dimensions—*language proficiency* and *content proficiency*. Academic performance of bilinguals should be seen as a continuum that is related to a continuum of English acquisition; in this view, the language in the tests of subject-matter content is adapted according to the place along the continuum in which the student might be situated.

Duverger (2005) has suggested that another way of disentangling the effects of language proficiency on content proficiency is to have a double scale of criteria: criteria relating to the *content* being delivered and criteria relating to the *language* being used. When content learning takes place through a student's weaker language, which is English in the case of emergent bilinguals, subject-matter knowledge should have a higher coefficient and language should not mask satisfactory handling of the content.

Assessing Students in Their Home Language

A much more equitable practice would be to assess students in their home languages. In this section, we address why this does not happen and the ideological and technical obstacles that stand in the way. The current debate over assessment of emergent bilinguals in the United States largely results from the lack of clarity over the goal of their education, which is whether educating emergent bilinguals should focus only on English language development or on their intellectual, academic, and social development. The education of English language learners—as the naming indicates—often focuses narrowly on the acquisition of *English language skills* and not on the acquisition of content knowledge. Houser (1995) explains that if content-area knowledge were the primary goal, students would be assessed in their home language. However, assessing students in their home language is generally considered inappropriate because educational policy attends narrowly to fluency in English. Furthermore, developing translations and transadaptations of assessments in the home language is complicated.

　　Test translations. Translating tests is not always feasible or appropriate. Because the testing industry is a market-driven operation, it might be possible to develop translations into Spanish, since the numbers of Spanish-speaking emergent bilinguals would merit it, but developing them into less commonly used languages could be difficult and expensive. Furthermore, assessments conducted in different languages may not be psychometrically equivalent (Anderson, Jenkins, & Miller, 1996). Maintaining construct equivalence is difficult when the test is either translated directly from one language to another or when tests in two languages are constructed. The nonequivalence of vocabulary difficulty between languages makes comparisons for content proficiency between tests given in different languages inappropriate (August & Hakuta, 1998). The Standards for Educational and Psychological Testing put forth conjointly by the American Educational Research Association, the American Psychological Association, and the National Council on Measurement in Education (1985) state:

> Psychometric properties cannot be assumed to be comparable across languages or dialects. Many words have different frequency rates or difficulty levels in different languages or dialects. Therefore, words in two languages that appear to be close in meaning may differ radically in other ways important for the test use intended. Additionally, test content may be inappropriate in a translated version. (p. 73)

Sometimes, emergent bilinguals are allowed to use both the home language version and the English language version of the test. But developing and validating equivalent versions of a test (two monolingual versions side by side) is difficult and costly (Anderson, Jenkins, & Miller, 1996). Furthermore, research on this issue has repeatedly shown substantial psychometric discrepancies in students' performance on the same test items across languages (August & Hakuta, 1997). This means that test items are not measuring the same underlying knowledge.

In addition, translations are only viable when emergent bilinguals have been effectively educated in their home languages. And even then, translations may privilege the standard variety of the language, which often has features that differ from contact varieties used in bilingual contexts (Solano-Flores, 2008). If students have limited literacy in the standard variety, an assessment that tests content proficiency is also invalid. Furthermore, translations are only appropriate if the students have been taught through the language of the test.

An additional concern is that even appropriate translation of tests would not obviate the cultural uniqueness and register of high-stakes tests, which might not be familiar to immigrant students—the format, layout, bubbling in multiple-choice answers, and discursive styles that are specific to tests (Solano-Flores, 2008). If the language is not used for instruction, then assessment for content proficiency in the students' home language also may be counterproductive. In short, the language of the assessment must match students' primary language of instruction (Abedi & Lord, 2001; Abedi, Lord, & Plummer, 1997).

Transadaption of tests. Transadaptation is a strategy with promise. Transadapted tests adapt test items to fit the cultural or linguistic requirement of the students who are being tested. For example, an English test item may ask about "mountain climbing," but the Spanish test may adapt this to say "*excursión*," a more relevant cultural experience. Transadapted test items are not simple translations. They are written from the linguistic and cultural perspective of the group being tested. Transadapted tests work to eliminate cultural biases, which are prevalent in many assessments because they refer to cultural experiences or historical backgrounds to which many emergent bilinguals have not been exposed (Johnston, 1997). As a result, they have more validity than do tests that are simply translated. This type of testing is now being used in some states—for example, Texas, where transadapted Spanish versions of the state's test, called STAAR, are developed. However, even transadapted tests, because they are monolingual, do not take into account the full range of linguistic practices of emergent bilingual students, whose full capabilities are enmeshed with their bilingualism.

Assessing Bilingually

The most valid way to assess the content proficiency of emergent bilinguals (not solely their English proficiency) is to develop large-scale assessments that build on their bilingual abilities. One example of a bilingual mode instrument designed to assess the verbal-cognitive skills of bilingual students is the Bilingual Verbal Ability Test. All subtests of the assessment are first administered in English. Any item failed is then readministered in the student's home language and the score added in order to measure the test-taker's knowledge and reasoning ability using both languages (Muñoz-Sandoval, Cummins, Alvarado, & Ruef, 1998).

Students also could be assessed via a *bilingual mode*, a way of rendering learners' bilingual competence visible. For example, spoken questions can be given in one language and responses requested in another. Or written tests can have the question in English, and the responses may be produced in the home language, or vice versa. Alternatively, the written text could be supplied in English and the oral presentation in the home language, or vice versa, thereby providing the teacher with a measure of students' productive skills across two modes and for all languages, while at the same time giving emergent bilinguals the opportunity to use all of their resources. Thus, this bilingual mode of assessment would not only give educators a more accurate picture of what students really know without having language as an intervening variable, but it also would offer a clearer picture of students' English language capacities.

In cases where school authorities are interested exclusively in students' progress in learning English, students might also be assessed via a *bilingual tap* mode, a way of tapping into or drawing on their home languages in order to produce English. This type of assessment would, for example, give instructions and questions in the students' home languages and ask students to respond solely in English. In this way, the home language would be used to activate knowledge for assessment in much the same that bilingual children use their home language and culture to make sense of what they know. This bilingual tap assessment builds on work on bilingual language processing by Dufour and Kroll (1995), Kecskes and Martínez Cuenca (2005), and Jessner (2006).

Translanguaging in Assessment

Leveraging translanguaging in assessment is the only way to level the playing field between bilingual and monolingual students, giving bilingual students the opportunity that monolingual children have—to be able to show what they know and can do using all their linguistic resources. Teachers who leverage translanguaging in instruction can design formative and summative assessments in which students are given the opportunity to show what they know by using their full language and communicative repertoire (García, Johnson, & Seltzer, 2017; Gottlieb, 2017).

A translanguaging design for assessments ensures that students can perform using all the features of their language repertoire; at the same time, the design tracks whether students are performing independently or with moderate assistance from other people or other resources. For just these purposes, García, Johnson, and Seltzer (2017) have developed a Teacher's Assessment Tool for Translanguaging Classrooms. Teachers who are bilingual can apply such a tool readily. The challenge for monolingual teachers, however, is greater, because they have to rely on other individuals (peers, parents, or other colleagues) and other resources for help in interpreting students' test responses. Even so, technology is making this easier, and electronic translations are an indispensable resource for teachers today.

Translanguaging in standardized assessments is still rare, although technology is enabling more possibilities: Alexis López and his associates in the Educational Testing Service have been developing a middle school math translanguaging assessment for Latinx bilingual students. Students are first asked to select a bilingual avatar who is a bilingual friend or assistant, and who provides a model of how to translanguage in assessments. Next, on this computer-based platform, students have the opportunity to see or hear items in two languages, English and Spanish. This way, they can write or say responses using all their linguistic resources (López, Guzmán-Orth, & Turkan, 2014; López, Turkan, & Guzmán-Orth, 2017). The intent is to ensure that language and content, as well as general language and language-specific capacities, are disentangled.

EDUCATING EMERGENT BILINGUALS:
ACCOUNTING FOR FAIR ASSESSMENT

The data-driven frenzy of accountability that was first spurred by NCLB (2001) puts assessments rather than teaching at the center of education today. The issue of assessment is particularly important for emergent bilinguals, for whom some of these high-stakes tests are invalid (Menken, 2008). There are, however, ways of improving the construction of valid assessments for this population, and this chapter has considered some of these alternative practices.

In sum, we see that misunderstandings about bilingualism in the United States create obstacles to developing assessment mechanisms that are fair and valid for all students. Monolingual high-stakes tests administered to emergent bilinguals have negative consequences, not only for the individual students, but also for the teachers who teach them, the leaders of the schools in which they are educated, the communities in which they live, and the states in which they reside. Scores on assessments are not only driving the kinds of instruction and programmatic opportunities that emergent bilinguals can access, but also the salary that their teachers receive, the funding that their schools and the states in which they reside obtain, and the real-estate value of the communities in which they live. This creates a cycle in which the victims will surely be the emergent bilinguals, as teachers, principals, communities, and states will drive these students out of the school system, excluding them from all opportunities to learn. Developing fair and valid assessments for emergent bilinguals emerges as the most critical issue in education during this era of increased accountability. Continuing down the path we are on has the potential not only to exclude children from educational opportunities but also to undermine the entire public school system on which our U.S. democracy rests.

STUDY QUESTIONS

1. Why are assessments so powerful?
2. Why are assessments not always valid and reliable for emergent bilinguals?
3. How do the different kinds of tests compare in the way they assess emergent bilinguals' language and content proficiencies?
4. What are some of the complications of establishing categories of proficiencies?
5. What is the difference between observing closely and assessing students? Discuss advantages and disadvantages.
6. Describe some of the test accommodations that can be used with emergent bilinguals. Identify issues to consider and practices that work best.
7. What are the issues that surround translations and transadaptions of tests?
8. Discuss ways of assessing bilingually. In your view, what are the difficulties with implementation of such assessments?
9. What does accounting for translanguaging in assessment entail? What are the benefits and the challenges of translanguaging in assessment?

CHAPTER 10

Signposts
Conclusion and Recommendations

In this concluding chapter, we will:

- Summarize what we have learned about:
  - ➤ Language theory and research,
  - ➤ Bilingual programs and practices,
  - ➤ Affordances of technology,
  - ➤ Curriculum and other practices,
  - ➤ Family and community engagement, and
  - ➤ Assessment; and
- Offer signposts: a set of detailed recommendations for advocates, policymakers, educators, and researchers to provide a more equitable education for emergent bilinguals.

Throughout this book, we have presented the case for reconceptualizing English language learners in American schools as *emergent bilinguals*. This concept recognizes the value of the students' home languages as resources for learning and as markers of their identity as individuals who have creative ways of knowing, being, and communicating. In repositioning these students from English Learners to emergent bilinguals, we have been able to expose the dissonance between research findings on best ways to educate them and the current educational policies and practices that have disregarded them.

WHAT HAVE WE LEARNED?

In Chapter 2, we began to address how emergent bilinguals have been identified and demonstrated the discrepancies in the way they have been counted and classified in federal, state, and even school district agencies. Despite problems with counting and sorting, what is clear is that the language-minoritized population is growing more rapidly than the English-speaking population; the number of emergent bilinguals has increased dramatically. What the data also show is that most emergent bilinguals attend schools in high-poverty urban school districts where classrooms are often crowded, material resources are lacking, and teachers are underqualified. Students in these schools have high incidences of health problems and absenteeism. Further, in spite of the assumption that these students are speakers of languages other than English, they are not all foreign born; three in four are native-born U.S. citizens. Finally, we know that the majority of emergent bilinguals in the United States are speakers of Spanish.

In Chapter 3, we charted the types of educational programs that have been available in the United States for emergent bilinguals. These range from programs that require the exclusive use of English in the classroom to those that provide instruction and support in the home language along with English. But over the 50-year history of language education policies, beginning with the Bilingual Education Act of 1968 through ESSA (2015), we have seen a shift away from the bilingual end of the continuum to a largely English-only language policy for ethnolinguistic minorities in U.S. schools.

Against this backdrop, in subsequent chapters, we explored theories and research that support ways in which emergent bilinguals can learn both English and subject-matter content optimally and be assessed equitably. We considered the gaps between the research evidence and language education policies and practices for emergent bilinguals. Most important of all, we advocated for alternative policies and practices that have the potential to educate these students more equitably.

Language Theory and Research

In Chapters 4 and 5, we discussed key theoretical frameworks for understanding the relationship between bilingualism and academic achievement. These interrelated frameworks have shown the cognitive, academic, and social benefits of drawing on all home language practices, including named languages such as English, as well as Haitian Creole, Korean, Mandarin Chinese, Russian, Spanish, and so on. Because there is a common underlying proficiency, as Jim Cummins (1979, 2000) has argued, this linguistic interdependence means that knowledge and proficiency in one language supports knowledge and proficiency in another and that language practices are interdependent. Further, translanguaging scholarship (for example, García & Wei, 2014; Otheguy, García, & Reid, 2015) has argued that this distinction between named languages is social, not linguistic or cognitive: Bilingual speakers have one complex language system or repertoire from which they select features guided by *social* understandings of which features might help them construct their message most successfully.

Scholars from an array of academic disciplines—including anthropology, education, linguistics, and psychology—have shown that language use varies in different contexts and have provided descriptive analyses of a wide range of language and literacy varieties. The research makes it clear that, in educational contexts, carrying on a conversation is not the same as discussing, reading, and writing about cognitively demanding ideas. We know from extensive research in schools in the United States and around the world that attaining competence in literacies for academic purposes requires sustained discussion, reflection, and practice. We also know that these literacies are bound up in relations of power and identity and that literacies entailing two or more named languages intensify questions of power and negotiations of identity. Skilled teachers can provide space in the classroom that empowers students to affirm their linguistic and cultural funds of knowledge even as they add to their repertoire of knowledge and communicative practices. It is through these linguistic and literacy processes that students engage in identity work: They develop a sense of self through multiple languages in different social situations (Norton, 2013). This is precisely what the notion of pluriliteracies addresses. As we discussed in Chapter 4, the term *pluriliteracies* describes the complex language practices that take place in multilingual communities (see García, Bartlett, & Kleifgen, 2007). It helps us understand young people's diverse and hybrid literacy practices and values in and out of school; it also takes into account the intermingling of multiple languages and scripts as well as rapidly changing new technologies that further shape their use.

Added to this understanding is the recognition that the path to bilingualism is a dynamic process, and not a linear one, as had been previously argued. So, we introduced the concept of translanguaging, an understanding that bilinguals have *one* complex linguistic system, a communicative repertoire made up of linguistic and other semiotic features, although society and schools identify these features as constituting one language or another (García, 2009a; García & Wei, 2014). Emergent bilinguals expand their own repertoire, adding new features. Bilingual students then select features from their unitary repertoire guided by social cues. At times, they creatively use linguistic features that are socially categorized as belonging to one or another language to make meaning. By understanding what makes up a bilingual's repertoire and bringing this flexible and subtle understanding of language practices into the classroom, teachers open new spaces for optimal meaning-making, identity formation, and eventual academic achievement.

Large-scale evaluations and meta-analyses of studies on bilingual programs beginning in the 1970s and continuing into the present have borne out these theoretical frameworks, showing that judicious use of different language practices in the classroom results in high achievement levels in both content and English and other languages, sometimes exceeding national norms, provided that teachers and students are given adequate time to develop how students "do" language. Bilingual education has been maligned in the United States despite the fact that the most carefully designed reviews of programs have shown positive educational outcomes. The political climate has overshadowed these empirical findings, and language has been treated as a problem rather than a resource. The problem does not reside in students or their languages, but rather in classroom practices that have been shaped by misguided educational policies.

Language and Classroom Practice

We have seen that emergent bilinguals generally have not been in classrooms that apply theory and research findings on the benefits of using the home language to support learning. In addition, in classrooms where both languages are used, the home language and English generally are kept strictly separated (what we called compartmentalization in Chapter 5), ignoring what we know about the benefits of dynamic bilingualism and translanguaging. Unfortunately, bilingual education programs themselves have decreased dramatically, and most emergent bilinguals today are in English-only programs. Even ESL support is being curtailed in some states.

Our response to this sad state of affairs is to put forth a strong argument for all students—majority- and minority-language speakers—to be given the opportunity to reap the benefits of bilingualism in their education.

Affordances of Technology

Over the past several years, there has been a conceptual shift in understanding literacy, not as a static, standardized, and monomodal (written) *product*, but as a plural, creative, and multimodal *practice*. Multimodality entails many semiotic resources: both spoken and written communication in multiple languages, along with other modes on which people draw to make meaning. This expanded notion of literacy practices has its impact in classrooms, where students can use multiple modes to study and learn.

As we have seen in Chapter 6, digital competence is essential for learning, working, and living in today's world (Kinzer, 2010; Llomaki et al., 2016). Yet, poor and minoritized students still have less access to computers and the internet than their more privileged counterparts. Despite advances in the availability of multimodal resources as a result of the expansion of new media technologies, some emergent bilingual students still do not have access to these tools to support their learning (Darling-Hammond, 2010; Poushter, 2016). This is truly unfortunate and inequitable, especially for emergent bilingual students, as many of the nonlinguistic modes or resources for learning can act as scaffolds for the development of the linguistic modes—speaking and writing. But more important, multiple linguistic modes also can be mutually elaborative for learning, particularly for emergent bilingual students. New technologies can provide the affordances of accessibility, retrievability, interactivity, and creativity to promote the educational achievement of emergent bilinguals.

Curriculum and Other Practices

If we cast a light of social justice and linguistic human rights on typical curricular and pedagogical designs for emergent bilinguals, we see the inequities, because the elements of rigor and creativity are missing. We described these inequities and considered alternative practices in Chapter 7.

Courtney Cazden (1986) pointed to the fact that two kinds of curricula exist in U.S. schools: one kind of curriculum that has well-designed, challenging content and engages students in creative and collaborative work, and another that only pays attention to basic skills. The latter is often the kind of curriculum that emergent bilinguals are taught. They are subject to deficit models of instruction—"remediation," tracking, mistaken placement into special education, exclusion from gifted programs, and reduced curricular choices because of a narrow focus on English language skills. Moreover, inequities begin early. Emergent bilinguals seldom get an early start through early childhood programs, despite the fact that these programs can contribute to later educational achievement.

Challenging and creative curricula can give emergent bilinguals access to rich classroom discourse and literacy experiences across subject-matter areas. It is through sustained social interactions that "foster collaborative relations of power" (Cummins, 2000, p. 253) that students' identities are affirmed while students learn at the same time.

Teacher preparation is crucial to a high-quality education for emergent bilinguals. We know that effective teachers of these students have a thorough understanding about how language works. These teachers have acquired the knowledge that is necessary to teach these students explicitly about how language is used in different content areas (Wong-Fillmore & Snow, 2000), they have studied child language development and bilingualism, and they have the pedagogical tools to enhance students' translanguaging in social interaction and in literacy events. In addition, effective teachers have received preparation to reach out to parents of emergent bilinguals to form a partnership in students' education.

Family and Community Engagement

Effective teachers know that they cannot go it alone. As we discussed in Chapter 8, research tells us that parents are emergent bilinguals' primary advocates for an equitable education; their engagement leads to students' improved attitudes about learning and to higher educational achievement. This is true especially for low-income, language-minoritized students in both primary and secondary school. Moreover, these students' parents and community members possess distinctive funds of knowledge—ways of knowing that their children learn at home (Gonzalez et al., 2005; Moll et al., 1992). These too often go unrecognized in the school; worse, these endogenous competencies—home language and literacy practices, practical skills, and values—are considered inferior and inconsequential to schooling. A deficit view of home language practices requires intervention in teacher education and ongoing professional development for critical reassessment based on research and best practices demonstrating that students' home language practices are a powerful resource for learning.

Even in cases where schools recognize the value of students' funds of knowledge, including linguistic knowledge, they may avoid applying some of the more "difficult" or uncomfortable funds of knowledge, which are perceived either to be too sensitive or to clash with the curriculum. In fact, such experiences can be a source of dialogue and an educative tool for problem solving.

Often, parental education programs are designed to "teach" parents how to educate their children; some of these programs betray a deficit model of their parenting skills. Alternative models view family engagement as a responsibility shared among the school, the community, and the family (Olivos et al., 2011; Rosenberg et al., 2009). These models of family and community engagement address learning both inside and outside the school. Teachers and administrators also become learners about the families and communities they serve. Community-organizing groups can help bring schools and families together in a more equitable partnership (Arias, 2015). In brief, learning becomes bidirectional, and this is to the benefit of emergent bilingual students.

Assessment

Testing is the gatekeeping device that often prevents emergent bilingual students from gaining access to further education and eventually an excellent quality of life. All students, including emergent bilinguals, are overtested under current government mandates, but for emergent bilinguals, testing is especially burdensome because they are essentially being tested for their academic language proficiency rather than for their knowledge of subject-matter content. Moreover, not only are the tests given in English, but they also have been normed on monolingual student populations; they do not take into account English learners' developing bilingualism. In Chapter 9, we suggested several alternatives to the way emergent bilinguals are currently tested. They involve changing the ways that students take the tests or how others score them, or taking different assessments altogether, such as tests in the home language or tests that use the students' translanguaging practices as a way to tap into and assess what students know (García et al., 2017; Gottlieb, 2017). The most promising alternatives continue to be close observations of student learning in the classroom and dynamic bilingual assessments, as well as performance assessments.

Our analysis of a wide variety of issues in the education of emergent bilinguals shows an ever-growing dissonance between the research and inappropriate educational programs and instruction, limited resources and funding, exclusion of parents and community, and faulty assessment procedures. We now conclude this book by offering a series of hopeful signposts—a set of recommendations for a more equitable education for emergent bilinguals.

SIGNPOSTS: POLICY RECOMMENDATIONS

The following recommendations for transforming the education of emergent bilinguals take on greater urgency today given the increase in the number of students—citizens and noncitizens alike—coming into classrooms speaking a language other than English. Some of these recommendations can be carried out by advocacy groups and grassroots organizations; some need the leadership of government at the federal, state, and local levels, and school officials, to move forward; others can be enacted by educators in their schools and classrooms; yet others belong to the realm of researchers.

For Advocates

Many people from outside the field of education—citizens, parents, other professionals, and grassroots organizations—are important advocates for emergent bilinguals and can take steps such as the following to transform education.

- Educate the American public through the media about the nature of bilingualism.

There are folk theories in the United States that "other" languages and speakers of "other" languages are somehow abnormal and in need of repair. The media and the internet could play an important role in disseminating essential knowledge about language and bilingualism to the general public. Advocates could post online articles, start blogs, and/or use other social media to offer discussions about ways in which bilingualism facilitates learning in school and creates work and social opportunities in life. In this way, people would come to an understanding that in acquiring English, language-minority students become bilingual, and thus, English language teaching develops bilingualism. And language majorities would understand the advantages of bilingualism in their own lives and those of their children. Furthermore, through the portrayal of bilingual Americans in movies and television shows, and the representation of bilingual language minorities as loyal and hardworking Americans, the public would come to recognize bilingualism as a characteristic of U.S. society. The mainstream media can play an important role in bringing the sounds of languages other than English and bilingualism to all Americans.

- Educate the American public through the media about the benefits of bilingualism as a national resource.

With the help of a wide range of media, the public can come to an understanding about the cognitive and creative value of bilingualism. People's use of the internet is ubiquitous, and they can easily be persuaded about the advantages of multilingual communication for work and education in today's globalized world, where the movement of people, goods, information, and services is no longer bound by national borders.

- Publicize the efforts of good schools and programs for emergent bilinguals, including the role of school leaders, educators, and community in this work.

Advocates can promote exposés on schools where emergent bilinguals are learning and where school leaders and educators are making a difference. The media can be convinced that portraits of school success can pique the public's interest, perhaps more than stories of failure and conflict. These and similar media presentations can help dispel folk theories about bilingualism and linguistic diversity.

- Urge federal funding for high-quality schools, educational programs and resources, and teacher education programs for emergent bilinguals.

Advocates can emphasize that fair funding needs to be given to educate emergent bilinguals. They can also urge that funding not be tied entirely to test results and that other factors be taken into account so that schools, programs, and teachers who serve language-minoritized communities can be adequately supported. High-quality schools are not always those that have the best test results, but high-quality schools are safe, clean, and have adequate instructional material and resources. They enjoy teams of teachers generously committed to teaching emergent bilinguals and prepared with knowledge about how students learn and develop proficiency in English for academic purposes. Equal educational opportunity for emergent bilinguals should be the focus of the advocacy.

- Keep the federal government and state and local educational authorities accountable for the education of emergent bilinguals.

Although there has been a major focus on accountability for school leaders and teachers, there are weak accountability measures for federal and state government and educational authorities. Questions can be raised about the irrationality of the federal government imposing unfunded mandates on state governments. Questions can also be raised about the ways in which state governments and local educational authorities report their services to emergent bilinguals, as well as how they assess them and report the test scores.

- Urge federal funding for the development of valid and reliable assessment instruments for emergent bilinguals—assessment that takes into account the difference between testing academic knowledge and testing linguistic knowledge, while recognizing the value of multiple indicators of students' academic achievement.

Advocates can insist that the testing industry be made accountable and expose how testing scores are being used to exclude emergent bilinguals. Advocates can urge that assessment be put back into the hands of educators. To that end, they should call for funding tied to assessment development that is user-centered. If test-makers were to spend time in classrooms, they would learn from educators what it is that emergent bilinguals can do and how they learn. Thus, test-makers would be able to develop tests with teachers that can adequately evaluate emergent bilinguals and help teachers understand the students' strengths and weaknesses.

Advocates could urge federal funding for the development and testing of new assessment initiatives that use students' bilingualism. New assessment tools should differentiate between testing students' general linguistic performance for academic purposes and testing their understanding and application of specific linguistic features. Funding might also support projects that enable schools and teachers to design their own assessments, as well as research on how teachers are using the assessment data to develop understandings about their own teaching, and about emergent bilinguals' lives and learning potential.

For Policymakers

- Develop a definition of an English learner that is stable across federal and state lines. The federal government should require stable and accurate data reporting and classification.

It is imperative that agreement be reached as to what constitutes a learner of English. Policymakers could call on scholars of bilingualism to explore how to measure and assess the academic English practices needed for success in schools. To be accurate, the measure should include students' home languages and their bilingual abilities. Policymakers could demand that this measure not define a category from which students exit and move to a "proficient" category, but designate points on a continuum of emergent bilingualism that require different kinds of educational programs and different levels of academic intervention.

- Design educational policy based on current theory and research regarding the benefits of an equitable education for emergent bilinguals.

The research evidence supporting the use of emergent bilinguals' home languages in their education is incontrovertible. Policymakers could become well versed in this research and empirical evidence so that this takes center stage in developing policy.

- Support and expand educational programs that have demonstrated success in providing a challenging, high-quality education, and that build on the strengths children and youth bring to school, particularly their home linguistic and cultural practices.

Policymakers could discontinue portraying categories of educational programs as if they were in opposition to each other—ESL or bilingual, for example. Instead, informed policymakers could support the students' translanguaging and leverage it in educating emergent bilinguals. They could support and encourage educational programs that follow research findings to the extent that the community situation permits.

- Support and expand student access to high-quality materials, including new technologies, especially in high-poverty schools, to facilitate access to the changing communication mediascape and give students a better chance to reach academic attainment.

Policymakers need to provide schools with multimodal, including multilingual, resources—books as well as digital audio and video materials. Access to technology infrastructure for fast connectivity to the internet, one-to-one access to computers, high-quality interactive tools with translation and voice recognition capabilities are especially important for emergent bilinguals. Policymakers should ensure that these resources are readily available in all classrooms so that students can read, write, and carry out research and creative design using all the languages at their disposal.

- Start bilingual educational support early through meaningful bilingual early childhood programs.

Policymakers should ensure that multilingual early childhood programs are available and that early assessment and intervention, when appropriate, are done in the children's home languages. Language-majority children could also benefit from these multilingual early childhood programs, participating and becoming familiar with different linguistic and cultural practices early in life.

- Pay particular attention to the middle school years.

Emergent bilinguals who are supported in elementary schools—through either ESL or bilingual programs—most often receive fewer services when they reach middle school. Policymakers must pay particular attention to the middle school years, because students who continue to be categorized as English learners after having received 5 to 6 years of education may face serious educational barriers. These students cannot be educated in the same ways as emergent bilinguals who are newcomers; educational programs have to be designed to meet the needs of these middle school emergent bilinguals.

- Support strong programs for emergent bilinguals at the secondary level.

Emergent bilinguals need challenging educational programs at all levels, but especially at the secondary level. Policymakers should require that schools provide these adolescents with the challenging academic content they need. A rigorous academic program that can also develop advanced English literacy is essential to make these adolescents college ready.

- Support ethnolinguistic communities and bilingual families in the development of more flexible structures for bilingual education programs.

Bilingual families often prefer a bilingual education program for all their children. Bilingual education programs hold much promise in developing the bilingualism of those classified as English learners, but also of English-speaking children growing up in bilingual homes or of those who identify with ancestors who spoke languages other than English, and even of those who don't. But because of the ways in which many dual-language bilingual education programs in the United States have been constructed with a strict definition of what is considered "two-way," many children are left out of a bilingual education experience. Flexibility is needed in implementation of bilingual education programs. Policymakers need to support all families in the development of bilingual education programs for all American children.

- Require all school leaders, teachers, and other school personnel to be well versed in issues of bilingualism and to understand the importance of the home language and culture for children.

Policymakers could make understandings of bilingualism and emergent bilinguals a requirement for teacher certification and employment. Beyond teachers who specialize in ESL and bilingual programs, all teachers should be required by policymakers to demonstrate an ability to work with emergent bilinguals and their families.

- Promote strong preservice/inservice education and professional development that prepares teachers to work with emergent bilinguals.

Given the growing numbers of emergent bilingual children in American schools, policymakers could require that all teacher education programs include coursework on bilingualism and the education of emergent bilinguals. Policymakers could also require that all teachers receive professional development that specifically targets emergent bilinguals as part of their professional commitment.

- Provide incentives for the preparation and hiring of additional bilingual staff—from school leaders and teachers to paraprofessionals, school psychologists, school counselors, therapists, and the like.

Because it is more difficult to recruit, prepare, and retain bilingual school staff, policymakers should provide financial incentives to those institutions of higher education that prepare bilingual staff and to schools that hire them. Financial incentives should be targeted to members of language-minoritized groups who are particularly needed in the teaching profession. Incentives for community members to become paraprofessionals are especially important, as are programs in which these paraprofessionals could then extend their preparation and eventually become teachers. The inclusion of family and community members who can contribute their endogenous knowledge to the life of the school would be a value-added policy measure.

- Provide incentives for bilinguals to join specialized professional organizations such as Teaching English to Speakers of Other Languages (TESOL) or to enter the bilingual teaching profession.

Bilingual individuals who can become ESL and bilingual teachers need to be offered incentives to join the profession. Different states and regions may offer incentives to different language groups whose language expertise is sorely needed by school systems.

- Require all teachers to develop some learning experience as emergent bilinguals themselves.

Academic study of an additional language is a worthy aim. However, a richer experience could be considered. Teacher education programs could arrange for prospective teachers to experience a period of time abroad or in an ethnolinguistic community in the United States other than the teacher's own.

- Promote the integration of ESL/bilingual education programs so that all ESL teachers would know about bilingualism and all bilingual teachers would be experts in working with bilingual students.

Policymakers could require that, with the exception of the coursework required of bilingual teachers in teaching content in the home language, the preparation of ESL and bilingual teachers be the same. Being in classes together would ameliorate the divisions between programs that often exist. All should know how to teach content in English to emergent bilinguals, as well as support the development of their academic English practices. Additionally, all should understand how to leverage the students' translanguaging in educating them.

- Require schools to recognize the funds of knowledge that exist in emergent bilingual students' families and communities, be accountable to them, and achieve closer mutual engagement for a higher-quality education.

Policymakers could also require that all teachers have coursework on how to work with families of emergent bilinguals who do not speak English and how to provide translation services to parents. This coursework might also include information on how community-based organizations (CBOs) can serve as catalysts in building school-family-community partnerships. The coursework ideally would require that all teachers learn an additional language to maximize the bilingualism of the U.S. teaching force in the 21st century. In addition, the coursework would make teachers aware of what they could learn from the funds of knowledge of the community and parents by developing the prospective teachers' ethnographic skills. This specialized coursework would help teachers develop assignments that build on parents' existing knowledge, whatever that might be, while extending the children's understandings in ways that would not require the parents to be knowledgeable of the same content or linguistic practices.

For Educators

- Consider the whole child.

To be effective, teachers would not focus narrowly on the language of the student, but instead "cast [their] inner eye on a particular child," as Carini (2000a, p. 57) would say. Teachers can follow Carini's advice about paying attention to students' physical presence and gesture, their disposition and temperament, their connection to other people, their strong interests and preferences, and their modes of thinking and learning.

- Consider students in the context of their communities.

Effective teachers become familiar with the community in which the children live and with the histories of the cultural practices in which the children and youth are immersed at home and in the community. If the community has a large immigrant population, educators should understand their histories of (im)migration, their cultural practices, their religion, and their language practices. They could also become familiar with community-based organizations that support language-minoritized groups and with after-school and weekend community bilingual programs that the students might attend.

- Observe and listen to language practices closely.

Effective teachers are listeners and observers of their students. Teachers should listen to the students on the playground, in the gym, and in the cafeteria. They might also listen to the parents as they pick up their children or to the youth as they make their way home when the school day is over. What languages are they speaking? What are they saying? Teachers could pay attention to the signage in the community and around the school. Are signs written in other languages? Other scripts? They might also inquire about TV programs, computer games, social media, and other digital forms that children and youth engage with, sometimes in languages other than English.

- Learn something about the home languages of students.

Teachers could ask parents to teach them how to say simple phrases such as "Good morning," "Good afternoon," "Thank you," "Please," and "Good-bye." They might experience what it means to write in a nonalphabetic script. Elementary school teachers can try to learn a short song (or obtain a recording) in an additional language to teach the children in the class to sing. Families can be asked to bring in multilingual materials and devise classroom signage in different languages so that the classroom can become a multilingual setting.

- Speak, speak, speak. Read, read, read. Write, write, write.

Language is learned through practice in different contexts. Teachers can give students opportunities to use the English language richly—by listening to different discourses on various media, by reading broadly both fiction and nonfiction, and by writing different genres frequently. Teachers should give students opportunities to leverage their home language practices by taking up translanguaging pedagogy. A school's access to the internet can facilitate these practices; teachers can use computers and whiteboards in the classroom to promote digital literacy and collaborative online research and projects using multiple language resources. Finally, teachers should encourage generative dialogue and opportunities to engage in lively, thoughtful, high-quality interactions.

- Encourage students to think about language practices and the power of language.

Emergent bilinguals need to become linguists—comfortable analyzing language practices, developing metalinguistic skills, comparing named languages, thinking aloud about languages, and critiquing the way languages are used in print and digital media, as well as in public life. They also need to have sustained practice learning content, and practicing how to select the features from their repertoire that are most appropriate in academic contexts. In addition, emergent bilinguals need to become aware of the different power of named languages in society and in their schools. Teachers can support this development by ensuring that their pedagogy is collaborative and culturally and linguistically relevant. A critical multilingual awareness curriculum would help students develop the ability to analyze social issues of language that are relevant to their lives.

- Use bilingual instructional practices and translanguaging pedagogy as a sense-making mechanism.

Instead of compartmentalizing English and excluding the home language practices from instruction, educators should engage in bilingual instructional practices—to render one assignment in the other language, to find research in any language, to use what they have learned in one language in the service of the other, to discuss and think in any language as they read and write in another. Furthermore, educators should understand the implications of the concept of translanguaging for the instruction of bilingual students. Teachers need to view bilingual students' language system as unitary, helping students add new linguistic features and appropriate them, and helping them select those that are most appropriate to successfully participate in the academic task at hand. Teachers should empower emergent bilingual students to use their translanguaging as sense-making in the service of deeper understandings and more advanced development of English for academic purposes.

- Provide a challenging and creative curriculum with challenging and relevant material.

Teachers should elaborate the lesson for emergent bilinguals by providing different scaffolds. This does not mean teachers should simplify; they should search for instructional material that is challenging. Whenever possible, they should provide opportunities to read and write in the students' home languages, enabling the development of complex ideas that can be expressed better in a language one knows while the target language is still being developed. Teachers should encourage the use of technology and the internet, because these can be important resources for students to find challenging material written in their home languages, material that is relevant to students' lives, and because this encourages positive identity development and engages them in complex ideas.

- Provide differentiated instruction for emergent bilingual students with different educational profiles.

Some emergent bilinguals are new to the school language; they have come to school from homes in which English is not spoken or from schools in other countries where instruction was in a language other than English. Some of the newcomer students have well-developed literacy practices in their home language, but others do not. Others have had their education interrupted by war, poverty, and other social conditions. Still other emergent bilinguals have been in U.S. classrooms for a long time, and yet have failed to develop academic literacy in English. Educators need to be aware of these differences and provide students with appropriate lessons and pedagogy. They should also include computer use in their classrooms to enable online access for differential learning and to unleash students' diverse interests and creativity.

- Become an advocate of emergent bilinguals and their instruction.

Individual and groups outside the school system are not the only ones who can become advocates. Besides parents, effective teachers know what the best academic path is for emergent bilinguals. Teachers should use the data generated from standardized assessments, but supplement it with their own close observations, performance assessments, and professional judgments. They should resist educational decisions made for emergent bilinguals that are based on one score on a standardized test. They should be advocates for what these students need with other school professionals, other teachers, the school leadership team, and the community.

- Develop a strong relationship with students' families.

Teachers should learn as much as they can about and from families of emergent bilinguals and the community's funds of knowledge. When it comes to newcomers to the United States, teachers need information regarding whether the family or other relatives were separated because of immigration, with whom the children/youth immigrated, and who was left behind. They can encourage parents and other community members to participate in classroom activities, inviting them to give presentations about their cultural and linguistic histories and practices. Above all, they can promote greater family and community engagement by inviting parents to learn more about the school's structures and processes, and by listening to parents' and the community's ideas for alternative educational practices.

- Inculcate in emergent bilingual students a hunger for inquisitiveness, and model dreams of tolerance, equity, and social justice.

Teachers should be particularly focused on high expectations for emergent bilingual students, as well as ways of releasing their imagination. At the same time, teachers should convey their convictions about the need for tolerance and social justice to build a more inclusive and just world.

For Researchers

- Study the cognitive and creative advantages of bilingualism.

Neurolinguistic research that focuses on the cognitive and creative consequences of bilingualism has just begun to emerge. This research needs to be advanced.

- Develop assessments that differentiate between language and content knowledge, and that distinguish between general linguistic performances and language-specific performances; as well as take translanguaging into account in the design of assessments.

Assessment is the most serious gap in research on emergent bilinguals' education. Researchers—in particular, neurolinguists, psycholinguists, and sociolinguists—need to join with educators in developing assessments for bilingual children that reflect their language practices and not simply monolingual practices.

- Develop measures of dynamic bilingual proficiency.

As researchers recognize the fallacy of a linear conception of bilingualism, it becomes necessary to develop ways of assessing the complex dynamic nature of language practices and bilingualism. Research in this area needs to be strengthened.

- Conduct research on the effects of translanguaging for the teaching and learning of emergent bilinguals.

Past conceptions of bilingualism have been constructed based on monolingual notions of language practices. As a result, English compartmentalization has been a preferred instructional approach in the United States. But, as studies of bilingualism begin to rest on heteroglossic (Bakhtin, 1981) notions of language use, translanguaging has become a more accepted concept. More research is needed in this area.

- Strengthen research on bilingual acquisition and evaluation of education for emergent bilinguals by conducting, for example, more multidisciplinary and mixed-method studies that will help educators and school officials in making informed decisions about the fit between children and programs and practices.

Research on the education of emergent bilinguals, focused on the students themselves and the teachers' pedagogies and practices (rather than on whether bilingual or ESL programs are more adequate), needs to be encouraged.

EDUCATING EMERGENT BILINGUALS: ALTERNATIVE PATHS

As we have tried to demonstrate in this book, current policies and practices for the education of emergent bilinguals are misguided. They contradict what theory and research have concluded and what scholars and educators have maintained. They also diverge from the realities of engagement in a globalized world with its growing multilingualism. However, despite restrictive educational policies, we see, on the ground, reflective educators who continue to use a commonsense approach in teaching the growing number of these students by building on the strengths of their home languages and cultures. American educators, however, should not be left alone—or even worse, forced to hide what they are doing—when implementing practices that make sense for the students and the communities they are educating. For emergent bilinguals to move forward, and not be left behind, educators need to be supported by policy and resources that bolster their expertise and advance their teaching. Educators need to be given time and space at school to observe students closely and document their work and learning *with* and *through* language, instead of being required to focus only on their performance through poorly designed tests and assessments. They need the opportunity to teach individual students, instead of seeing teaching as a master plan of scores. With better preparation on the nature of bilingualism, teachers can find ways to work with the good aspects of governmental policy at the federal, state, and local levels.

Educators, and all who are concerned about this growing student population, should advocate for changes in aspects of the policy that make no sense for emergent bilinguals. For changes to be effective, the different levels of policy must work in tandem with educators and language-minority communities. Only then will we begin to close the gap between levels of abstract policies and local realities through which most disadvantaged students, such as emergent bilinguals, fall. We must start closing the gap of inequity for emergent bilinguals by naming the inequities, as we have done in this book, and then taking action to support their meaningful education.

Notes

Chapter 1

1. We use the term *emergent bilingual* in this book for students who are speakers of *one or more languages* other than English and who are developing English literacy in school. Some might say that students who are already bilingual and who are learning in English in school might be better called *emergent multilinguals*. But we use the term *bilingual* because of its ties to sociopolitical struggles that surrounded the civil rights era in the United States. Although in this book we use *emergent bilingual* to call attention to those learning English who are minoritized in U.S. society, in fact, the term can be also used to designate those who are acquiring languages other than English—for example, English speakers in two-way dual-language bilingual programs.

2. Throughout this book, we prefer the term *home language practices* to *mother tongue, native language,* or *first language. Mother tongue* is extensively used, especially to refer to the language of minoritized communities, although it has been called inaccurate (Baker & Prys Jones, 1998; Kaplan & Baldauf, 1997; Skutnabb-Kangas, 1981). Skutnabb-Kangas (1981) reminds us that one can identify a mother tongue based on different criteria—the language one learned first, the language one knows best, the language one uses most, the language one identifies with, and the language with which others identify one. The term *native language* has also been discredited because of its ties to exclusivity, privilege, and Whiteness (see, for example, Bonfiglio, 2010). Our preference for the use of *language practices*, rather than simply *language*, has to do with the epistemological understandings of language that are clarified throughout the book.

3. We prefer to use *additional language* instead of *second language* because English may not necessarily be the second language acquired, but rather a third or fourth. It is also a more equitable way of expressing the complex acquisition and use of many languages.

4. Sometimes, building on home language practices is accomplished through bilingual education, about which we say more in subsequent chapters. At other times, this can be accomplished in programs where only English is formally used as a medium of instruction, but where teachers acknowledge and build on the language practices that the students bring to the classroom.

Chapter 2

1. The WIDA consortium consists of member states (38 at the time of this writing and the District of Columbia) that support WIDA's high-quality standards for emergent bilinguals and assessments that measure what these students can do.

2. At the time of this writing, 11 states belong to the ELPA21 consortium: Arkansas, Florida, Iowa, Kansas, Louisiana, Nebraska, Ohio, Oregon, South Carolina, Washington, and West Virginia.

3. As in all cases where we use U.S. census figures, we calculate emergent bilinguals by adding up all those who claim to speak English less than "very well."

4. *Indo-European* is not synonymous with European languages. In this survey, the category Indo-European includes all languages of this linguistic family except for English and Spanish. French, German, Hindi, and Persian are all classified as Indo-European. Hungarian, a European language that belongs to the Uralic language family, is included in the "other language" category.

5. Asian/Pacific languages include languages indigenous to Asia and Pacific Island areas that are not also Indo-European languages. Chinese, Japanese, Telugu, and Hawaiian are all in this category.

6. Scholars point out that categories of race and ethnicity are confounded in the U.S. census as well as in educational policy, where the terms *linguistic minority*, *race*, and *ethnicity* are often ambiguously used (Macías, 1994; Wiley, 1996).

7. High-LEP schools are those that have 25% or more LEP students. Low-LEP schools are those in which LEP students represent less than a quarter of all students.

8. *Temporary sojourners* are usually business persons who are on a short-term visit.

9. The term *migrant workers* usually refers to persons who work at seasonal jobs and move around; in the United States, it usually describes low-wage laborers in the field of agriculture.

Chapter 3

1. Some of the history in this section is taken from O. García (2009a). A valuable source for this information is Crawford (2004). See also Baker and Wright (2017).

2. Otheguy and Otto (1980) argue that a simple maintenance bilingual education is not possible because language always has to be developed. Thus, we prefer to call these programs *developmental bilingual education programs*.

3. The original model for international high schools in New York mixed newcomers of different language backgrounds. However, in scaling up the

model, they were confronted with the reality that some neighborhoods were almost exclusively Spanish speaking. Two schools in New York that are exclusively for Spanish-speaking newcomers were then established, following the same pedagogical principles of collaborative grouping and use of home languages to support English language development. At the time of this writing, the Internationals Network for Public Schools consisted of 22 schools—15 in New York City, two in Maryland, two in California, two in Virginia, and one in Washington, D.C.

4. The subgroups of students were: racial and ethnic groups (Asian/Pacific Islander, Black, Hispanic, American Indian, White), economically disadvantaged, (those receiving) free/reduced-price lunch, students with disabilities, and limited English proficient.

5. Title I, Improving the Academic Achievement of the Disadvantaged, provides financial assistance to schools with high numbers or high percentages of poor children to help ensure that all children meet challenging state academic standards.

Chapter 4

1. Notice that we are not using the term *academic English*, but *English for academic purposes* or *academic English practices* in this volume. The term *academic English* is problematic because it implies a set of static autonomous features that describe it and that students can "have" (see, for example, Valdés, 2017). Our use of *English for academic purposes* makes it clear that these features change depending on what students are doing with language.

2. Sociolinguist John Gumperz (1992) explains that paralinguistic cues or signs in conversation include "tempo, pausing and hesitation, . . . and other 'tone of voice' expressive cues" (p. 231).

3. The term *decontextualized* has been considered controversial because no language, however abstract, can truly be considered separated from a context.

4. It is important to understand that the Canadian immersion bilingual education programs resulted from an initiative of Anglophone-majority parents to support their children's' acquisition of French in Francophone Québec—that is, to make their children bilingual. Thus, the use of *immersion*, or more precisely, *submersion* for English-only programs in the United States has little to do with Canadian immersion programs. Furthermore, today Canada has to respond to much more than the two "official languages" of Canada, as per the 1972 Official Languages Act. The great number of speakers of languages of Canadian First Nations, as well as the high influx of immigrants in Canada, have also disrupted the orthodoxy of Canadian immersion programs in using only French to teach Anglophone children (see, for example, Cummins, 2008).

5. It is well known that immigrants to the United States have traditionally shifted to English by the third generation (see, for example, Fishman, 1966).

6. These included the ITBS, CTBS, Stanford 9, and Terra Nova tests.

Chapter 5

1. For more on the structure of CUNY-NYSIEB, see García and Kleyn, 2016; García and Menken, 2015; and García and Sánchez, 2015. The project has created teaching guides in different areas: general strategies (Celic & Seltzer, 2012), curriculum (Seltzer, Hesson, & Woodley, 2014), writing (Espinosa, Ascenzi-Moreno, & Vogel, 2016), and Latino literature (Pérez Rosario, 2014). These guides and other resources and videos can be downloaded from the website.

2. Two important websites with resources for teachers of emergent bilinguals are: ¡Colorín, Colorado! (http://www.colorincolorado.org/new-teaching-ells) and Edutopia (https://www.edutopia.org/article/resources-for-teaching-english-language-learners-ashley-cronin).

Chapter 6

1. For a description of the web-based system design and instructional approach developed for this intervention, along with a detailed example of its use in the classroom, see Kleifgen, Kinzer, Hoffman, Gorski, Kim, Lira, and Ronan (2014).

2. Although most iEARN learning group exchanges are in English, many teacher-initiated projects are in other languages such as French, Kiswahili, and Spanish (https://iearn.org).

3. Examples of research exploring children's and adolescents' use of these internet spaces include Hung (2011), Kleifgen and Kinzer (2009), Knobel and Lankshear (2009), Lam (2004), Lam and Rosario-Ramos (2009), and Mazur (2005).

Chapter 7

1. According to Zehler et al. (2003), the percentage of ELL students reported to be in special education (all classifications) was smaller than the percentage of all students in special education (9% versus 13%). This may have to do with an underidentification of ELL students in need of special education services in many categories.

2. Eight percent of emergent bilinguals in special education were in multilevel classrooms and thus are not included in this count. The lower rate of emergent bilingual students in high school is indicative of the higher dropout rate among this population.

3. Typically, state and local tax revenues provide most of the money in the United States for public education, 92% of the total on average, but this has not always been so for English learners and not for all states where the funding often comes from federal initiatives, as do other categorical programs to serve "disadvantaged" students.

4. NCLB defined these immigrant children and youth as 3- to 21-year-olds who were not born in the United States and had not been in school attendance for more than 3 full academic years.

5. This section owes a great deal to the work done by Lori Falchi for the report written for the Center for Educational Equity (García, Kleifgen, & Falchi, 2008). We are grateful to her for this invaluable contribution.

6. These numbers include the cost of the base education plus any additional costs.

Chapter 8

1. We use the terms *parent* and *family* interchangeably in this chapter, with a view toward a broader definition of what constitutes a parent or a family in today's diverse society. Our use of these terms encompasses other adults such as stepparents, grandparents, guardians, and caretakers, and varied family structures such as families with single- or same-sex parents. See also Yosso (2005) on community cultural capital.

2. Kreider et al. (2007) do not address the advantages of parental agency and leadership in the school and community.

3. Shifting the focus away from the school to local communities, Compton-Lilly (2007) describes the tension between the "official reading capital" and local communities' reading capital, which schools ignore.

References

Abedi, J. (2004). The No Child Left Behind Act and English language learners: Assessment and accountability issues. *Educational Researcher, 33*(1), 4–14.

Abedi, J. (2010). *Performance assessments for English language learners.* Stanford, CA: Stanford University, Stanford Center for Opportunity Policy in Education.

Abedi, J., Hofstetter, C. H., & Lord, C. (2004). Assessment accommodations for English language learners: Implications for policy-based empirical research. *Review of Educational Research, 74*(1), 1–28.

Abedi, J., & Lord, C. (2001). The language factor in mathematics tests. *Applied Measurement in Education, 14*(3), 219–234.

Abedi, J., Lord, C., & Plummer, J. R. (1997). *Final report of language background as a variable in NAEP mathematics performance* (CSE Tech. Rep. No. 429). Los Angeles, CA: University of California at Los Angeles, National Center for Research on Evaluation, Standards, and Student Testing.

Abutalebi, J., Della Rosa, P. A., Green, D. W., Hernández, M., Scifo, P., Keim, R., Cappa, S. F., & Costa, A. (2012). Bilingualism tunes the anterior cingulate cortex for conflict monitoring. *Cerebral Cortex, 22*(9), 2076–2086. doi:10.1093/cercor/ bhr287

Ackerman, D. J., & Tazi, Z. (2015). *Enhancing young Hispanic dual language learners' achievement: Exploring strategies and addressing challenges* (Policy Information Report, ETS Research Report No. RR-15-01). Princeton, NJ: Educational Testing Service. doi:10.1002/ets2.12045

Adams, M., Blumenfeld, W., Castañeda, C. R., Hackman, H. W., Peters, M. L., & Zúñiga, X. (Eds.). (2013). *Readings for diversity and social justice* (3rd ed.). New York, NY: Routledge.

Alim, S., Rickford, R., & Ball, A. (Eds.) (2016). *Raciolinguistics: How language shapes our ideas about race.* Oxford, UK: Oxford University Press.

Alvarez, L., Ananda, S., Walqui, A., Sato, E., & Rabinowitz, S. (2014). *Focusing formative assessment on the needs of English language learners.* San Francisco, CA: WestEd.

American Educational Research Association, American Psychological Association, & National Council on Measurement in Education (AERA, APA, & NCME). (1985). *Standards for educational and psychological testing.* Washington, DC: American Psychological Association.

American Educational Research Association, American Psychological Association, & National Council on Measurement in Education (AERA, APA, & NCME).

(2014). *The standards for educational and psychological testing.* Washington, DC: American Psychological Association.

American Institutes for Research (AIR). (2004). *Determining the cost of providing all children in New York an adequate education.* Available at https://www.air.org/resource/determining-cost-providing-all-children-new-york-adequate-education

Amrein, A. L., & Berliner, D. C. (2002, March 28). High-stakes testing, uncertainty, and student learning. *Education Policy Analysis Archives, 10*(18). Available at http://epaa.asu.edu/epaa/v10n18/

Anderson, N. E., Jenkins, F. F., & Miller, K. E. (1996). *NAEP inclusion criteria and testing accommodations: Findings from the NAEP 1995 fieldtest in mathematics.* Washington, DC: National Center for Education Statistics.

Angay-Crowder, T., Choi, J., & Yi, Y. (2013). Multimodal literacies and technology: Digital storytelling for multilingual adolescents in a summer program. *TESL Canada Journal, 30*(2), 36–45.

Anstrom, K. (1997). *Academic achievement for secondary language minority students: Standards, measures, and promising practices.* Washington, DC: National Clearinghouse for Bilingual Education.

Anyon, J. (1997). *Ghetto schooling. A political economy of urban educational reform.* New York, NY: Teachers College Press.

Anyon, J. (2005). *Radical possibilities: Public policy, urban education, and a new social movement.* New York, NY: Routledge.

Anzaldúa, G. (2012). *Borderlands/La Frontera. The new mestiza* (4th ed.). San Francisco, CA: Aunt Lute Books.

Arias, B. (2007). School desegregation, linguistic segregation and access to English for Latino students. *Journal of Educational Controversy, 2*(1), Article 7. Available at http://cedar.wwu.edu/jec/vol2/iss1/7

Arias, B. (2015). Parent and community involvement in bi/multilingual education. In W. Wright, B. Sovicheth, & O. García (Eds.), *The handbook of multilingual education* (pp. 282–298). Malden, MA: Wiley.

Arizona Proposition 203. (2000). Arizona Revised Statues 15-751-755.

Arthur, J., & Martin, P. (2006). Accomplishing lessons in postcolonial classrooms: Comparative perspectives from Botswana and Brunei Darussalam. *Comparative Education, 42*, 177–202.

Artiles, A. J. (1998). The dilemma of difference: Enriching the disproportionality discourse with theory and context. *The Journal of Special Education, 32*(1), 32–36.

Artiles, A. J., & Ortiz, A. A. (Eds.). (2002). *English language learners with special education needs: Identification, assessment, and instruction.* Washington, DC, and McHenry, IL: Center for Applied Linguistics and Delta System.

Artiles, A. J., Rueda, R., Salazar, J., & Higareda, I. (2002). English-language learner representation in special education in California urban school districts. In D. Losen & G. Orfield (Eds.), *Racial inequity in special education* (pp. 117–136). Cambridge, MA: Harvard Education Press.

Au, K. H. (1993). *Literacy instruction in multicultural settings.* Orlando, FL: Harcourt Brace.

Au, K. H. (2005). *Multicultural issues and literacy achievement.* Mahwah, NJ: Erlbaum.

Auer, P. (2005). A postscript: Code-switching and social identity. *Journal of Pragmatics, 37*(3), 403–410.

Auerbach, E. A. (1995). Deconstructing the discourse of strengths in family literacy. *Journal of Reading Behavior, 27*(4), 643–661.

August, D., & Hakuta, K. (1997). *Improving schooling for language-minority children: A research agenda.* Washington, DC: National Research Council, National Academies Press.

August, D., & Hakuta, K. (Eds.). (1998). *Educating language-minority children.* Washington, DC: Committee on Developing a Research Agenda on the Education of Limited-English-Proficient and Bilingual Students, National Research Council, Institute of Medicine, and National Academies Press.

August, D., & Shanahan, T. (Eds.). (2006). *Developing literacy in second-language learners: Report of the National Literacy Panel on language-minority children and youth.* Mahwah, NJ: Lawrence Erlbaum Associates.

Ayers, W., Hunt, J. A., & Quinn, T. (Eds.). (1998). *Teaching for social justice: A democracy and education reader.* New York, NY: New Press.

Baca, G., & Gándara, P. (2008). *NCLB and California's English language learners: The perfect storm.* New York, NY: Springer Science Business and Media B.V.

Bachman, L. F. (2001). *Fundamental considerations in language testing* (5th ed.). Oxford, UK: Oxford University Press.

Bachman, L. F. (2002). Alternative interpretations of alternative assessments: Some validity issues in educational performance assessments. *Educational Measurement: Issues and Practice, 21*(3), 5–18.

Baetens Beardsmore, H. (2018). Plurilingualism et créativité. In J. Erfurt, E. Carporal, & A. Weirich (Eds.), *L'éducation bi-/plurilingue pour tous. Enjeux politiques, sociaux et éducatifs.* New York, NY: Peter Lang.

Bailey, A. L., & Heritage, M. (2014). The role of language learning progressions in improved instruction and assessment of English language learners. *TESOL Quarterly, 48*, 480–506.

Bailey, A. L., & Kelly, K. R. (2013). Home language survey practices in the initial identification of English learners in the United States. *Educational Policy, 27*, 770–804.

Baker, B. D., Green, P. C., & Markham, P. (2004). *Legal and empirical analysis of state financing of programs for children with English language communication barriers.* Paper presented at the annual meeting of the National Association for Bilingual Education, Albuquerque, NM. Available at http://www.ku.edu/%7Ebdbaker/papers/nabe04.pdf

Baker, C. (2001). *Foundations of bilingual education and bilingualism* (3rd ed.). Clevedon, UK: Multilingual Matters.

Baker, C. (2011). *Foundations of bilingual education and bilingualism* (5th ed.). Clevedon, UK: Multilingual Matters.

Baker, C., & Lewis, G. (2015). A synthesis of research on bilingual and multilingual education. In W. E. Wright, S. Boun, & O. García (Eds.), *The handbook of bilingual and multilingual education* (pp. 109–126). Malden, MA: Wiley-Blackwell.

Baker, C., & Prys Jones, S. (1998). *Encyclopedia of bilingualism and bilingual education.* Bristol, UK: Multilingual Matters.

Baker, C., & Wright, W. (2017). *Foundations of bilingual education and bilingualism* (6th ed.). Clevedon, UK: Multilingual Matters.

Bakhtin, M. (1981). *The dialogic imagination. Four essays.* Houston, TX: The University of Texas Press.

Ballenger, C. (1997). Social identities, moral narratives, scientific argumentation: Science talk in a bilingual classroom. *Language and Education, 11*(1), 1–14.

Barac, R., & Bialystok, E. (2012). Bilingual effects on cognitive and linguistic development: Role of language, cultural background, and education. *Child Development, 83*(2), 413–422.

Barnett, W. S., & Masse, L. N. (2007). Comparative benefit-cost analysis of the Abecedarian program and its policy implications. *Economics of Education Review, 26,* 113–125.

Bartlett, L. (2007). Bilingual literacies, social identification, and educational trajectories. *Linguistics and Education, 18,* 214–231.

Batalova, J., Fix M., & Murray, J. (2007). *Measures of change: The demography and literacy of adolescent English learners—A report to Carnegie Corporation of New York.* Washington, DC: Migration Policy Institute.

Batalova, J., & McHugh, M. (2010). *Number and growth of students in U.S. schools in need of English instruction.* Washington, DC: Migration Policy Institute. Available at http://www.migrationpolicy.org/research/number-and-growth-students-us-schools-need-english-instruction-2009

Beeman, K., & Urrow, C. (2013). *Teaching for biliteracy. Strengthening bridges between languages.* Philadelphia, PA: Caslon.

Ben-Zeev, S. (1977). The effect of bilingualism in children from Spanish-English low-income neighborhoods on cognitive development and cognitive strategy. *Working Papers on Bilingualism,* 14. Toronto, Canada: Ontario Institute for Studies in Education, Bilingual Education Project.

BEST (Building Educational Success Together). (2006). *Growth and disparity: A decade of U.S. public school construction.* Washington, DC: BEST.

Bezemer, J., & Kress, G. (2016). *Multimodality, learning and communication: A social semiotic frame.* New York, NY: Routledge.

Bialystok, E. (2004). Language and literacy development. In T. K. Bhatia & W. C. Ritchie (Eds.), *The handbook of bilingualism* (pp. 577–601). Malden, MA: Blackwell.

Bialystok, E. (2007). Cognitive effects of bilingualism: How linguistic experience leads to cognitive change. *International Journal of Bilingual Education and Bilingualism, 10*(3), 210–223.

Bialystok, E. (2011). Reshaping the mind: The benefits of bilingualism. *Canadian Journal of Experimental Psychology, 65*(4), 229–235.

Bialystok, E. (2015). Bilingualism and the development of executive function: The role of attention. *Child Development Perspectives, 9*, 117–121.

Bialystok, E. (2016). Bilingual education for young children: review of the effects and consequences. *International Journal of Bilingual Education and Bilingualism.* Available at http://dx.doi.org/10.1080/13670050.2016.1203859

Bialystok, E., Craik, F. I., & Luk, G. (2012). Bilingualism: Consequences for mind and brain. *Trends in Cognitive Sciences, 16*(4), 240–250.

Bilingual Education Act. (1968). Title VII, Bilingual Education, Language Enhancement, and Language Acquisition Programs of Elementary and Secondary Education Act. P.L. 90-247.

Bilingual Education Act. (1974). Title VII of Elementary and Secondary Education Act, 1974 reauthorization, P. L. 93-380.

Bilingual Education Act. (1978). Title VII of Elementary and Secondary Education Act, 1978 reauthorization, P.L. 95-561.

Bilingual Education Act. (1984). Title VII of Elementary and Secondary Education Act, 1984 reauthorization, P. L. 98-511.

Bilingual Education Act. (1988). Title VII of Elementary and Secondary Education Act, 1988 reauthorization, P. L.100-297

Bilingual Education Act. (1994). Title VII of Improving America's Schools Act of 1994. P.L. 103-382.

Birch, B. M. (2002). *English L2 Reading: Getting to the bottom.* Mahwah, NJ: Lawrence Erlbaum.

Blackledge, A., & Creese, A. (2010). *Multilingualism: A critical perspective.* London, UK: Continuum Press.

Blanc, M., & Hamers, J. (Eds.). (1985). Theoretical and methodological issues in the study of languages/dialects in contact at macro- and micro-logical levels of analysis. London: *Proceedings of the International Conference DALE* (University of London)/ICRB (Laval University, Quebec).

Blase, J., & Blase, J. (2001). *Empowering teachers: What successful principals do* (2nd ed.). Thousand Oaks, CA: Corwin Press.

Block, D. (2014). Moving beyond "lingualism": Multilingual embodiment and multimodality in SLA. In S. May (Ed.), *The multilingual turn: Implications for SLA, TESOL and Bilingual Education* (pp. 54–77). New York, NY: Routledge.

Blommaert, J. (2010). *The sociolinguistics of globalization.* Cambridge, UK: Cambridge University Press.

Blommaert, J., & Rampton, B. (2011). Language and superdiversity. *Diversities, 13*(2), 1–22.

Bonfiglio, T. H. (2010). *Mother tongues and nations. The invention of the native speaker.* New York, NY: Mouton de Gruyter.

Booher-Jennings, J. (2006). Rationing education in an era of accountability. *Phi Delta Kappan, 87*(10), 756–761.

Borlase, K., & Haines, D. (n.d.). Mr. Darwin music video. Available at https://www.youtube.com/watch?v=SSFL1Z1rMoE)

Bos, B. (2007). The effect of the Texas Instrument interactive instructional environment on the mathematical achievement of eleventh grade low achieving students. *Journal of Educational Computing Research, 37*(4), 351–368.

Bos, B. (2009). Technology with cognitive and mathematical fidelity: What it means for the math classroom. *Computers in the Schools, 26,* 107–114. doi: 10.1080/07380560902906088

Bourdieu, P. (1985). The forms of capital. In J. G. Richardson (Ed.), *Handbook of theory and research for the sociology of education* (pp. 241–258). New York, NY: Greenwood.

Bransford, J. D., Sherwood, R. D., Hasselbring, T. S., Kinzer, C. K., & Williams, S. M. (1990). Anchored instruction: Why we need it and how technology can help. In D. Nix & R. Spiro (Eds.), *Cognition, education, and multimedia: Exploring ideas in high technology* (pp. 115–141). New York, NY: Routledge.

Brown v. Board of Educ., 347 U.S. 483 (1954).

Browning-Aiken, A. (2005). Border crossing: Funds of knowledge within an immigrant household. In N. González, L. C. Moll, & C. Amanti (Eds.), *Funds of knowledge: Theorizing practices in households, communities, and classrooms* (pp.167–181). Mahwah, NJ: Lawrence Erlbaum Associates.

Bruce, B. C., Bishop, A. P., & Budhathoki, N. R. (Eds.). (2014). *Youth community inquiry: New media for community and personal growth.* New York, NY: Peter Lang.

California Department of Education. (2006a). *Number of English learner students enrolled in specific instructional settings.* Available at http://dq.cde.ca.gov/dataquest/ElP2_State.asp?RptYear=2005-

California Department of Education. (2006b). *English learners, instructional settings and services.* Available at www.dq.cde.ca.gov/dataquest/ELP2_State.asp?RptYear=200405&RPTType=ELPart2_1a

California Department of Education. (2012). *California English language development standards: Kindergarten through grade 12.* Sacramento, CA: Author.

California Proposition 227. (1998). California Education Code, Sections 300–311.

Calkins, L. (1994). *The art of teaching writing* (2nd ed.). Portsmouth, NH: Heinemann.

Callahan, R. (2003). *Tracking and English language proficiency: Variable effects on academic achievement of high school ELs.* Unpublished doctoral dissertation, University of California, Davis.

Callahan, R. (2005). Tracking and high school English learners: Limiting opportunities to learn. *American Educational Research Journal, 42*(2), 305–328.

Callahan, R. (2016). Equitable access for secondary English learner students: Course taking as evidence of EL program effectiveness. *Educational Administration Quarterly, 52*(3), 463–496.

Callahan, R., & Gándara, P. (2014). *The Bilingual advantage. Language, literacy and the US labor market.* Bristol, UK: Multilingual Matters.

Cammarota, J., & Fine, M. (2008). *Revolutionizing education: Youth participatory action research in motion.* New York, NY: Routledge.

Canagarajah, S. (1999). *Resisting linguistic imperialism in English teaching.* Oxford, UK: Oxford University Press.

Canagarajah, S. (2011). Translanguaging in the classroom: Emerging issues for research and pedagogy. *Applied Linguistics Review, 2,* 1–27.

Canale, M., & Swain, M. (1980). Theoretical bases of communicative approaches to second language teaching and testing. *Journal of Applied Linguistics, 1*(1), 1–47.

Capps, R., Fix, M., Murray, J., Ost, J., Passel, J. S., & Herwantoro, S. (2005). *The new demography of America's schools: Immigration and the No Child Left Behind Act.* Washington, DC: Urban Institute.

Carini, P. (2000a). A letter to parents and teachers on some ways of looking at and reflecting on children. In M. Himley & P. Carini (Eds.), *From another angle: Children's strengths and school standards. The Prospect Center's descriptive review of the child* (pp. 56–64). New York, NY: Teachers College Press.

Carini, P. (2000b). Prospect's descriptive processes. In M. Himley & P. Carini (Eds.), *From another angle: Children's strengths and school standards. The Prospect Center's descriptive review of the child* (pp. 8–20). New York, NY: Teachers College Press.

Carlo, M. S., August, D., McLaughlin, B., Snow, C. E., Dressler, C., & Lippman, D. N. (2004). Closing the gap: Addressing the vocabulary needs of English-language learners in bilingual and mainstream classrooms. *Reading Research Quarterly, 39*(2), 188–215.

Carnock, J. T., & Ege, A. (2015, November 17). The "triple segregation" of Latinos, ELLs. What can we do? Post from New America's Dual Language Learner National Work Group. Available at https://www.newamerica.org/education-policy/edcentral/latinos-segregation/

Carrasquillo, A., & Rodriguez, V. (2002). *Language minority students in the mainstream classroom* (2nd ed.). Clevedon, UK: Multilingual Matters.

Caspe, M., Lopez, M. E., & Wolos, C. (2007). *Family involvement makes a difference: Family involvement in elementary school children's education.* Cambridge, MA: Harvard Family Research Project. Available at http://www.hfrp.org/publications-resources/browse-our-publications/family-involvement-in-elementary-school-children-s-education

Castañeda v. Pickard. (1981). 648 F.2d 989 (5th Cir., 1981).

Castells, M. (2007). Communication, power and counter-power in the network society. *International Journal of Communication, 1,* 238–266.

Cazden, C. (1986). ESL teachers as advocates for children. In P. Rigg & D.S. Engirgh (Eds.), *Children and ESL: Integrating perspectives* (pp. 7–21). Washington, DC: TESOL.

CCSSO (Council of Chief State School Officers). (2016, February). *Major provisions of Every Student Succeeds Act (ESSA) related to the education of English Learners.* Available at http://www.ccsso.org/Documents/2016/ESSA/CCSSOResourceonESSAELLs02.23.2016.pdf

Celic, C. (2009). *English language learners day by day K–6.* Portsmouth, NH: Heinemann.

Celic, C., & Seltzer, K. (2012) *Translanguaging: A CUNY-NYSIEB guide for educators.* New York, NY: CUNY-NYSIEB, The Graduate Center, CUNY. Available at http://www.cuny-nysieb.org

Cenoz, J., & Gorter, D. (Eds.) (2015), *Multilingual Education: Between language learning and translanguaging.* Cambridge, UK: Cambridge University Press.

Center for Applied Linguistics (CAL). (2009). *Foreign language teaching in U.S. Schools: Results of a national survey.* Washington, DC: Center for Applied Linguistics.

Center on Education Policy. (2005, July). *NCLB: Narrowing the curriculum?* (NCLB Policy Brief 3). Available at file:///Users/ogarcia/Downloads/CEPPB3_070105

Center on Education Policy. (2016, May). *Listen to us: Teachers' views and voices.* Washington, DC: George Washington University. Available at http://files.eric.ed.gov/fulltext/ED568172.pdf

Cervantes-Soon, C. G. (2014). A critical look at dual language immersion in the new Latin@ diaspora. *Bilingual Research Journal, 37*(4), 64–82. Available at http://doi.org/10.1080/15235882.2014.893267

Cerat, M. L. (2017). *Haitian linguistic and cultural practices.* Doctoral dissertation, The Graduate Center, City University of New York.

Chamot, A. U., & O'Malley, J. M. (1994). *The CALLA handbook: Implementing the cognitive academic language learning approach.* Reading, MA: Addison-Wesley.

Chappell, S. V., & Faltis, C. J. (2013). *The arts and emergent bilingual youth: Building culturally responsive, critical and creative education in school and community contexts.* New York, NY: Routledge.

Chatterji, M. (2003). *Designing and using tools for educational assessment.* Boston, MA: Allyn & Bacon/Pearson.

Cheng, L., Watanabe, Y., & Curtis, A. (Eds.). (2004). *Washback in language testing: Research contexts and methods.* Mahwah, NJ: Lawrence Erlbaum.

Chrispeels, J. H., & Gonz, M. (2004). *Do educational programs increase parents' practices at home?: Factors influencing Latino parent involvement.* Cambridge, MA: Harvard Family Research Project. Available at http://www.hfrp.org/family-involvement/publications-resources/do-educational-programs-increase-parents-practices-at-home-factors-influencing-latino-parent-involvement#_ftnref1

Chrispeels, J. H., & Rivero, E. (2001). Engaging Latino families for student success: How parent education can reshape parents' sense of place in the education of their children. *Peabody Journal of Education, 76*(2), 119–169.

Chumak-Horbatsch, R. (2012). *Linguistically appropriate practice. A guide for working with young immigrant children.* Toronto, Canada: University of Toronto Press.

Civil Rights Act, Title VI, Section 601. (1964).

Clewell, B., & Campbell, P. (2004). *Highly effective USI schools: An outlier study.* Washington, DC: The Urban Institute/Campbell-Kibler Associates, Inc.

Clewell, B. C., & Villegas, A. M. (2001). *Absence unexcused: Ending teacher shortages in high-need areas.* Washington, DC: The Urban Institute.

Cloud, N., Genesee, F., & Hamayan, E. (2000). *Dual language instruction. A handbook for enriched education.* Boston, MA: Heinle and Heinle.

Cochran-Smith, M. (Ed.). (2004). *Walking the road: Race, diversity and social justice in teacher education.* New York, NY: Teachers College Press.

Collier, V. P., & Thomas, W. (2017). Validating the power of bilingual schooling: Thirty-two years of large-scale, longitudinal research. *Annual Review of Applied Linguistics.* doi:10.1017/S0267190517000034

Collins, B., & Cioè-Peña, M. (2016). Declaring freedom: Translanguaging in the social studies classroom to understand complex texts. In O. García & T. Kleyn (Eds.), *Translanguaging with multilingual students. Learning from classroom moments* (pp. 118–139). New York, NY: Routledge.

Common Core State Standards. (2010). Available at http://www.corestandards.org/

Compton-Lilly, C. (2007). The complexities of reading capital in two Puerto Rican families. *Reading Research Quarterly, 42*(1), 72–98.

Condliffe, B., Visher, M. G., Banger, M. R., Drohojowska, S., & Saco, L. (2016). *Project-based learning: A literature review.* New York, NY: MDRC.

Connecticut State Department of Education. (2015). *Connecticut English language proficiency (CELP) standards.* Available at http://www.sde.ct.gov/sde/cwp/view.asp?a=2618&q=320848

Conteh, J., & Meier, G. (Eds.) (2014). *The multilingual turn in languages education: Opportunities and challenges for individuals and societies.* Clevedon, UK: Multilingual Matters.

Cook, V. (2002). Background to the L2 user. In V. Cook (Ed.), *Portraits of the L2 User* (pp. 1–28). Clevedon, UK: Multilingual Matters.

Cook, V. (2008). *Second language learning and language teaching* (4th ed.). London, UK: Hodder.

Cope, B., & Kalantzis, M. (Eds.) (2000). *Multiliteracies: Literacy learning and the design of social futures.* New York, NY: Routledge.

Cope, B., & Kalantzis, M. (2013). Towards a new learning: The Scholar social knowledge workspace, in theory and practice. *E-Learning and Digital Media, 10*(4), 332–356.

Council of Europe. (2000). *Common European framework of reference for languages: Learning, teaching, assessment.* Strasbourg, France: Language Policy Division. Available at www.coe.int/t/dg4/linguisic/CADRE_EN.asp

Council of the Great City Schools. (2004, fall). *Title III of No Child Left Behind: A status report from the Great City Schools.* Available at http://www.cgcs.org/pdfs/Title%20III%20Survey%20Report%202004--Final.pdf

Council of the Great City Schools. (2015). *Student testing in America's Great City Schools: An inventory and preliminary analysis.* Available at http://www.cgcs.org/cms/lib/DC00001581/Centricity/ Domain/87/Testing%20Report.pdf

Crawford, J. (2003). *A few things Ron Unz would prefer you didn't know about English learners in California*. Available at http://ourworld.compuserve.com/homepages/ JWCRAWFORD/castats.htm

Crawford, J. (2004). *Educating English learners: Language diversity in the classroom* (5th ed.). Los Angeles, CA: Bilingual Educational Services.

Crawford, J. (2007). The decline of bilingual education in the USA: How to reverse a troubling trend? *International Multilingual Research Journal, 1*(1), 33–37.

Crawford, J., & Krashen. S. (2007). *English learners in American classrooms. 101 questions. 101 answers*. New York, NY: Scholastic.

Creese, A., & Blackledge, A. (2010). Translanguaging in the bilingual classroom: A pedagogy for learning and teaching? *Modern Language Journal, 94*, 103–115.

Cronbach, L. J. (1989). Construct validation after thirty years. In R. L. Linn (Ed.), *Intelligence: Measurement theory and public policy* (pp. 147–171). Urbana, IL: University of Illinois Press.

Cummins, J. (1979). Cognitive/academic language proficiency, linguistic interdependence, the optimum age question, and some other matters. *Working Papers on Bilingualism, 19*, 121–129.

Cummins, J. (1981). *Bilingualism and minority language children*. Toronto, Canada: Ontario Institute for Studies in Education.

Cummins, J. (1984). *Bilingualism and special education: Issues in assessment and pedagogy*. Clevedon, UK: Multilingual Matters.

Cummins, J. (2000). *Language, power, & pedagogy: Bilingual children caught in the cross-fire*. Clevedon, UK: Multilingual Matters.

Cummins, J. (2003). *Biliteracy, empowerment and transformative pedagogy.* Available at http://www.iteachilearn.com/cummins/biliteratempowerment.html

Cummins, J. (2006). Identity texts: The imaginative construction of self through multiliteracies pedagogy. In O. García, T. Skutnabb-Kangas, & M. Torres-Guzmán (Eds.), *Imagining multilingual schools: Languages in education and glocalization* (pp. 51–68). Clevedon, UK: Multilingual Matters.

Cummins, J. (2007). Rethinking monolingual instructional strategies in multilingual classrooms, *The Canadian Journal of Applied Linguistics, 10*(2), 221–240.

Cummins, J. (2008). Teaching for transfer: Challenging the two solitudes assumption in bilingual education. *Encyclopedia of Language and Education, 5*, 65–75.

Cummins, J. (2009). Foreword. In D. Fu (Ed.), *Writing between languages: How English language learners make the transition to fluency, grades 4–12* (pp. ix–xii). Portsmouth, NH: Heinemann.

Cummins, J. (2017). Teaching minoritized students: Are additive approaches legitimate? *Harvard Educational Review, 87*(3), 404–425.

Cummins, J., Brown, K., & Sayers, D. (2007). *Literacy, technology and diversity: Teaching for success in changing times*. Boston, MA: Allyn & Bacon.

Darling-Hammond, L. (1999). *Teacher quality and student achievement: A review of state policy evidence*. Seattle, WA: Center for the Study of Teaching Policy, University of Washington.

Darling-Hammond, L. (2010). *The flat world and education: How America's commitment to equity will determine our future.* New York, NY: Teachers College Press.

Darling-Hammond, L., Zielezinski, M. B., & Goldman, S. (2014). *Using technology to support at-risk students' learning.* Stanford, CA: Stanford Center for Opportunity Policy in Education (SCOPE) and Alliance for Excellent Education.

De Cohen, C. C., Deterding, N., & Chu Clewell, B. (2005). *Who's left behind? Immigrant children in high and low LEP schools.* Washington, DC: Program for Evaluation and Equity Research. Urban Institute. Available at http://www.urban.org/UploadedPDF/411231_whos_left_behind.pdf

DeGraff, M. (2005). Linguists' most dangerous myth: The fallacy of Creole exceptionalism. *Language in Society, 34*(4), 533–591.

DeGraff, M. (2009). Creole exceptionalism and the (mis)-education of the Creole speaker. In J. Kleifgen & G. C. Bond (Eds.), *The languages of Africa and the diaspora: Educating for language awareness* (pp. 124–144). Bristol, UK: Multilingual Matters.

DeGraff, M. (2013). MIT-Haiti initiative uses Haitian Creole to make learning truly active, constructive, and interactive. *Educational Technology Debate.* Available at https://edutechdebate.org/cultural-heritage-and-role-of-education/mit-haiti-initiative-uses-haitian-creole-to-make-learning-truly-active-constructive-and-interactive/

DeGraff, M. (2016). Kreyòl, pedagogy and technology for opening up quality education in Haiti. Manuscript submitted for publication.

de Jong, E. J., & Bearse, C. (2011). The same outcomes for all? High school students reflect on their two-way immersion program experiences. In D. J. Tedick, D. Christian, & T. W. Fortune (Eds.), *Immersion education: Practices, policies, possibilities* (pp. 104–122). Bristol, UK: Multilingual Matters.

Delgado-Gaitán, C. (1990). *Literacy for empowerment: The role of parents in children's education.* London, UK: Falmer Press.

Delgado-Gaitán, C. (1992). School matters in the Mexican-American home: Socializing children to education. *American Educational Research Journal, 29*(3), 495–513.

Delgado-Gaitán, C. (2001). *The power of community: Mobilizing for family and schooling.* Blue Ridge Summit, PA: Rowman & Littlefield.

Delgado-Gaitán, C., & Trueba, H. (1991). *Crossing cultural borders: Education for immigrant families in America.* New York, NY: Falmer Press.

Dewey, J. (1938). *Experience and education.* New York, NY: Macmillan.

Díaz, R., & Klinger, C. (1991). Towards an explanatory model of the interaction between bilingualism and cognitive development. In E. Bialystok (Ed.), *Language processing in bilingual children* (pp. 167–192). Cambridge, UK: Cambridge University Press.

Doerr, N. M. (Ed.) (2009). *The native speaker concept: Ethnographic investigations of native speaker effect.* Berlin, Germany: De Gruyter/Mouton.

Dufour, R., & Kroll, J. F. (1995). Matching words to concepts in two languages: A test of the concept mediation model of bilingual representation. *Memory & Cognition, 23*(2), 166–180.

Duncan, J. (2013, February 7). *No Child Left Behind: Early lessons from state flexibility waivers.* Testimony of Secretary of Education Arne Duncan to the U.S. Senate Committee on Health, Education, Labor and Pensions. Available at http://www.ed.gov/news/speeches/no-child-left-behind-early-lessons-state-flexibility-waivers

Dunn, L. (1987). *Bilingual Hispanic children on the U.S. mainland: A review of research on their cognitive, linguistic and scholastic development.* Circle Pines, MN: American Guidance Service.

Duverger, J. (2005). *L'Enseignment en classe bilingue [Teaching in a bilingual class].* Paris, France: Hachette.

Ebe, A. E. (2016). Student voices shining through: Exploring translanguaging as a literary device. In O. García & T. Kleyn (Eds.), *Translanguaging with multilingual students. Learning from classroom moments* (pp. 57–82). New York, NY: Routledge.

Eccles, J. S., & Harold, R. D. (1993). Parent–school involvement during the early adolescent years. *Teachers College Record, 94*(3), 568–587.

Echevarría, J., Vogt, M. E., & Short, D. J. (2004). *Making content comprehensible for English learners. The SIOP model* (2nd ed.). Boston, MA: Allyn & Bacon.

EDFacts. (2015, September 4). Data groups 695 and 696, School year 2013–14.

Education Law Center. (2007). *Starting at 3: Securing access to preschool education.* Available at http://www.startingat3.org/news/Sa3news_070323_ECE_HispanicsReport.htm)

Eisner, E. W. (2001). What does it mean to say a school is doing well? *The Phi Delta Kappan, 82*(5), 367–372.

English Language Learners Sub-Committee of the Massachusetts Board of Elementary and Secondary Education's Committee on the Proficiency Gap. (2009). *Halting the race to the bottom: Urgent interventions for the improvement of English language learners in Massachusetts and selected districts.* Boston, MA: Gastón Institute Publications.

Epstein, J. L. (1987). What principals should know about parent involvement. *Principal, 66*(3), 6–9.

Epstein, J. L. (1990). School and family connections: Theory, research, and implications for integrating sociologies of education and family. In D. G. Unger & M. B. Sussman (Eds.), *Families in community settings: Interdisciplinary perspectives* (pp. 99–126). New York, NY: Haworth Press.

Epstein, J. L., & Dauber, S. L. (1991). School programs and teacher practices of parent involvement in inner-city elementary and middle schools. *The Elementary School Journal, 91*(3), 289–305.

Epstein, J. L., & Sheldon, S. B. (2006). Moving forward: Ideas for research on school, family, and community partnerships. In C. F. Conrad & R. Serlin (Eds.), *SAGE Handbook for research in education: Engaging ideas and enriching inquiry* (pp. 117–137). Thousand Oaks, CA: Sage Publications.

Escamilla, K., Hopewell, S., Butvilofsky, S., Sparrow, W., Soltero-González, L., Ruiz-Figueroa, O., & Escamilla, M. (2014). *Biliteracy from the start: Literacy squared in action.* Philadelphia, PA: Caslon Publishing.

Esch, C. E., Chang-Ross, C. M., Guha, R., Humphrey, D. C., Shields, P. M., Tiffany-Morales, J. D., Wechsler, M. E., & Woodworth, K. R. (2005). *The status of the teaching profession 2005.* Santa Cruz, CA: The Center for the Future of Teaching and Learning.

Esch, C. E., & Shields, P. M. (2002). *Who is teaching California's children? Teaching and California's future.* Santa Cruz, CA: Center for the Future of Teaching and Learning.

Espinosa, C., Ascenzi-Moreno, L., & Vogel, S. (2016). *A Translanguaging pedagogy for writing. A CUNY-NYSIEB guide for educators.* New York, NY: CUNY-NYSIEB, The Graduate Center, CUNY. Available at http://www.cuny-nysieb. org/wp-content/uploads/2016/05/TLG-Pedagogy-Writing-04-15-16.pdf

Espinosa, C., & Herrera, L. (2016). Reclaiming bilingualism: Translanguaging in a science class. In O. García, & T. Kleyn (Eds.), *Translanguaging with multilingual students. Learning from classroom moments* (pp. 160–178). New York, NY: Routledge.

Espinosa, L. (2013a). *Early education for dual language learners: promoting school readiness and early school success.* Washington, DC: Migration Policy Institute.

Espinosa, L. (2013b). *PreK-3rd: Challenging common myths about dual language learners. An update to the seminal 2008 report. No. 10.* New York, NY: Foundation for Child Development.

Esteban-Guitart, M., & Moll, L. C. (2014). Funds of identity: A new concept based on the funds of knowledge approach. *Culture & Psychology, 20*(1), 31–48.

Estrin, E. T., & Nelson-Barber, S. (1995). Bringing Native American perspectives to mathematics and science teaching. *Theory into Practice, 34*(3), 174–185.

Every Student Succeeds Act of 2015 (ESSA). (2015). Pub.L.No. 114-95 § 114 Stat.1177 (2015-2016).

Fairclough, N. (Ed.). (1992). *Critical language awareness.* London, UK: Longman.

Fairclough, N. (1999). Global capitalism and critical awareness of language. *Language Awareness, 8*(2), 71–83.

Ferguson, G. (2006). *Language planning and education.* Edinburgh, Scotland: Edinburgh Press.

Fishman, J. A. (1966). *Language loyalty in the United States. The maintenance and perpetuation of non-English mother tongues by American ethnic and religious groups.* The Hague, Netherlands: Mouton.

Fitts, S. (2006). Reconstructing the status quo: Linguistic interaction in a dual-language school. *Bilingual Research Journal, 30*(2), 337–365.

Fix, M., & Passel, J. (2003). *U.S. immigration—Trends and implications for schools.* Washington, DC: Immigration Studies Program, Urban Institute.

Fleischman, H. F., & Hopstock, P. J. (1993). *Descriptive study of services to limited English proficient students: Volume I. Summary of findings and conclusions.*

Report submitted to the U.S. Department of Education. Arlington, VA: Development Associates, Inc.

Flores, N. (2013). The unexamined relationship between neoliberalism and plurilingualism: A cautionary tale. *TESOL Quarterly, 47*(3), 500–521.

Flores, N. (2016). A tale of two visions: Hegemonic whiteness and bilingual education. *Educational Policy, 30*(1), 13–38. Available at http://doi. org/10.1177/0895904815616482

Flores, R., & Rosa, J. (2015). Undoing appropriateness: Raciolinguistic ideologies and language diversity in Education. *Harvard Educational Review, 85* (2), 149–171.

Foucault, M. (1979). *Discipline and punish: The birth of the prison.* New York, NY: Vintage Books.

Foulger, T. S., & Jimenez-Silva, M. (2007). Enhancing the writing development of English Learners: Teacher perceptions of common technology in project-based learning. *Journal of Research on Childhood Education, 22*(2), 109–124.

Freeman, Y., & Freeman, D. (2008). *Academic language for English language learners and struggling readers.* New York, NY: Heinemann.

Freire, P. (1970). *Pedagogy of the oppressed.* New York, NY: Herder and Herder.

Fry, R. (2003). *Hispanic youth dropping out of US schools: Measuring the challenge.* Washington, DC: Pew Hispanic Center.

Fry, R., & Gonzales, F. (2008, August 25). *One-in-five and growing fast: A profile of Hispanic public school students.* Available at http://www.pewhispanic. org/2008/08/26/one-in-five-and-growing-fast-a-profile-of-hispanic-public-school-students/.

Fry, R., & López, M. H. (2012). *Hispanic student enrollments reach new highs in 2011.* Available at http://www.pewhispanic.org/2012/08/20/hispanic-student-enrollments-reach-new-highs-in-2011/

Fu, D. (2003). *An island of English: Teaching ESL in Chinatown.* Portsmouth, NH: Heinemann.

Fu, D. (2009). *Writing between languages: How English language learners make the transition to fluency.* Portsmouth, NH: Heinemann.

Gándara, P. (1999). *Review of research on the instruction of Limited English proficient Students: A report to the California legislature.* Santa Barbara, CA: University of California at Santa Barbara, Linguistic Minority Research Institute.

Gándara, P., & Contreras. F. (2009). *The Latino education crisis. The consequences of failed social policies.* Cambridge, MA: Harvard University Press.

Gándara, P., & Hopkins, M. (Eds.). (2010). *Forbidden language: English learners and restrictive language policies.* New York, NY: Teachers College Press.

Gándara, P., Maxwell-Jolly, J., & Driscoll, A. (2005). *Listening to teachers of English language learners.* Santa Cruz, CA: Center for the Future of Teaching and Learning.

Gándara, P., O'Hara, S., & Gutiérrez, D. (2004). The changing shape of aspirations: Peer influence on achievement behavior. In G. Gibson, P. Gándara, & J. Koyama (Eds.), *School connections: U.S. Mexican youth, peers, and achievement* (pp. 39–62). New York, NY: Teachers College Press.

Gándara, P., & Orfield, G. (2010). A return to the "Mexican room." The segregation of America's English learners. University of California, Los Angeles: The Civil Rights Project. Available at https://files.eric.ed.gov/fulltext/ED511322.pdf

Gándara, P., Rumberger, R., Maxwell-Jolly, J., & Callahan, R. (2003). English learners in California schools: Unequal resources, unequal outcomes. *Education Policy Analysis Archives*. Available at http://epaa.asu.edu/epaa/v11n36/

Garcia, E. (2005). *Teaching and learning in two languages. Bilingualism and schooling in the United States*. New York, NY: Teachers College Press.

Garcia, E., & Frede, E. (Eds.) (2010). *Young English language learners. Current research and emerging directions for practice and policy*. New York, NY: Teachers College Press.

Garcia, E., & Gonzalez, D. (2006, July). *Pre-K and Latinos: The foundation for America's future*. Washington, DC: Pre-K Now Research Series.

Garcia, E., & Jensen, B. (2009). Early educational opportunities for children of Hispanic origins. *Social Policy Report, 23*(2), 1–19.

García, G., & Pearson, P. D. (1994). Assessment and diversity. *Review of Research in Education, 20*, 337–391.

García, O. (1999). Educating Latino high school students with little formal schooling. In C. J. Faltis & P. Wolfe (Eds.), *So much to say: Adolescents, bilingualism, & ESL in the secondary school* (pp. 61–82). New York, NY: Teachers College Press.

García, O. (2006a). Lost in transculturation: The case of bilingual education in New York City. In M. Putz, J. A. Fishman, & N. V. Aertselaer (Eds.), *Along the routes to power: Exploration of the empowerment through language* (pp. 157–178). Berlin, Germany: Mouton de Gruyter.

García, O. (2006b, fall). Equity's elephant in the room. Multilingual children in the U.S. are being penalized by current education policies. *TC Today, 40*.

García, O. (2009a). *Bilingual education in the 21st century: A global perspective*. Malden, MA: Wiley-Blackwell.

García, O. (2009b). Emergent bilinguals and TESOL. What's in a name? *TESOL Quarterly, 43*(2), 322–326.

García, O. (2016). The language valued at school. In G. Valdés, K. Menken, & M. Castro (Eds.), Common core bilingual and English language learners. A resource for educators (pp 47–48). Philadelphia, PA: Caslon Publishing.

García, O. (2017). Critical multilingual awareness and teacher education. In J. Cenoz, D. Gorter, & S. May (Eds.), *Encyclopedia of language and education: Language awareness and multilingualism* (pp. 263–279). Cham, Switzerland: Springer International Publishing Switzerland. DOI 10.1007/978-3-319-02325-0_30-1 1

García, O., Bartlett, L., & Kleifgen, J. (2007). From biliteracy to pluriliteracies. In P. Auer & L. Wei (Eds.), *Multilingualism and multilingual communication: Handbook of applied linguistics* (Vol. 5, pp. 207–228). Berlin, Germany: Mouton de Gruyter.

García, O., & Flores, N. (2014). Multilingualism and Common Core State Standards in the US. In S. May (Ed.), *Addressing the multilingual turn:*

Implications for SLA, TESOL and Bilingual Education (pp. 147–166). New York, NY: Routledge.

García, O., Flores, N., & Chu, H. (2011). Extending bilingualism in U.S. secondary education: New variations. *International Multilingual Research Journal, 5*(1), 1–18.

García, O., Flores, N., & Spotti, M. (Eds.) (2017). *Oxford handbook of language and society.* New York, NY, and London, UK: Oxford University Press.

García, O., Flores, N., & Woodley, H. H. (2015). Constructing in-between spaces to "do" bilingualism: A tale of two high schools in one city. In J. Cenoz & D. Gorter (Eds.), *Multilingual education: Between language learning and translanguaging* (pp. 199–224). Cambridge, UK: Cambridge University Press.

García, O., Johnson, S., & Seltzer, K. (2017). *The translanguaging classroom. Leveraging student bilingualism for learning.* Philadelphia, PA: Caslon.

García, O., Kleifgen, J., & Falchi, L. (2008). *Equity perspectives: From English language learners to emergent bilinguals.* New York, NY: Teachers College, Campaign for Educational Equity.

García, O., & Kleyn, T. (Eds.) (2016). *Translanguaging with multilingual students: Learning from classroom moments.* New York, NY: Routledge.

García, O., & Li Wei (2014). *Translanguaging: Language, bilingualism and education.* London, UK: Palgrave Macmillan Pivot.

García, O., & Menken, K. (2015). Cultivating an ecology of multilingualism in schools. In B. Spolsky, O. Inbar, & M. Tannenbaum (Eds.), *Challenges for language education and policy: Making space for people* (pp. 95–108). New York, NY: Routledge.

García, O., & Sánchez, M. (2015). Transforming schools with emergent bilinguals: The CUNY-NYSIEB Project. In I. Dirim, I. Gogolin, D. Knorr, M. Krüger-Potratz, D. Lengyel, H. Reich, & W. Weiße (Eds.), *Intercultural education: Festchrift for Ulla Neumann* (pp. 80–94). Berlin, Germany: Waxmann-Verlag.

García, O., Seltzer, K., & Witt, D. (2018). Disrupting linguistic inequalities in US urban classrooms: The role of translanguaging. In S. Slembrouck, K. Van Gorp, S. Sierens, K. Maryns, & P. Van Avermaet (Eds.), *The multilingual edge of education* (pp.414–456). Oxford, UK: Palgrave Macmillan UK.

García, O., & Sylvan, C. (2011). Pedagogies and practices in multilingual classrooms: Singularities in pluralities. *Modern Language Journal, 95*(iii), 385–400.

García, O., & Traugh, C. (2002). Using descriptive inquiry to transform the education of linguistically diverse U.S. teachers and students. In L. Wei, J. Dewaele, & A. Housen (Eds.), *Opportunities and challenges of (societal) bilingualism* (pp. 311–328). Berlin, Germany: Walter de Gruyter.

García, O., Velasco, P., Menken K., & Vogel, S. (forthcoming). Dual language bilingual education in NYC: A potential unfulfilled. In M. B. Arias & M. Fee (Eds.), *Perspectives on dual language programs.* Washington, DC, and Bristol, UK: Center for Applied Linguistics and Multilingual Matters.

García, O., Zakharia, Z., & Otcu, B. (Eds.). (2013). *Bilingual community education and multilingualism: Beyond heritage languages in a global city.* Bristol, UK: Multilingual Matters.

Gay, G. (2002). Preparing for culturally responsive teaching. *Journal of Teacher Education, 53*(2), 106–116.

Genesee, F., Lindholm-Leary, K., Saunders, W. M., & Christian, D. (Eds.). (2006). *Educating English language learners.* New York, NY: Cambridge University Press.

Genishi, C., & Borrego Brainard, M. (1995). Assessment of bilingual children: A dilemma seeking solutions. In E. Garcia & B. McLaughlin (Eds.), *Meeting the challenge of linguistic and cultural diversity in early childhood education* (pp. 49–63). New York, NY: Teachers College Press.

Gibbons, P. (2002). *Scaffolding language, scaffolding learning. Teaching second languages in the mainstream classroom.* Portsmouth, NH: Heinemann.

Gibbons, P. (2009). *English learners' academic literacy and thinking. Learning in the challenge zone.* Portsmouth, NH: Heinemann.

Gibson, M. A., Gándara, P., & Koyama, J. P. (2004). The role of peers in the schooling of U.S. Mexican youth. In M. A. Gibson, P. Gándara, & J. P. Koyama (Eds.), *School connections: U.S. Mexican youth, peers, and school achievement* (pp. 1–17). New York, NY: Teachers College Press.

Gil, L. S. (2016, May 21). *A new future for English Learners.* Presentation to New York State Association for Bilingual Education.

Gilmore, P. (2016). *Kisisi (our language): The story of Colin and Sadiki.* Malden, MA: Wiley-Blackwell.

Giroux, H. (1988). *Teachers as intellectuals.* Westport, CT: Bergin and Garvey.

Goh, D. S. (2004). *Assessment accommodations for diverse learners.* Boston, MA: Pearson.

Gold, E., Simon, E., & Brown, C. (2002). *Strong neighborhoods, strong schools: The indicators project on education organizing.* Chicago, IL: Cross City Campaign for Urban School Reform.

Goldenberg, C. (2008). Teaching English language learners. What the research does—and does not—say. *American Educator, 32*(2), 8–23, 42–44.

Goldenberg, C., & Coleman, R. (2010). *Promoting academic achievement among English learners. A guide to the research.* Thousand Oaks, CA: Corwin Press.

González, N. (2005). Beyond culture: The hybridity of funds of knowledge. In N. González, L. C. Moll, & C. Amati (Eds.), *Funds of knowledge: Theorizing practices in households, communities, and classrooms* (pp. 29–46). Mahwah, NJ: Lawrence Erlbaum.

González, N., Moll, L. C., & Amanti, C. (2005). *Funds of knowledge. Theorizing practices in households, communities, and classrooms.* Mahwah, NJ: Lawrence Erlbaum.

Goodall, J., & Montgomery, C. (2014). Parental involvement to parental engagement. A continuum. *Educational Review, 66*(4), 399–410.

Gormley, Jr., W. (2008). The effects of Oklahoma's pre-K program on Hispanic children. *Social Science Quarterly, 89*(4), 916–936.

Gort, M. (2015). *International Multilingual Research Journal, 9*(1). doi: 10.1080/19313152.2014.988030

Gort, M. (Ed.). (2018). *The complex and dynamic languaging practices of emergent bilinguals. Translanguaging across diverse educational and community contexts.* New York, NY: Taylor and Francis.

Gort, M., & Sembiante, S. F. (2015). Navigating hybridized language learning spaces through translanguaging pedagogy: Dual language preschool teachers' languaging practices in support of emergent bilingual children's performance of academic discourse. *International Multilingual Research Journal, 9*(1), 7–25. doi: 10.1080/19313152.2014.981775

Gorter, D., Marten, H. F., & Van Mensel, L. (Eds.) (2012). *Minority languages in the linguistic landscape.* Basingstoke, UK: Palgrave Macmillan.

Gottlieb, M. (2006). *Assessing English language learners: Bridges from language proficiency to academic achievement.* Thousand Oaks, CA: Corwin Press.

Gottlieb, M. (2016). *Assessing English language learners: Bridges to educational equity. Connecting academic language proficiency to student achievement.* Thousand Oaks, CA: Corwin Press.

Gottlieb, M. (2017). *Assessing multilingual learners. A month-by-month guide.* Alexandria, VA: ASCD.

Grant, E. A., & Wong, S. D. (2003). Barriers to literacy for language-minority learners: An argument for change in the literacy education profession. *Journal of Adolescent & Adult Literacy, 46,* 386–394.

Grantmakers for Education. (2013). *Educating English language learners: Grantmaking strategies for closing America's other achievement gap.* Available at https://edfunders.org/sites/default/files/Educating%20English%20 Language%20Learners_April%202013.pdf

Grapin, S. (forthcoming). Multimodality in the new content standards era: Implications for English learners. *TESOL Quarterly.*

Graves, M. (2006). *The vocabulary book: Learning and instruction.* New York, NY: Teachers College Press.

Gray, L., Thomas, N., & Lewis, L. (2010). *Teachers' use of educational technology in U.S. public schools: 2009* (NCES 2010-040). Washington, DC: National Center for Education Statistics, Institute of Education Sciences, U.S. Department of Education.

Green, D. W. (2011). Bilingual worlds. In V. Cook & B. Bassetti (Eds.), *Language and bilingual cognition* (pp. 229–240). New York, NY: Psychology Press.

Greenberg, J. (1989, June). *Funds of knowledge: Historical constitution, social distribution, and transmission.* Paper presented at the annual meeting of the Society for Applied Anthropology, Santa Fe, NM.

Greenberg, J. (1990). Funds of knowledge: Historical constitution, social distribution, and transmission. In W. T. Pink, D. S. Ogle, & B. F. Jones (Eds.), *Restructuring to promote learning in America's schools: Selected readings*

(Vol. 2, pp. 317–326), Elmhurst, IL: North Central Regional Educational Laboratory.

Greene, J. (1997). A meta-analysis of the Rossell and Baker review of bilingual education research. *Bilingual Research Journal, 21*, 103–122.

Greene, M. (1995). *Releasing the imagination. Essays on education, the arts and social change.* San Francisco, CA: Jossey-Bass.

Grimes, D., & Warschauer, M. (2008). Learning with laptops: A multi-method case study. *Journal of Educational Computing Research, 38*(3), 305–332.

Grosjean, F. (1982). *Life with two languages.* Cambridge, MA: Harvard University Press.

Grosjean, F. (1985). The bilingual as a competent but specific speaker-hearer. *Journal of Multilingual and Multicultural Development, 6*, 467–477.

Grosjean, F. (1989). Neurolinguists, beware! The bilingual is not two monolinguals in one person. *Brain and Language, 36*, 3–15.

Gumperz, J. J. (1976). The sociolinguistic significance of conversational code-switching. *Working Papers of the Language Behavior Research Laboratory, 46.* Berkeley, CA: University of California, Berkeley.

Gumperz, J. J. (1992). Contextualization and understanding. In A. Duranti & C. Goodwin (Eds.), *Rethinking context: Language as an interactive phenomenon* (pp. 229–252). Cambridge, UK: Cambridge University Press.

Gutiérrez, K. D., Asato, J., Pacheco, M., Moll, L. C., Olson, K., Horng, E., Ruiz, R., Garcia, E., & McCarty, T. L. (2002). "Sounding American": The consequences of new reforms on English language learners. *Reading Research Quarterly, 37*(3), 328–343.

Gutierrez-Clellen, V., & Peña, E. (2001). Dynamic assessment of diverse children: A tutorial. *Language, Speech and Hearing Services in Schools, 32*, 212–224.

Hakuta, K. (1986). *Cognitive development of bilingual children.* Los Angeles, CA: University of California at Los Angeles, Center for Language, Education, & Research.

Hakuta, K., Goto Butler, Y., & Witt, D. (2000). *How long does it take English learners to attain proficiency?* Berkeley, CA: University of California, Linguistic Minority Research Institute.

Hale, J. (2011). The student as a force for social change: The Mississippi Freedom Schools and student engagement. *Journal of African American History, 96*(3), 325–347.

Halliday, M. A. K. (1978). *Language as social semiotic: The social interpretation of language and meaning.* Baltimore, MD: University Park Press.

Halliday, M. A. K. (1993). Towards a language-based theory of learning. *Linguistics and Education, 5*, 93–116.

Harklau, L. (1994). Tracking and linguistic minority students: Consequences of ability grouping for second language learners. *Linguistics and Education, 6*(3), 217–244.

Harmer, J. (1998). *How to teach English.* Essex, UK: Pearson.

Haskins, R., & Rouse, C. (2005). Closing achievement gaps. *The Future of Children, 15*, 1–7.

Heath, S. B. (1983). *Ways with words.* Cambridge, UK: Cambridge University Press.

Heller, M. (1999). *Linguistic minorities and modernity: A sociolinguistic ethnography.* London, UK: Longman.

Henderson, A. T. (Ed.). (1987). *The evidence continues to grow: Parent involvement improves student achievement.* Columbia, MD: National Committee for Citizens in Education.

Henderson, A. T., & Berla, N. (1994). *A new generation of evidence: The family is critical to student achievement.* Washington, DC: National Committee for Citizens in Education.

Henderson, A. T., & Mapp, K. L. (2002). *A new wave of evidence: The impact of school, family, and community connections on student achievement.* Austin, TX: Southwest Educational Development Laboratory.

Herdina, P., & Jessner, U. (2002). *A dynamic model of multilingualism: Changing the psycholinguistic perspective.* Clevedon, UK: Multilingual Matters.

Heritage, M., Walqui, A., & Linquanti, R. (2015). *English language learners and the new standards. Developing language, content knowledge, and analytical practices in the classroom.* Cambridge, MA: Harvard Education Press.

Hidalgo, N. M., Siu, S. F., & Epstein, J. L. (2004). Research on families, schools, and communities: A multicultural perspective. In J. Banks & C. Banks (Eds.), *Handbook of research on multicultural education* (2nd ed., pp. 631–655). San Francisco, CA: Jossey-Bass.

Hobson v. Hansen. (1967). 269 F. Supp. 401, 490; DDC 1967.

Honig, B. (1996). *Teaching our children to read: The role of skills in a comprehensive reading program.* Thousand Oaks, CA: Corwin Press.

Hoover-Dempsey, K. V., & Sandler, H. M. (1997). Why do parents become involved in their children's education? *Review of Educational Research, 67*, 3–42.

Hopstock, P. J., & Stephenson, T. G. (2003a). *Descriptive study of services to LEP students and LEP students with disabilities.* Special Topic Report #1: Native Languages of LEP Students. OELA, U.S. Department of Education. Available at http://www.ncela.gwu.edu/resabout/research/descriptivestudyfiles/native_languages1.pdf

Hopstock, P. J., & Stephenson, T. G. (2003b). *Descriptive study of services to LEP students and LEP students with disabilities.* Special Topic Report #2: Analysis of Office for Civil Rights Data related to LEP students. Washington, DC: U.S. Department of Education, OELA.

Hornberger, N. (1990). Creating successful learning contexts for bilingual literacy. *Teachers College Record, 92*(2), 212–229.

Hornberger, N. (Ed.). (2003). *Continua of biliteracy. An ecological framework for educational policy, research, and practices in multilingual settings.* Clevedon, UK: Multilingual Matters.

Hornberger, N. (2005). Opening and filling up implementational and ideological spaces in heritage language education. *Modern Language Journal, 89*(4), 605–609.

Hornberger, N. (2006). Nichols to NCLB: Local and global perspectives on U.S. language education policy. In O. García, T. Skutnabb-Kangas, & M. Torres-Guzmán. (Eds.), *Imagining multilingual schools: Languages in education and glocalization* (pp. 223–237). Clevedon, UK: Multilingual Matters.

Hornberger, N., & Link, H. (2012). Translanguaging and transnational literacies in multilingual classrooms: A bilingual lens. *International Journal of Bilingual Education and Bilingualism, 15*(3), 261–278.

Hornberger, N., & Skilton-Sylvester, P. (2003). Revisiting the Continua of biliteracy: International and critical perspectives. In N. Hornberger (Ed.), *Continua of biliteracy. An ecological framework for educational policy, research, and practices in multilingual settings* (pp. 35–70). Clevedon, UK: Multilingual Matters.

Houser, J. (1995). Assessing students with disabilities and Limited English Proficiency. *Working Paper Series. Working Paper 95-13*. Washington, DC: National Center for Education Statistics.

Hudicourt-Barnes, J. (2003). The use of argumentation in Haitian Creole science classrooms. *Harvard Educational Review, 73*(1), 73–93.

Hull, G., & Nelson, M. (2005). Locating the semiotic power of multimodality. *Written Communication, 22*(2), 224–261.

Hung, A. (2011). *The work of play: Meaning making in video games*. New York, NY: Peter Lang.

Iedema, R. (2003). Multimodality, resemiotization: Extending the analysis of discourse as multi-semiotic practice. *Visual Communication, 2*(1), 29–57.

Jacobson, R., & Faltis, C. (1990). *Language distribution issues in bilingual schooling*. Clevedon, UK: Multilingual Matters.

Jaumont, F. (2017). *The bilingual revolution: The future of education is in two languages*. New York, NY: TBR Books.

Jensen, L. (2001). The demographic diversity of immigrants and their children. In R. Rumbaut & A. Portes (Eds.), *Ethnicities: Children of immigrants in America* (pp. 21–56). New York, NY: Russell Sage Foundation.

Jessner, U. (2006). *Linguistic awareness in multilinguals: English as a third language*. Edinburgh, Scotland: Edinburgh University Press.

Jewitt, C. (2002). The move from page to screen: The multimodal reshaping of school English. *Journal of Visual Communication, 1*(2), 171–196.

Jewitt, C. (Ed.). (2009). *The Routledge handbook for multimodal analysis*. London, UK: Routledge.

Jewitt, C., & Kress, G. (Eds.) (2003). *Multimodal literacy*. New York, NY: Peter Lang.

Jeynes, W. H. (2005). A meta-analysis of the relation of parental involvement to urban elementary school student academic achievement. *Urban Education, 40*(3), 237–269.

Jeynes, W. H. (2007). The relationship between parental involvement and urban secondary school student academic achievement. *Urban Education, 42*(1), 82–110.

Jeynes, W. H. (2011). *Parent involvement and academic success.* New York, NY: Routledge.

Jeynes, W. H. (2012). A meta-analysis of the efficacy of different types of parental involvement programs for urban students. *Urban Education, 47*(4), 706–742.

Jiménez-Castellanos, O., & Topper, A. M. (2012). The cost of providing an adequate education to English language learners. A review of the literature. *Review of Educational Research, 82*(2), 179–232. doi:10.3102/0034654312449872

Johnson, E. J., & Johnson, D. C. (2015). Language policy and bilingual education in Arizona and Washington State. *International Journal of Bilingual Education and Bilingualism, 18*(1), 92–112. doi:10.1080/13670050.2014.882288

Johnson, L. R. (2009). Challenging "best practices" in family literacy and parent education programs: The development and enactment of mothering knowledge among Puerto Rican and Latina mothers in Chicago. *Anthropology & Education Quarterly, 40*(3), 257–276.

Johnston, P. (1997). *Knowing literacy: Constructive literacy assessment.* York, ME: Stenhouse Publishers.

Jordan, C., Orozco, E., & Averett, A. (2001). *Emerging issues in school, family, and community connections.* Austin, TX: Southwest Educational Development Laboratory.

Kagan, S. (1986). Cooperative learning and sociocultural factors in schooling. In California State Department of Education (Ed.) *Beyond language: Social and cultural factors in schooling language minority students* (pp. 231–298). Los Angeles, CA: Evaluation, Dissemination and Assessment Center, California State University at Los Angeles.

Kagan, S., & McGroarty, M. (1993). Principles of cooperative learning for language and content gains. In D. D. Holt (Ed.), *Cooperative learning: A response to linguistic and cultural diversity* (pp. 47–66). McHenry, IL, and Washington, DC: Delta Systems and Center for Applied Linguistics.

Kaplan, R., & Baldauf, R. (1997). *Language planning from practice to theory.* Bristol, UK: Multilingual Matters.

Karoly, L., & Bigelow, J. (2005). *The economics of investing in universal preschool education in California.* Santa Monica, CA: RAND Labor and Population Program.

Karp, F., & Uriarte, M. (2010). *Educational Outcomes of English language learners in Massachusetts: A focus on Latino/a students.* Boston, MA: Gastón Institute publications. Paper 159. Available at http://scholarworks.umb.edu/gaston_pubs/159

Katz, A., Low, P., Stack, J., & Tsang, T. (2004). *A study of content area assessment for English language learners.* Prepared for the Office of English Language Acquisition and Academic Achievement for Limited English Proficient Students, U.S. Department of Education. San Francisco, CA: ARC Associates.

Kecskes, I., & Martínez Cuenca, I. (2005). Lexical choice as a reflection of conceptual fluency. *International Journal of Bilingualism, 9*(1), 49–69.

Kelly, L. B. (2016). Interest convergence and hegemony in dual language programs: Bilingual education, but for whom and why? *Language Policy*. Available at https://doi.org/10.1007/s10993-016-9418-y

Kena, G., Hussar W., McFarland J., de Brey C., Musu-Gillette, L., Wang, X., Zhang, J., Rathbun, A., WilkinsonFlicker, S., Diliberti M., Barmer, A., Bullock Mann, F., & Dunlop Velez, E. (2016). *The Condition of Education 2016* (NCES 2016-144). Washington, DC: U.S. Department of Education, National Center for Education Statistics. Available at http://nces.ed.gov/pubsearch.

KewalRamani, A., Gilbertson, L., Fox, M., & Provasnik, S. (2007). *Status and trends in the education of racial and ethnic minorities (NCES 2007-039)*. Washington, DC: National Center for Education Statistics, Institute of Education Sciences, U.S. Department of Education. Available at http://files.eric.ed.gov/fulltext/ED498259.pdf

Kharkhurin, A. (2015). Bilingualism and creativity. An educational perspective. In W. Wright, S. Boun, & O. García (Eds.), *The handbook of bilingual and multilingual education* (pp. 109–126). Malden, MA: Wiley-Blackwell.

Kieffer, M. J., & Lesaux, N. K. (2007). Breaking down words to build meaning: Morphology, vocabulary, and reading comprehension in the urban classroom. *The Reading Teacher, 61*, 134–144.

Kindler, A. (2002). *Survey of the states' limited English proficient students and available educational programs and services: 2000–2001 summary report*. Report prepared for the U.S. Department of Education, Office of English Language Acquisition, Language Enhancement and Academic Achievement for Limited English proficient Students (OELA). Washington, DC: National Clearinghouse for English Language Acquisition and Language Instruction Educational Programs. Available at http://www.ncela.gwu.edu/policy/states/reports/seareports/0001/sea0001.pdf

Kinzer, C. K. (2010). Considering literacy and policy in the context of digital environments. *Language Arts, 88*(1), 51–61.

Kleifgen, J. (1991). Kreyòl ekri, Kreyòl li: Haitian children and computers. *Educational Horizons, 59*(3), 152–158.

Kleifgen, J. (2006). Variation in multimodal literacies: How new technologies can expand or constrain modes of communication. *WORD, 57*(3), 303–324.

Kleifgen, J. (2009). Discourses of linguistic exceptionalism and linguistic diversity in education. In J. Kleifgen & G. C. Bond (Eds.), *The languages of Africa and the diaspora: Educating for language awareness* (pp. 1–21). Bristol, UK: Multilingual Matters.

Kleifgen, J. (2013). *Communicative Practices at Work: Multimodality and learning in a high-tech firm*. Bristol, UK: Multilingual Matters.

Kleifgen, J. (2017a). *BRIDGE evaluation progress report: Analysis and findings for Group B teacher online training class*. New York, NY: iEARN.

Kleifgen, J. (2017b). *BRIDGE evaluation progress report: Analysis for Group A students "My Identity, Your Identity" project*. New York, NY: iEARN.

Kleifgen, J., & Kinzer, C. (2009). Alternative spaces for education with and through technology. In H. Varenne & E. Gordon (Eds.), *Theoretical perspectives on comprehensive education: The way forward* (pp. 139–186). Lewiston, NY: Mellen Press.

Kleifgen, J., Kinzer, C. K., Hoffman, D. L., Gorski, K., Kim, J., Lira, A., & Ronan, B. (2014). An argument for a multimodal, online system to support English learners' writing development. In R. S. Anderson & C. Mims (Eds.), *Digital tools for writing instruction in k-12 settings: Student perceptions and experiences* (pp. 171–192). Hershey, PA: IGI Global.

Kleifgen, J., Lira, A., & Ronan, B. (2014, December). Developing content knowledge and science literacy in a transitional bilingual classroom. In C. Kinzer (Chair), *Collaborative design and implementation of alternative spaces for Latina/o Adolescent writers: The STEPS to Literacy intervention.* Symposium organized for the annual meeting of the Literacy Research Association, Marco Island, FL.

Klein, A. (March 13, 2017). Trump Education Dept. Releases New ESSA Guidelines. *Education Week.* Retrieved from http://blogs.edweek.org/edweek/campaign-k-12/2017/03/trump_education_dept_releases_new_essa_guidelines.html

Klein, E., & Martohardjono, G. (2009). *Students with interrupted formal education in New York City.* New York, NY: New York City Department of Education.

Kleyn, T. (2016). The grupito flexes their listening and learning muscles. In O. García & T. Kleyn (Eds.), *Translanguaging with multilingual students. Learning from classroom moments* (pp. 100–117). New York, NY: Routledge.

Knobel, M., & Lankshear, C. (2009). Wikis, digital literacies, and professional growth. *Journal of Adolescent & Adult Literacy, 52*(7), 631–634.

Koelsch, N. (n.d.). *Improving literacy outcomes for English language learners in high school: Considerations for states and districts in developing a coherent policy framework.* Available at http://www.betterhighschools.org/docs/NHSC_AdolescentS_110806.pdf

Kramsch, C. (1997). The privilege of the nonnative speaker. *Publications of the Modern Language Association of America, 112*(3), 359–369.

Kreider, H., Caspe, M., Kennedy, S., & Weiss, H. (2007). *Family involvement makes a difference: Family involvement in middle and high school students' education.* Cambridge, MA: Harvard Family Research Project. Available at http://www.hfrp.org/publications-resources/browse-our-publications/family-involvement-in-middle-and-high-school-students-education

Kress, G. (1995). *Writing the future: English and the making of a culture of innovation.* Sheffield, UK: National Association for the Teaching of English.

Kress, G. (2000a). Design and transformation: New theories of meaning. In B. Cope & M. Kalantzis (Eds.), *Multiliteracies: Literacy learning and the design of social futures* (pp. 153–161). London, UK: Routledge.

Kress, G. (2000b). A curriculum for the future. *Cambridge Journal of Education, 30*(1), 133–145.

Kress, G. (2003). *Literacy in the new media age.* New York, NY: Routledge.

Kress, G. (2010). *Multimodality.* New York, NY: Routledge.

Kress, G., Jewitt, C., Bourne, J., Franks, A., Hardcastle, J., Jones, K., & Reid, E. (2005). *English in urban classrooms. A multimodal perspective on teaching and learning.* New York, NY: RoutledgeFalmer.

Kress, G., Jewitt, C., Ogborn, J., & Tsatsarelis, C. (2001). *Multimodal teaching and learning: The rhetorics of the science classroom.* London, UK: Continuum.

Kress, G., & van Leeuwen, T. (1996.) *Reading images: The grammar of visual design.* London, UK: Routledge.

Kress, G., & van Leeuwen, T. (2001). *Multimodal discourse.* London, UK: Arnold.

Krizman, J., Marian, V., Shook, A., Skoe, E., & Kraus, N. (2012). Subcortical encoding of sound is enhanced in bilinguals and relates to executive function advantages. *Proceedings of the National Academy of Sciences of the United States of America, 109*(20), 7877–7881.

Kroll, J., & Bialystok, E. (2013). Understanding the consequences for bilinguals for language processing and cognition. *Journal of Cognitive Psychology, 25*(5), 497–514. Available at http://dx.doi.org/10.1080/20445911.2013.799170

Kukulska-Hulme, A., & Wible, D. (2008). Context at the crossroads of language learning and mobile learning. *Proceedings from ICCE 2008,* 27–31 October 2008, Taiwan.

Lachat, M. (1999). *What policymakers and school administrators need to know about assessment reform for English language learners.* Providence, RI: Brown University, Northeast and Islands Regional Education Laboratory.

Ladson-Billings, G. (1994). *The dreamkeepers: Successful teachers of African-American children.* San Francisco, CA: Jossey-Bass.

Ladson-Billings, G. (1995). Toward a theory of culturally relevant pedagogy. *American Educational Research Journal, 32*(3), 465–491.

Lam, W. S. E. (2004). Second language socialization in a bilingual chat room: Global and local considerations. *Language Learning & Technology, 8,* 44–65.

Lam, W. S. E., & Rosario-Ramos, E. (2009). Multilingual literacies in transnationally digitally mediated contexts: An exploratory study of immigrant teens in the United States. *Language and Education, 23,* 171–190.

Lambert, W. E. (1974). Culture and language as factors in learning and education. In F. E. Aboud & R. D. Meade (Eds.), *Cultural factors in learning and education* (pp. 91–122). Bellingham, WA: Western Washington State College.

Lambert, W. E. (1984). An overview of issues in immersion education. In California State Department of Education (Ed.), *Studies on immersion education: A collection for United States educators.* (pp. 8–30). Sacramento: California State Department of Education.

Lanauze, M., & Snow, C. (1989). The relation between first- and second-language writing skills: Evidence from Puerto Rican elementary school children in bilingual programs. *Linguistics and Education, 1*(4), 323–329.

Landry, R., & Bourhis, R. Y. (1997). Linguistic landscape and ethnolinguistic vitality. An empirical study. *Journal of Language and Social Psychology, 16*(1), 23–49. doi:10.1177/0261927X970161002

Language Instruction for Limited English Proficient and Immigrant Students. (2001). Public Law 107-110. Title III of No Child Left Behind (NCLB), Section 3001.

Larsen-Freeman, D., & Cameron, L. (2008). *Complex systems and applied linguistics.* Oxford, UK: Oxford University Press.

Lau Remedies. (1975). Task-force findings specifying remedies available for eliminating past educational practices ruled unlawful under *Lau v. Nichols.* Washington, DC: Office for Civil Rights. Available at http://www.stanford.edu/~kenro/LAU/LauRemedies.htm

Lau v. Nichols, 414 U.S. 563 (1974).

Lave, J., & Wenger, E. (1991). *Situated learning: Legitimate peripheral participation.* Cambridge, UK: Cambridge University Press.

Lee, J. S., & Oxelson, E. (2006). "It's not my job": K–12 teacher attitudes toward students' heritage language maintenance. *Bilingual Research Journal, 30*(2), 453–477.

Lemke, J. (1998). Multiplying meaning: Visual and verbal semiotics in scientific text. In J. R. Martin & R. Veel (Eds.), *Reading science* (pp. 87–113). London, UK: Routledge.

Lenhart, A., & Madden, M. (2005). *Teens content creators and consumers.* Washington, DC: Pew Internet and American Life Project.

Leu, D., Kinzer, C. K., Coiro, J., Castek, J., & Henry, L. A. (2013). New literacies: A dual level theory of the changing nature of literacy, instruction, and assessment. In D. E. Alvermann, N. J. Unrau, & R. B. Ruddell (Eds.), *Theoretical models and processes of reading* (6th ed., pp. 1150–1181). Newark, DE: International Reading Association.

Lewis, G., Jones, B., & Baker, C. (2012a). Translanguaging: Developing its conceptualisation and contextualisation. *Educational Research and Evaluation, 18*(7), 655–670.

Lewis, G., Jones, B., & Baker, C. (2012b). Translanguaging: Origins and development from school to street and beyond. *Educational Research and Evaluation, 18*(7), 641–654.

Li Wei (2011). Moment analysis and translanguaging space: Discursive construction of identities by multilingual Chinese youth in Britain. *Journal of Pragmatics, 43,* 1222–1235.

Li Wei (2014). Who's teaching whom? Co-learning in multilingual classrooms. In S. May (Ed.), *The multilingual turn: Implications for SLA, TESOL and bilingual education* (pp. 167–190). New York, NY: Routledge.

Li Wei (2017). Translanguaging as a practical theory of language. *Applied Linguistics, 2017*: 1–23. doi:10.1093/applin/amx039

Lin, A. M. Y. (2013) Classroom code-switching: three decades of research. *Applied Linguistic Review, 4*(1), 195–218.

Lindholm-Leary, K. (2001). *Dual language education.* Clevedon, UK: Multilingual Matters.

Lindholm-Leary, K., & Genesee, F. (2014). Student outcomes in one-way and two-way immersion and indigenous language education. *Journal of Immersion and Content-Based Language Education, 2*(2), 165–180.

Linquanti, R. (2001). *The redesignation dilemma: Challenges and choices in fostering meaningful accountability for English learners.* Santa Barbara, CA: University of California, Linguistic Minority Research Institute.

Linquanti, R., & Bailey, A.L. (2014). *Reprising the home language survey: Summary of a national working session on policies, practices, and tools for identifying potential English learners.* Washington, DC: Council of Chief State School Officers. Available at http://www.ccsso.org/Documents/2014/CCSSO%20Common%20EL%20Definition%20Reprising%20the%20Home%20Language%20Survey%2001242014.pdf

Linquanti, R., & Cook, H. G. (2013). *Toward a "common definition of English learner": Guidance for states and state assessment consortia in defining and addressing policy and technical issues and options.* Washington, DC: Council of Chief State School Officers.

Lippi-Green, R. (1997). *English with an accent: Language, ideology, and discrimination in the United States.* New York, NY: Routledge.

Llomaki, L., Paavola, S., Lakkala, M., & Kantosalo, A. (2016) Digital competence—an emergent boundary concept for policy and educational research. *Education and Information Technologies, 21*(3), 655–679.

Llopart, M., & Esteban-Guitart, M. (2016). Funds of knowledge in 21st century societies: inclusive educational practices for under-represented students. A literature review. *Journal of Curriculum Studies.* doi: 10.1080/00220272.2016.1247913

López, A. A., Guzmán-Orth, D., & Turkan, S. (2014, March). *A study on the use of translanguaging to assess the content knowledge of emergent bilingual students.* Paper presented at the Invited Colloquium, Negotiating the Complexities of Multilingual Assessment at the 2014 AAAL Conference. Portland, United States.

López, A. A., Turkan, S., & Guzman-Orth, D. (2017). *Conceptualizing the use of translanguaging in initial content assessments for newly arrived emergent bilingual students* (Research Report). Princeton, NJ: Educational Testing Service. Available at http://onlinelibrary.wiley.com/doi/10.1002/ets2.12140/full

López, G. L. (2001). The value of hard work: Lessons on parent involvement from an (im)migrant household. *Harvard Educational Review, 71*(3), 416–437.

López, M. P. (2005). Reflections on educating Latino and Latina undocumented children: Beyond *Plyler v. Doe. Seton Hall Law Review, 35*, 1373–1406.

Lucas, T., & Grinberg, J. (2008). Responding to the linguistic reality of mainstream classrooms: Preparing all teachers to teach English language learners. In M. Cochran-Smith, S. Feiman-Nemser, & J. McIntyre (Eds.), *Handbook of research in teacher education: Enduring issues in changing contexts* (3rd ed., pp. 606–636). Mahwah, NJ: Lawrence Earlbaum.

Lucas, T., & Katz, A. (1994). Reframing the debate: The roles of native languages in English-only programs for language minority students. *TESOL Quarterly, 28*, 537–562.

Macías, R. F. (1994). Inheriting sins while seeking absolution: Language diversity and national statistical data sets. In D. Spener (Ed.), *Adult biliteracy in the*

United States (pp. 15–45). Washington, DC, and McHenry, IL: Center for Applied Linguistics and Delta Systems.

MacSwan, J. (2017). A multilingual perspective on translanguaging. *American Educational Research Journal, 54*(1), 167–201. doi:10.3102/0002831216683935

Madden, M., Lenhart, A., Duggan, M., Cortesi, S., & Gasser, U. (2013). *Teens and technology*. Washington, DC: Pew Research Center. Available at http://www.pewinternet.org/Reports/2013/03/teens-and-tech.aspx

Magadán, C. (2015). *Integración de la technología educativa en el aula. Enseñar lengua y literatura con las TIC*. Buenos Aires, Argentina: Cenage Learning.

Makoni, S., & Pennycook, A. (2007). *Disinventing and reconstituting languages*. Clevedon, UK: Multilingual Matters.

Maninger, R. M. (2006). Successful technology integration: Student test scores improved in an English literature course through the use of supportive devices. *TechTrends: Linking Research and Practice to Improve Learning, 50*(5), 37–45.

Manyak, P. (2004). What did she say? Translation in a primary-grade English immersion class. *Multicultural Perspectives, 6*(1), 12–18.

Marshall, F., & Toohey, K. (2010). Representing family. Community funds of knowledge, bilingualism and multimodality. *Harvard Education Review, 80*(2), 221–241.

Martínez, E. (2002). Fragmented community, fragmented schools: The implementation of educational policy for Latino immigrants. In S. Wortham, E. G. Murillo Jr., & E. T. Hamann (Eds.), *Education in the new Latino diaspora: Policy and the politics of identity* (pp. 143–168). Westport, CT: Ablex Publishing.

Martiniello, M. (2008). Language and the performance of English language learners in math word problems. *Harvard Educational Review, 98*(2), 333–368.

Massachusetts Question 2. (2002). G.L. C. 71A.

Maxwell-Jolly, J., Gándara, P. (2012). Teaching all our children well. Teachers and teaching to close the academic achievement gap. In T. Timar & J. Maxwell Jolly (Eds.), *Narrowing the achievement gap: Perspectives and strategies for challenging times* (pp. 163–186). Cambridge, MA: Harvard Education Press.

May, S. (2011). *Language and minority rights: Ethnicity, nationalism and the politics of language*. New York, NY: Routledge.

May, S. (Ed.) (2015). *Addressing the multilingual turn: Implications for SLA, TESOL and bilingual education* (2nd ed.). New York, NY: Routledge.

Mazak, C., & Carroll, K. (Eds.). (2017). *Translanguaging in higher education. Beyond monolingual ideologies*. Bristol, UK: Multilingual Matters.

Mazur, E. (2005). Online and writing: Teen blogs as mines of adolescent data. *Teaching of Psychology, 32*(3), 180–182.

McIntyre, E., Rosebery, A., & González, N. (Eds.). (2001). *Classroom diversity: Connecting curriculum to students' lives*. Portsmouth, NH: Heinemann.

Mediratta, K., Fruchter, N., & Lewis, A. (2002). *Organizing for school reform: How communities are finding their voice and reclaiming their public schools*. New York, NY: New York University Institute for Education and Social Policy. Available at http://steinhardt.nyu.edu/iesp/papers#2002

Mehan, H., Datnow, A., Bratton, E., Tellez, C., Friedlander, D., & Ngo, T. (1992). *Untracking and college enrollment* (Cooperative Agreement No. R117G10022). San Diego, CA: University of California, San Diego, National Center for Research on Cultural Diversity and Second Language Learning.

Menken, K. (2008). *English language learners Left Behind: Standardized testing as language policy.* Clevedon, UK: Multilingual Matters.

Menken, K. (2013). Emergent bilingual students in secondary school: Along the academic language and literacy continuum. *Language Teaching, 46,* 438–476.

Menken, K., & García, O. (Eds.). (2010). *Negotiating language policies in schools. Educators as policymakers.* New York, NY: Routledge.

Menken, K., & Kleyn, T. (2009). The difficult road for long-term English learners. *Educational Leadership, 66*(7). Available at http://doi.org/10.1080/15348431.20 11.605686 and http://www.ascd.org/publications/educational_leadership/apr09/ vol66/num07/The_Difficult_Road_for_Long-Term_English_Learners.aspx.

Menken, K., Kleyn, T., & Chae, N. (2012). Spotlight on long-term English language learners: Characteristics and prior schooling experiences of an invisible population. *International Multilingual Research Journal, 6*(2), 121–142.

Menken, K., & Solorza, C. (2013). Where have all the bilingual programs gone?!: Why prepared school leaders are essential for bilingual education. *Journal of Multilingual Education Research, 4,* 9–39.

Menken, K., & Solorza, C. (2014). No child left bilingual: Accountability and the elimination of bilingual education programs in New York City schools. *Educational Policy, 8*(1), 96–125.

Mercado, C. (2005a). Reflections on the study of households in New York City and Long Island: A different route, a common destination. In N. González, L. C. Moll, & C. Amanti (Eds.), *Funds of knowledge: Theorizing practices in households, communities, and classrooms* (pp. 233–255). Mahwah, NJ: Lawrence Erlbaum.

Mercado, C. (2005b). Seeing what's there: Language and literacy funds of knowledge in New York Puerto Rican homes. In A. C. Zentella (Ed.), *Building on strength: Language and literacy in Latino families and communities* (pp. 134–147). New York, NY: Teachers College Press.

Mercer, J. R. (1989). Alternative paradigms for assessment in a pluralistic society. In J. A. Banks & C. M. Banks (Eds.), *Multicultural education* (pp. 289–303). Boston, MA: Allyn & Bacon.

Messick, S. (1989). Validity. In R. L. Linn (Ed.), *Educational measurement* (3rd ed., pp. 13–103). New York, NY: Macmillan.

Millard, M. (2015). *State funding mechanisms for English language learners.* Denver, CO: Education Commission of the States. Available at http://www.ecs.org/ clearinghouse/01/16/94/11694.pdf

Miller, H. (2016). The MIT-Haiti Initiative: An international engagement. *MIT Faculty Newsletter, 29*(1). Available at http://web.mit.edu/fnl/volume/291/ miller.html

Minicucci, C., & Olsen, L. (1992, Spring). *Programs for secondary limited English proficient students: A California study* (Occasional Papers in Bilingual Education, No. 5). Washington, DC: National Clearinghouse for Bilingual Education.

MIT-Haiti Initiative. (n.d.). *Resources/STEM tools*. Available at https://haiti.mit.edu/resources/

Moll, L. C., Amanti, C., Neff, D., & Gonzalez, N. (1992). Funds of knowledge for teaching: Using a qualitative approach to connect homes and classrooms. *Theory into Practice, 31*, 132–141.

Moll, L. C., & Greenberg, J. B. (1990). Creating zones of possibilities: Combining social contexts for instruction. In L. C. Moll (Ed.), *Vygotsky and education: Instructional implications and applications of sociohistorical psychology* (pp. 319–348). New York, NY: Cambridge University Press.

Montero, K., Newmaster, S., & Ledger, S. (2014) Exploring early reading instructional strategies to advance the print literacy development of adolescent SLIFE. *Journal of Adolescent and Adult Literacy, 58*(1), 59–69.

Morrell, E. (2008). *Critical literacy and urban youth: Pedagogies of access, dissent, and liberation*. New York, NY: Routledge.

Muñoz-Sandoval, A. F., Cummins, J., Alvarado, C. G., & Ruef, M. L. (1998). *Bilingual verbal abilities test: Comprehensive manual*. Itasca, IL: The Riverside Publishing Company.

Murnane, R. J., & Phillips, R. R. (1981). Learning by doing, vintage, and selection: Three pieces of the puzzle relating teaching experience and teaching performance. *Economics of Education Review, 1*(4), 453–465.

Myers-Scotton, C. (2005). *Multiple voices: An introduction to bilingualism*. Malden, MA: Wiley.

Nagy, W., & Anderson, R. (1984). How many words are there in printed school English? *Reading Research Quarterly, 19*, 304–330.

National Clearinghouse for English Language Acquisition and Language Instruction Educational Programs (NCELA). (2006). *Frequently asked questions*. Available at http://www.ncela.gwu.edu/faqs/

National Research Council (NRC). (2011). *Allocating federal funds for state programs for English language learners*. Panel to review alternative sources for the limited English proficiency allocation formula under Title III, Part A., Elementary and Secondary Education Act, Committee on National Statistics and Board Testing and Assessment. Washington, DC: National Academies Press.

National Task Force on Early Childhood Education for Hispanics. (2007). *Para nuestros niños: Expanding and improving early education for Hispanics*. Washington, DC: Author. Available at http://www.ecehispanic.org/

National Telecommunications and Information Administration (NTIA). (2011). *Digital nation: Expanding internet usage*. Washington, DC: US Department of Commerce.

Navarrete, C., & Gustke, C. (1996). *A guide to performance assessment for linguistically diverse students*. Albuquerque, NM: Evaluation Assistance Center—Western Region, New Mexico Highlands University.

New London Group. (1996). A pedagogy of multiliteracies: Designing social futures. *Harvard Educational Review, 66*, 60–92.

Nichols, S. L., & Berliner, D. C. (2007). *Collateral damage: How high stakes testing corrupts America's schools*. Cambridge, MA: Harvard University Press.

No Child Left Behind Act of 2001 (NCLB). (2001). 20 U.S.C. 6301 et seq. (2002).

Nores, M., Belfield, C., Barnett, W., & Schweinhart, L. (2005). Updating the economic impacts of the High/Scope Perry Preschool Program. *Educational Evaluation and Policy Analysis, 27*(3), 245–261.

Norton, B. (2013). *Identity and language learning: Extending the conversation* (2nd ed.) Bristol, UK: Multilingual Matters.

NYCDOE Department of English Language Learners and Student Support. (2013–2014). *School Year 2013–2014. Demographic Report.* New York, NY: New York City Department of Education.

Oakes, J. (1985). *Keeping track: How schools structure inequality.* New Haven, CT: Yale University Press.

Oakes, J. (1990). *Multiplying inequalities: The effects of race, social class, and tracking on opportunities to learn mathematics and science.* Santa Monica, CA: Rand.

Oakes, J., & Saunders, M. (2002). *Access to textbooks, instructional materials, equipment, and technology: Inadequacy and inequality in California's public schools, found in the Williams Watch Series (wws-rr001-1002).* Los Angeles, CA: UCLA/IDEA.

Office of English Language Acquisition (OELA). (2006). Biennial Evaluation Report to Congress on the Implementation of Title III, Part A of the ESEA.

Office of English Language Acquisition (OELA). (2015, October). English learner students who are Hispanic/Latino. *Fast Facts.* Available at https://www2.ed.gov/about/offices/list/oela/fast-facts/index.html

Office of English Language Acquisition (OELA). (2017, February). Languages spoken by English learners. *Fast Facts.* Available at https://www2.ed.gov/about/offices/list/oela/fast-facts/index.html

O'Halloran, K. L. (2008). Systemic functional-multimodal discourse analysis (SF-MDA): Constructing ideational meaning using language and visual imagery. *Visual Communication, 7*(4), 443–475. doi:https://doi.org/10.1177/1470357208096210

Olivos, E. M. (2006). *The power of parents: A critical perspective of bicultural parent involvement in public schools.* Bern, Switzerland: Peter Lang.

Olivos, E. M., Jiménez-Castellanos, O., & Ochoa, A. M. (2011). *Bicultural parent engagement: Advocacy and empowerment.* New York, NY: Teachers College Press.

Olsen, L. (1997). *Made in America.* New York, NY: The Free Press.

Olsen, L. (2014). *Meeting the unique needs of long term English learners: A guide for educators.* Washington, DC: National Education Association.

Orfield, G. (2001). *Schools more separate: Consequences of a decade of resegregation.* Cambridge, MA: The Civil Rights project, Harvard University.

Orfield. G., & Frankenberg, E. (May 15, 2014). Brown at 60: Great progress, a long retreat and an uncertain future. *The Civil Rights Project.* Available at https://civilrightsproject.ucla.edu/research/k-12-education/integration-and-diversity/brown-at-60-great-progress-a-long-retreat-and-an-uncertain-future/Brown-at-60-051814.pdf

Organisation for Economic Co-operation and Development (OECD). (2005). The definition and selection of key competencies: Executive summary. *The DeSeCo Project.* Available at http://www.oecd.org/dataoecd/47/61/35070367.pdf

Ortega, L. (2014). Ways forward for a bi/multilingual turn in SLA. In S. May (Ed.), *The multilingual turn: Implications for SLA, TESOL and bilingual education* (pp. 32–53). New York, NY, and London, UK: Routledge.

Ortiz, A. (2001). *English language learners with special needs: Effective instructional strategies.* Arlington, VA: Center for Applied Linguistics. Available at www.cal.org/resources/digest/0808ortiz.html

Otheguy, R., García, O., & Reid, W. (2015). Clarifying translanguaging and deconstructing named languages: A perspective from linguistics. *Applied Linguistics Review, 6*(3), 281–307.

Otheguy, R., & Otto, R. (1980). The myth of static maintenance in bilingual education. *Modern Language Journal, 64,* 350–357.

Ovando, C., & Collier, V. (1998). *Bilingual and ESL classrooms: teaching in multicultural contexts* (2nd ed.). Boston, MA: McGraw-Hill.

Padrón, Y. N., & Waxman, H. C. (1999). Classroom observations of the Five Standards for Effective Teaching in urban classrooms with ELLs. *Teaching and Change, 7,* 79–100.

Palmer, D. (2010). Race, power, and equity in a multiethnic urban elementary school with a dual language "strand" program. *Anthropology & Education Quarterly, 41*(1), 94–114.

Palmer, D. K., Martínez, R. A., Mateus, S. G., & Henderson, K. (2014). Reframing the debate on language separation: Toward a vision for translanguaging pedagogies in the dual language classroom. *The Modern Language Journal, 98*(3), 757–772. doi:10.1111/modl.12121

Paris, D., & Alim, S. (2014). What are we seeking to sustain through culturally sustaining pedagogy? *Harvard Education Review, 84*(1), 85–100.

Parrish, T. B. (1994). A cost analysis of alternative instructional models for limited English proficient students in California. *Journal of Education Finance, 19,* 256–278.

Parrish, T. B., Linquanti, R., Merickel, A., Quick, H. E., Laird, J., & Esra, P. (2002). *Effects of the implementation of Proposition 227 on the education of English learners K–12: Year Two Report.* Palo Alto, CA: American Institutes for Research. Available at http://lmri.ucsb.edu/resdiss/pdf files/062802yr2finalreport.pdf

Passel, J., Capps, R., & Fix, M. (2004). *Undocumented immigrants: Facts and figures.* Washington, DC: Urban Institute.

Passel, J., & Cohn, D. V. (2009). A portrait of unauthorized immigrants in the United States. *Pew Hispanic Center.* Available at http://www.pewhispanic. org/2009/04/14/a-portrait-of-unauthorized-immigrants-in-the-united-states/

PDK International. (2015, September). Testing doesn't measure up for Americans: 47th annual PDK/Gallup poll of the public's attitudes about the public schools. *Phi Delta Kappan.* Available at http://pdkpoll2015.pdkintl.org

Peal, E., & Lambert, W. (1962). The relation of bilingualism to intelligence. *Psychological Monographs, 76*(546), 1–23.

Pedraza, P., & Rivera, M. (Eds.) (2005). *Latino education: An agenda for community action research*. New York, NY: Routledge.

Pennock-Román, M. (1994). *Background Characteristics and future plans of high-scoring GRE general test examinees*. Research report ETS-RR9412 submitted to EXXON Education Foundation. Princeton, NJ: Educational Testing Service.

Pennycook, A. (2006). *Global Englishes and transcultural flows*. London, United Kingdom, and New York, NY: Routledge.

Pennycook, A. (2007). The myth of English as an international language. In S. Makoni & A. Pennycook (Eds.), *Disinventing and reconstituting languages* (pp. 90–115). Clevedon, UK: Multilingual Matters.

Pennycook, A. (2010). *Language as a local practice*. New York, NY: Routledge.

Pérez Carreón, G., Drake, C., & Calabrese Barton, A. (2005). The importance of presence: Immigrant parents' school engagement experiences. *American Educational Research Journal, 42*(3), 465–498.

Pérez Rosario, V. (2014). *The CUNY-NYSIEB Guide to translanguaging in Latino literature*. New York, NY: CUNY-NYSIEB, The Graduate Center, The City University of New York. Available at www.nysieb.ws.gc.cuny.edu/files/2015/02/CUNY-NYSIEB-Latino-Literature-Guide-Final-January-2015.pdf

Petrovic, J. E. (2005). The conservative restoration and neoliberal defenses of bilingual education. *Language Policy, 4*(4), 395–416. Available at http://doi.org/10.1007/s10993-005-2888-y

Peyton, J. K., Ranard, D. A., & McGinnis, S. (Eds.). (2001). *Heritage languages in America: Preserving a national resource*. Washington, DC: CAL/ERIC/Delta Systems Inc.

Philips, S. (1983). *The invisible culture*. Prospect Heights, IL: Waveland.

Phillipson, R. (1992). *Linguistic imperialism*. Oxford, UK: Oxford University Press.

Pimentel, C. (2011). The color of language: The racialized educational trajectory of an emerging bilingual student. *Journal of Latinos and Education, 10*(4), 335–353. Available at http://doi.org/10.1080/15348431.2011.605686

Pitt, A., & Britzman, D. (2003). Speculations on qualities of difficult knowledge in teaching and learning: an experiment in psychoanalytic research. *Qualitative Studies in Education, 16*(6), 755–776.

Poehner, M. E. (2007). Beyond the test: L2 dynamic assessment and the transcendence of mediated learning. *The Modern Language Journal, 91*(iii), 323–340.

Portes, A. (1998). Social capital: Its origins and applications in modern sociology. *Annual Review of Sociology, 24*, 1–24.

Poushter, J. (2016, February 22). *Smartphone ownership and internet usage continues to climb in emerging economies*. Washington, DC: Pew Research Center. Available at http://www.pewglobal.org/2016/02/22/smartphone-ownership-and-internet-usage-continues-to-climb-in-emerging-economies/

Poza, L., Brooks, M., & Valdés, G. (2014). Entre familia: Immigrant parents' strategies for involvement in children's schooling. *The School Community Journal, 24*(1), 119–148.

Purcell, K., Heaps, A., Buchanan, J., & Friedrich, L. (2013). *How teachers are using technology at home and in their classrooms.* Washington, DC: Pew Research Center's Internet & American Life Project. Available at http://pewinternet.org/reports/2013/teachers-and-technology

Ramirez, A. Y. F. (2003). Dismay and disappointment: Parental involvement of Latino immigrant parents. *The Urban Review, 35*(2), 93–110.

Ramírez, J. D. (1992). Executive summary, final report: Longitudinal study of structured English immersion strategy, early-exit and late-exit transitional bilingual education programs for language-minority children. *Bilingual Research Journal, 16*(1–2), 1–62.

Rawls, J. (1971). *A theory of justice.* Cambridge, MA: Harvard University Press.

Rebell, M. (2007). Professional rigor, public engagement and judicial review: A proposal for enhancing the validity of education adequacy studies. *Teachers College Record, 109*(4). Available at http://www.tcrecord.org/content.asp?contentid=12743

Rebell, M. (2009). *Courts and kids. Pursuing educational equity through the state courts.* Chicago, IL: Chicago University Press.

Reyes, A. (2006). Reculturing principals as leaders for cultural and linguistic diversity. In K. Téllez & H. C. Waxman (Eds.), *Preparing quality educators for English language learners* (pp. 145–156). Mahwah, NJ: Lawrence Erlbaum.

Ricciardelli, L. A. (1992). Bilingualism and cognitive development in relation to threshold theory. *Journal of Psycholinguistic Research, 21*, 301–316.

Rice, J. K. (2003). *Teacher quality: Understanding the effectiveness of teacher attitudes.* Washington, DC: Economic Policy Institute.

Ricento, T. (2005). Problems with the "language as resource" discourse in the promotion of heritage languages in the U.S.A. *Journal of Sociolinguistics, 9*(3), 348–368. doi:10.1111/j.1360-6441.2005.00296.x

Riches, C., & Genesee, F. (2006). Cross-linguistic and cross-modal aspects of literacy development. In F. Genesee, K. Lindholm-Leary, W. Saunders, & D. Christian (Eds.), *Educating English language learners: A synthesis of research evidence* (pp. 64–108). New York, NY: Cambridge University Press.

Rios-Aguilar, C., González Canché, M. S., & Sabetghadam, S. (2012). Evaluating the impact of restrictive language policies: The Arizona 4-hour English language development block. *Language Policy, 11*(1), 47–80. Available at http://doi.org/10.1007/s10993-011-9226-3

Rivera, C., & Collum, E. (Eds.). (2006). *A national review of state assessment policy and practice for English language learners.* Mahwah, NJ: Lawrence Erlbaum.

Rivera, C., & Stansfield, C. W. (2001). Leveling the playing field for English language learners: Increasing participation in state and local assessments through accommodations. In R. Brandt (Ed.), *Assessing student learning: New rules, new realities* (pp. 65–92). Arlington, VA: Educational Research Service. Available at http://ceee.gwu.edu/standards_assessments/researchLEP_accommodintro.htm

Rodriguez, G. M. (2013). Power and agency in education: Exploring the pedagogical dimensions of funds of knowledge. *Review of Research in Education, 37,* 87–120.

Rolstad, K., Mahoney, K., & Glass, G. (2005). The big picture: A meta-analysis of program effectiveness research on English language learners. *Educational Policy Review, 19*(4), 572–594.

Ronan, B. (2014). *Moving across languages and other modes: Emergent bilinguals and their meaning making in and around an online space.* Unpublished doctoral dissertation, Teachers College, Columbia University.

Ronan, B. (2015). Intertextuality and dialogic interaction in students' online text construction. *Literacy Research: Theory, Method, and Practice, 64*(1), 379–397.

Ronan, B. (2017). Digital tools for supporting English language learners' content area writing. In M. Carrier, R. M. Damerow, & K. M. Bailey (Eds.), *Digital language learning and teaching: Research, theory and practice* (pp. 93–103). New York, NY: Routledge, Taylor & Francis.

Rosebery, A. S., Warren, B., & Conant, F. (1992). Appropriating scientific discourse: Findings from language minority classrooms. *Journal of the Learning Sciences, 2*(1), 61–94.

Rosebery, A. S., & Warren, B. (Eds.). (2008). *Teaching science to English language learners: Building on students' strengths.* Arlington, VA: NSTA Press.

Rosenberg, H., Lopez, M. E., & Westmoreland, H. (2009). *Family engagement: A shared responsibility.* Cambridge, MA: Harvard Family Research Project. Available at http://www.hfrp.org/family-involvement/publications-resources/family-engagement-a-shared-responsibility

Ruiz-De-Velasco, J., Fix, M, & Clewell, T. (2000). *Overlooked and underserved: Immigrant children in U.S. secondary schools.* Washington, DC: Urban Institute Press.

Ruiz Soto, A., Hooker, S., & Batalova, J. (2015a). States and districts with the highest number and share of English language learners. ELL Information Center Fact Sheet Series. *Migration Policy Institute.* Available at http://www.migrationpolicy.org/research/states-and-districts-highest-number-and-share-english-language-learners

Ruiz Soto, A., Hooker, S., & Batalova, J. (2015b). *Top languages spoken by English Language Learners Nationally and by State. Fact Sheet.* Available at http://www.migrationpolicy.org/research/top-languages-spoken-english-language-learners-nationally-and-state

Rumberger, R. W. (2002). Language minority students account for most of California's enrollment growth in past decade. *UC LMRI Newsletter, 12*(1), 1–2.

Rumberger, R. W., & Gándara, P. (2000). The schooling of English learners. In E. Burr, G. Hayward, & M. Kirst (Eds.), *Crucial issues in California education* (pp. 23–44). Berkeley, CA: Policy Analysis for California Education.

Rymes, B. (2014). *Communicating beyond language: Everyday encounters with diversity.* New York, NY: Routledge.

Sánchez, C. (2017, February 23). English language learners: How your state is doing. *NPREd. How Learning Happens.* Available at http://www.npr.org/sections/

ed/2017/02/23/512451228/5-million-english-language-learners-a-vast-pool-of-talent-at-risk

Sánchez, M. T., García, O., & Solorza, C. (2017). Reframing language allocation policy in dual language bilingual education. *Bilingual Research Journal*. doi: 10.1080/15235882.2017.1405098

Sanders, W. L., & Rivers, J. C. (1996). *Cumulative and residual effects of teachers on future student academic achievement*. Knoxville, TN: University of Tennessee Value-Added Research and Assessment Center.

Sayer, P. (2013). Translanguaging, TexMex, and bilingual pedagogy: Emergent bilinguals learning through the vernacular. *TESOL Quarterly, 47*(1), 63–88.

Seeley, D. S. (1993). Why home-school partnership is difficult in bureaucratic schools. In F. Smit, W. van Esch, & H. J. Walberg (Eds.), *Parental involvement in education* (pp. 49–58). Nijmegen, Netherlands: Institute for Applied Social Sciences.

Selinker, L. (1972). Interlanguage. *International Review of Applied Linguistics, 10*, 209–231.

Selinker, L., & Han, Z-H. (2001). Fossilization: Moving the concept into empirical longitudinal study. In C. Elder, A. Brown, E. Grove, K. Hill, N. Iwashita, T. Lumley, T. McNamara, & K. O'Loughlin (Eds.), *Studies in language testing: Experimenting with uncertainty* (pp. 276–291). Cambridge, UK: Cambridge University Press.

Seltzer, K., & Collins, B. (2016). Navigating turbulent waters: Translanguaging to support academic and socioemotional well-being. In O. García & T. Kleyn (Eds.), *Translanguaging with multilingual students. Learning from classroom moments* (pp. 140–159). New York, NY: Routledge.

Seltzer, K., Hesson, S., & Woodley, H. H. (2014). *Translanguaging in curriculum and instruction: A CUNY-NYSIEB guide for educators*. New York, NY: CUNY-NYSIEB, The Graduate Center, The City University of New York. Available at http://www.nysieb.ws.gc.cuny.edu/files/2014/12/Translanguaging-Guide-Curr-Inst-Final-December-2014.pdf

Shepard, L. A. (1996). *Research framework for investigating accommodations for language minority students*. Presentation made at CRESST Assessment Conference, UCLA, 1996.

Shirley, D. (1997). *Community organizing for urban school reform*. Austin, TX: University of Texas Press.

Shohamy, E. (2001). *The power of tests: A critical perspective on the uses of language tests*. Harlow, UK: Longman.

Shohamy, E. (2006). *Language policy: Hidden agendas and new approaches*. London, UK: Routledge.

Shohamy, E. (2011). Assessing multilingual competencies: Adopting construct valid assessment policies. *The Modern Language Journal, 95*, 418–429. doi:10.1111/j.1540-4781.2011.01210.x

Shohamy, E., Donitsa-Schmidt, S., & Ferman, I. (1996). Test impact revisited: Washback effect over time. *Language Testing, 13*(3), 298–317.

Shohamy, E., & Gorter, D. (Eds.) (2009). *Linguistic landscape: Expanding the scenery.* New York, NY: Routledge.

Short, D., & Fitzsimmons, S. (2007). *Double the work: Challenges and solutions to acquiring language and academic literacy for adolescent English language learners—A report to Carnegie Corporation of New York.* Washington, DC: Alliance for Excellent Education.

Skutnabb-Kangas, T. (1981). *Bilingualism or not. The education of minorities.* Clevedon, UK: Multilingual Matters.

Skutnabb-Kangas, T. (2000). *Linguistic genocide in education—or worldwide diversity and human rights?* Mahwah, NJ: Erlbaum.

Skutnabb-Kangas, T. (2006). Language policy and linguistic human rights. In T. Ricento (Ed.), *An introduction to language policy. Theory and method* (pp. 273–291). Malden, MA: Blackwell.

Skutnabb-Kangas, T., & Phillipson, R. (1994). *Linguistic human rights: Overcoming linguistic discrimination.* Berlin, Germany: Mouton.

Skutnabb-Kangas, T., & Phillipson, R. (2017). *Language rights.* New York, NY: Routledge.

Skutnabb Kangas, T., & Toukomaa, P. (1976). *Semilingualism and middle-class bias: A reply to Cora Brent-Palmer.* Working Papers on Bilingualism, 19. Toronto, Canada: Ontario Institute for Studies in Education, Bilingual Education Project.

Slama, R. (2014). Investigating whether and when English learners are reclassified into mainstream classrooms in the United States: A discrete-time survival analysis. *American Educational Research Journal, 51*(2), 220–252. doi: 10.3102/0002831214528277 2014 AERA.

Slavin, R., & Cheung, A. (2005). A synthesis of research on reading instruction for English language learners. *Review of Educational Research, 75*(7), 247–284.

Snow, C. E. (2017). The role of vocabulary versus knowledge in children's language learning: A fifty-year perspective. *Infancia y Aprendizaje, 40,* 1–18. Available at http://dx.doi.org/10.1080/02103702.2016.1263449

Solano-Flores, G. (2008). Who is given tests in what language by whom, when, and where? The need for probabilistic views of language in the testing of English language learners. *Educational Researcher, 37*(4), 189–199.

Steinberg, L. (1996). *Beyond the classroom: Why school reform has failed and what parents need to do.* New York, NY: Simon & Schuster.

Stolarick, K., & Florida, R. (2006) Creativity, connections and innovation: a study of linkages in the Montréal region. *Environment and Planning, 38,* 1799–1817.

Street, B. V. (1985). *Literacy in theory and practice.* Cambridge, UK: Cambridge University Press.

Street, B. V. (1996). Academic literacies. In D. Baker, J. Clay, & C. Fox (Eds.), *Alternative ways of knowing: Literacies, numeracies, sciences* (pp. 101–134). London, UK: Falmer Press.

Street, B. V. (2003). What's "new" in new literacy studies? Critical approaches to literacy in theory and practice. *Current Issues in Comparative Education, 5*(2), 77–91.

Street, B. V. (Ed.). (2005). *Literacies across educational contexts: Mediating, learning and teaching.* Philadelphia, PA: Caslon Press.

Suárez-Orozco, C., & Suárez-Orozco, M. (2001). *Children of immigration.* Cambridge, MA: Harvard University Press.

Suárez-Orozco, C., Suarez-Orozco, M., & Todorova, I. (2008). *Learning a new land: Immigrant students in American society.* Cambridge, MA: The Belknap Press of Harvard University Press.

Swinney, R., & Velasco, P. (2011). *Connecting content and academic language for English learners and struggling students.* Thousand Oaks, CA: Corwin Press.

Sylvan, C., & Romero, M. (2002). Reversing language loss in a multilingual setting: A native language enhancement program and its impact. In T. Osborn (Ed.), *The future of foreign language education in the United States* (pp. 139–166). New York, NY: Greenwood Publishing Group.

Takanishi, R. (2004). Leveling the playing field: Supporting immigrant children from birth to eight. *The Future of Children, 14*(2), 61–79. Available at http://www.futureofchildren.org/usr_doc/takanishi.pdf

Taylor, D. (1997). *Many families, many literacies: An international declaration of principles.* Portsmouth, NH: Heinemann.

Tazi, Z. (2014). Ready for la escuela: School Readiness and the languages of instruction in kindergarten. *Journal of Multilingual Education Research, 5*(3), 11–31.

Téllez, K., & Waxman, H. C. (Eds.). (2006). *Preparing quality educators for English language learners. Research, policies, and practices.* Mahwah, NJ: Lawrence Erlbaum.

Tenery, M. F. (2005). La visita. In N. González, L. C. Moll, & C. Amanti (Eds.), *Funds of knowledge: Theorizing practices in households, communities, and classrooms* (pp. 119–130). Mahwah, NJ: Lawrence Erlbaum.

Tharp, R. G., Estrada, P., Dalton, S. S., & Yamauchi, L. A. (2000). *Teaching transformed: Achieving excellence, fairness, inclusion and harmony.* Boulder, CO: Westview Press.

Thomas, J. W. (2000). *A review of research on project based learning.* Available at http://www.autodesk.com/foundation/news/pblpaper.htm

Thomas, W. P., & Collier, V. (1997). *School effectiveness for language minority students.* Washington, DC: National Clearinghouse for Bilingual Education, George Washington University, Center for the Study of Language and Education.

Thomas, W. P., & Collier, V. P. (2002). *A national study of school effectiveness for language minority students' long term academic achievement: Final report.* Available at http://www.crede.ucsc.edu/research/llaa/1.1_final.html

Torrance, E. P., Gowan, J. C., Wu, J., & Aliotti, N. C. (1970). Creative functioning of monolingual and bilingual children in Singapore. *Journal of Educational Psychology, 61,* 72–75.

Traugh, C. (2000). Whole-school inquiry: Values and practice. In M. Himley & P. Carini (Eds.), *From another angle: Children's strengths and school standards. The Prospect Center's descriptive review of the child* (pp. 182–198). New York, NY: Teachers College Press.

Tuck, E., & Yang, K. W. (2013). *Youth resistance research and theories of change.* New York, NY: Routledge.

Umansky, I., & Reardon, S. F. (2014). Reclassification patterns among Latino English Learner students in bilingual, dual immersion, and English immersion classrooms. *American Educational Research Journal, 51,* 879–912. doi: 10.3102/0002831214545110

UNESCO. (1960, December 14). Convention against Discrimination in education. Adopted by General Conference at 11th session. Paris, France.

U.S. Census Bureau. (1979). *Current population survey 1979.* Washington, DC: U.S. Government Printing Office.

U.S. Census Bureau. (1989). *Current population survey 1989, November supplement.* Washington, DC: U.S. Government Printing Office.

U.S. Census Bureau. (1995). *Current population survey, October supplement.* Washington, DC: U.S. Government Printing Office.

U.S. Census Bureau. (2005). *American Community Survey (ACS), 2000–2004,* previously unpublished tabulations (November, 2005). Washington, DC: U.S. Government Printing Office.

U.S. Census Bureau (2008). *American Community Survey (ACS), 2008.* Washington, DC: U.S. Government Printing Office.

U.S. Census Bureau. (2014). *American Community Survey (ACS), 2014.* Washington, DC: U.S. Government Printing Office.

U.S. Department of Education, National Center for Education Statistics (NCES). (2003). *The condition of education 2003.* Washington, DC: Author.

U.S. Department of Education, National Center for Education Statistics (NCES). (2006). Washington, DC: Author.

U.S. Department of Education (NCELA). (2015a). *English learner toolkit for state and local education agencies.* Washington, DC: Author. Available at http://www2.ed.gov/about/offices/list/oela/english-learner-toolkit/eltoolkit.pdf

U.S. Department of Education. (2015b, January 7). U.S. Departments of Education and Justice release joint guidance to ensure English learner students have equal access to high-quality education. Available at http://www.ed.gov/news/press-releases/us-departments-education-and-justice-release-joint-guidance-ensure-english-learn

U.S. Department of Education (2015c). National Assessment of Educational Progress (NAEP) National Center for Education Statistics. (2015). Available at http://www.nationsreportcard.gov/reading_math_2015/#?grade=4

U.S. Department of Education, National Center for Education Statistics. (2015d). *The condition of education 2015* (NCES 2015-144). English language learners. Available at http://nces.ed.gov/programs/coe/indicator_cgf.asp

U.S. Department of Education, National Center for Education Statistics (2015e). *Digest of education statistics,* Table 204.27. Available at http://nces.ed.gov/programs/digest/d15/tables/dt15_204.27.asp and Table 204.20. https://nces.ed.gov/programs/digest/d14/tables/dt14_204.20.asp

U.S. Department of Education, National Center for Education Statistics, 2016. *The condition of education.* Available at https://nces.ed.gov/pubsearch/pubsinfo.asp?pubid=2016144

U.S. Department of Education. (2016). Fiscal year 2017 budget summary. Available at http://www2.ed.gov/about/overview/budget/budget17/summary/17summary.pdf

U.S. Department of Education and Office for Civil Rights. (2016). *Key data highlights on equity and opportunity gaps in our nation's public schools.* Available at http://www2.ed.gov/about/offices/list/ocr/docs/2013-14-first-look.pdf

U.S. Department of Health and Human Services, Office of Refugee Resettlement. (2017). *Unaccompanied alien children released to sponsors by state.* Available at http://www.acf.hhs.gov/programs/orr/unaccompanied-childrenreleased-to-sponsors-by-county

U.S. Government Accountability Office (GAO). (July 2009). Teacher preparation. GOA-09.573 Available at http https://www.gao.gov/assets/300/294197.pdf

Valdés, G. (1996). *Con respeto. Bridging the distances between culturally diverse families and schools. An ethnographic portrait.* New York, NY: Teachers College Press.

Valdés, G. (1997). Dual-language immersion programs: A cautionary note concerning the education of language-minority students. *Harvard Educational Review* 67, 391–429.

Valdés, G. (2005). Bilingualism, heritage language learners and second language acquisition research: Opportunities lost or seized? *Modern Language Journal, 89*(3), 410–416.

Valdés, G. (2017). Entry visa denied: The construction of symbolic language borders in educational settings. In O. García, N. Flores, & M. Spotti (Eds.), *Handbook of language and society* (pp. 321–348). Oxford, UK: Oxford University Press.

Valdés, G., & Figueroa, R. A. (1994). *Bilingualism and testing: A special case of bias.* Westport, CT: Ablex Publishing.

Valdez, V. E., Delavan, G., & Freire, J. A. (2014). The marketing of dual language education in Utah print media. *Educational Policy*, 1–35.

Valenzuela, A. (1999). *Subtractive schooling: U.S. Mexican youth and the politics of caring.* Albany, NY: SUNY Press.

Valenzuela, A. (Ed.). (2005). *Leaving children behind: How "Texas-style" accountability fails Latino youth.* Albany, NY: State University of New York Press.

van Dijk, T. (2008). *Discourse and power.* Houndsmills, UK: Palgrave.

Van Hook, J., & Fix, M. (2000). A profile of the immigrant student population. In J. Ruiz-De-Velasco, M. Fix, & T. Clewell (Eds.), *Overlooked and underserved: Immigrant children in U.S. secondary schools* (pp. 9–33). Washington, DC: Urban Institute Press.

van Leeuwen, T. (1999). *Speech, music, sound.* London, UK: Macmillan.

van Leeuwen, T. (2011). *The language of colour: An introduction.* New York, NY: Routledge.

van Lier, L. (2000). From input to affordance: Social-interactive learning from an ecological perspective, In J. P. Lantolf (Ed.), *Sociocultural theory and second language learning* (pp. 245–260). Oxford, UK: Oxford University Press.

van Lier, L., & Walqui, A. (2012, January 13–14). *Language and the Common Core State Standards.* Paper presented at the Understanding Language Conference, Stanford, CA: Stanford University.

Varenne, H., & McDermott, R. (1998). *Successful failure: The schools America builds.* Boulder, CO: Westview Press.

Varghese, M. M., & Park, C. (2010). Going global: Can dual-language programs save bilingual students. *Journal of Latinos and Education, 10*(4), 335–353.

Velasco, P., & Johnson, H. (2014). New York State bilingual common core initiative: Creating scaffolds for the successful education of language learners. In L. Minaya-Rowe (Ed.), *A handbook to implement educational programs, practices, and policies for English language learners* (pp. 29–62). Charlotte, NC: Information Age.

Villegas, A., & Lucas, T. (2002). *Educating culturally responsive teachers.* Albany, NY: State University of New York Press.

Vogel, S., Ascenzi-Moreno, L., & García, O. (2017). An expanded view of translanguaging: Leveraging the dynamic interactions between a young multilingual writer and machine translation software. In J. Choi & S. Ollerhead (Eds.), *Plurilingualism in teaching and learning: Complexities across contexts* (pp. 89–106). New York, NY: Routledge.

Vygotsky, L. S. (1978). *Mind and society.* Cambridge, MA: Harvard University Press.

Walqui, A. (2006). Scaffolding instruction for English learners. A conceptual framework. *International Journal of Bilingual Education and Bilingualism, 9*(2), 159–180.

Walqui, A., García, O., & Hamburger, L. (2004). Quality teaching for English language learners. In *Classroom observation scoring manual.* San Francisco, CA: WestEd.

Walqui, A., & van Lier, L. (2010). *Scaffolding the academic success of adolescent English language learners: A pedagogy of promise.* San Francisco, CA: WestEd.

Ward, T. B., Smith, S. M., & Vaid, J. (1997). Conceptual structures and processes in creative thought. In T. B. Ward, S. M. Smith, & J. Vaid (Eds.), *Creative thought: An investigation of conceptual structures and processes* (pp. 1–27). Washington, DC: American Psychological Association.

Warren, M. R., Hong, S., Leung Rubin, C., & Uy, P. S. (2009). Beyond the bake sale: A community-based relational approach to parent engagement in schools. *Teachers College Record, 111*(9), 2209–2254.

Warriner, D. (2009). Continued marginalization: The social cost of exceptionalism for African refugee learners of English. In J. Kleifgen & G. C. Bond (Eds.), *The languages of Africa and the diaspora: Educating for language awareness* (pp. 199–213). Bristol, UK: Multilingual Matters.

Warschauer, M., & Matuchniak, T. (2010). New technology and digital worlds: Analyzing evidence of equity in access, use, and outcomes. *Review of Research in Education, 34*(1), 179–225.

Weiss, H., Caspe, M., & Lopez, M. E. (2006). *Family involvement makes a difference: Family involvement in early childhood education.* Cambridge, MA: Harvard Family Research Project. Available at http://www.hfrp.org/ publications-resources/browse-our-publications/family-involvement-in-early-childhood-education

Weiss, H., & Lopez, M. E. (2009). Redefining family engagement in education. *FINE Newsletter, 1*(3). Cambridge, MA: Harvard Family Research Project. Available at http://www.hfrp.org/family-involvement/publications-resources/ redefining-family-engagement-in-education

Wenglinsky, H. (2000). *How teaching matters: Bringing the classroom back into discussions of teacher quality.* Princeton, NJ: Educational Testing Service.

Wenglinsky, H. (2005). *Using technology wisely: The keys to success in schools.* New York, NY: Teachers College Press.

Wenworth, L., Pellegrin, N., Thompson, K., & Hakuta, K. (2010). Proposition 227 in California: A long-term appraisal of its impact on English learner student achievement. In P. Gándara & M. Hopkins (Eds.), *Forbidden language: English learners and restrictive language policies* (pp. 37–49). New York, NY: Teachers College Press.

Wible, D., Kuo, C., Chien, F., Liu, A., & Tsao, N. (2001). A web-based EFL writing environment: Integrating information for teachers, learners, and researchers. *Computers & Education, 37,* 297–315.

Wible, D., Kuo, C. Tsao, N., Liu, A., & Lin, H-L. (2003). Bootstrapping in a language learning environment. *Journal of Computer-Assisted Learning, 19*(1), 90–102.

Wiley, T. G. (1996). *Literacy and language diversity in the United States.* Washington, DC: Center for Applied Linguistics.

Wiley, T. G., & Lukes, M. L. (1996). English-only and standard English ideologies in the U.S. *TESOL Quarterly, 30*(3), 511–535.

Wiley, T. G., & Wright, W. (2004). Against the undertow: Language minority education policy and politics in the "Age of Accountability." *Educational Policy, 18*(1), 142–168.

Williams, C. (1994). *Arfarniad o Ddulliau Dysgu ac Addysgu yng Nghyd-destun Addysg Uwchradd Ddwyieithog* [*An evaluation of teaching and learning methods in the context of bilingual secondary education*]. Unpublished doctoral thesis, University of Wales, Bangor.

Williams, C. (2015, January 5). New America's dual language learner national work group sets up shop. Available at ttps://www.newamerica.org/education-policy/ edcentral/dllworkgrouplaunch/

Willig, A. C. (1985). A meta-analysis of selected studies on the effectiveness of bilingual education. *Review of Educational Research, 55*(3), 269–317.

Wong-Fillmore, L., & Fillmore, C. J. (n.d.) What does text complexity mean for English learners and language minority students? *Understanding Language.* Stanford, CA: Stanford University. Available at http://ell.stanford.edu/ sites/default/files/pdf/academic-papers/06-LWF%20CJF%20Text%20 Complexity%20FINAL_0.pdf

Wong-Fillmore, L., & Snow, C. (2000). *What teachers need to know about language.* Washington, DC: U.S. Department of Education, Office of Educational Research and Improvement.

Woodley, H. (2016). Balancing windows and mirrors: Translanguaging in a linguistically diverse classroom. In O. García & T. Kleyn (Eds.), *Translanguaging with multilingual students. Learning from classroom moments* (pp. 83–99). New York, NY: Routledge.

Wright, W. E. (2010). *Foundations for teaching English language learners: Research, theory, policy, and practice.* Philadelphia, PA: Caslon Publishing.

Wyman, L. T., McCarty, T. L., & Nicholas, S. E. (Eds.). (2013). *Indigenous youth and multilingualism: Language identity, ideology, and practice in dynamic cultural worlds.* New York, NY: Routledge.

Yates, J. R., & Ortiz, A. (1998). Issues of culture and diversity affecting educators with disabilities: A change in demography is reshaping America. In R. J. Anderson, C. E. Keller, & J. M. Karp, (Eds.), *Enhancing diversity: Educators with disabilities in the education enterprise* (pp. 21–37). Washington, DC: Gallaudet University Press.

Yip, J. (2016). *Educational histories of newcomer immigrant youth: From countries of origin to the United States.* Doctoral dissertation, The Graduate Center, City University of New York.

Yosso, T. (2005). Whose culture has capital? A critical race theory discussion of community cultural wealth. *Race Ethnicity and Education, 8*(1), 69–91.

Zehler, A., Fleischman, H., Hopstock, P., Stephenson, T., Pendizick, M., & Sapru, S. (2003). *Descriptive study of services to LEP students and LEP students with disabilities* (Vol. 1). Available at http://www.ncela.gwu.edu/resabout/research/descriptivestudyfiles/volI_research_fulltxt.pdf

Zentella, A. C. (1997). *Growing up bilingual.* Maiden, MA: Blackwell.

Zentella, A. C. (2005). Premises, promises, and pitfalls of language socialization research in Latino families and communities. In A. C. Zentella (Ed.), *Building on strength: Language and literacy in Latino families and communities* (pp. 13–30). New York, NY: Teachers College Press.

Zickuhr, K. (2012). *Digital differences.* Washington, DC: Pew Research Center. Available at http://www.pewinternet.org/2012/10/17/digital-differences-2/

Zielezinski, M. B., & Darling-Hammond, L. (2016). *Promising practices: A literature review of technology use by underserved* students. Stanford, CA: Stanford Center for Opportunity Policy in Education.

Zipin, L. (2009). Dark funds of knowledge, deep funds of pedagogy: Exploring boundaries between lifeworlds and schools. *Discourse: Studies in the Cultural Politics of Education, 30*(3), 317–331.

Zipin, L., Sellar, S., & Hattam, R. (2012). Countering and exceeding "capital": A "funds of knowledge" approach to re-imagining community. *Discourse: Studies in the Cultural Politics of Education, 33*(2), 179–192.

Zong, J., & Batalova, J. (2015a). Frequently requested statistics on immigrants and immigration in the United States. *Migration Policy Institute.* Available at http://

www.migrationpolicy.org/article/frequently-requested-statistics-immigrants-and-immigration-united-states-4#Current and Historical

Zong, J., & Batalova, J. (2015b). The limited English proficient population in the U.S. *Migration Policy Institute*. Available at http://www.migrationpolicy.org/article/limited-english-proficient-population-united-states06&RptType=ELPart2_1

Index

About the Authors

Ofelia García is a professor in the PhD programs of Urban Education and of Latin American, Iberian and Latino Cultures at The Graduate Center of The City University of New York. She has been professor of Bilingual Education at Teachers College, Columbia University, dean of the School of Education at the Brooklyn Campus of Long Island University, and professor of Education at The City College of New York. Among her best-known books are *Bilingual Education in the 21st Century: A Global Perspective* and *Translanguaging: Language, Bilingualism and Education* (with Li Wei, 2015, British Association of Applied Linguistics Book Award recipient). García is the general editor of the *International Journal of the Sociology of Language* and the coeditor of *Language Policy* (with H. Kelly-Holmes). García's extensive publication record on bilingualism and the education of bilinguals is grounded in her life experience living in New York City after leaving Cuba at the age of 11, teaching language-minority students bilingually, educating bilingual and ESL teachers, and working with doctoral students researching these topics. In 2017 she received the Charles Ferguson Award in Applied Linguistics from the Center of Applied Linguistics, and the Lifetime Career Award from the Bilingual Education SIG of the American Education Research Association.

Jo Anne Kleifgen is professor emerita of Linguistics and Education at Teachers College, Columbia University. She was a founder and co-director of the Center for Multiple Languages and Literacies at TC. She served twice as president of the International Linguistic Association and is its current vice president. Her research has focused on discourse practices in multilingual settings and the use of technologies to strengthen learners' bilingualism and biliteracy. Among her scholarly contributions are *Communicative Practices at Work: Multimodality and Learning in a High-tech Firm* (Multilingual Matters, 2013), which describes her multiple-year study of a multilingual workplace in Silicon Valley; the first edition of *Educating Emergent Bilinguals* with Ofelia García (Teachers College Press, 2010); and *The Languages of Africa and the Diaspora: Educating for Language Awareness* edited with George Bond (Multilingual Matters, 2009). Her articles have been published in book chapters and journals of linguistics and literacy. She was director and Co-PI of a research project funded by the Institute on

Educational Sciences (U.S. Department of Education) on using new media to support Latinos' language and literacy development (2009–2014). Currently, she consults for iEARN-USA, supervising the evaluation of *BRIDGE*, an online collaboration project between classrooms in the United States and the Middle East and North Africa (U.S. Department of State and Aspen Institute funding). She serves on several editorial boards and has been a visiting scholar at universities in the United States and abroad.